December 8, 1992

Guerrilla
in Striped Pants

To Carl with best wishes.

Walter W. Orebaugh

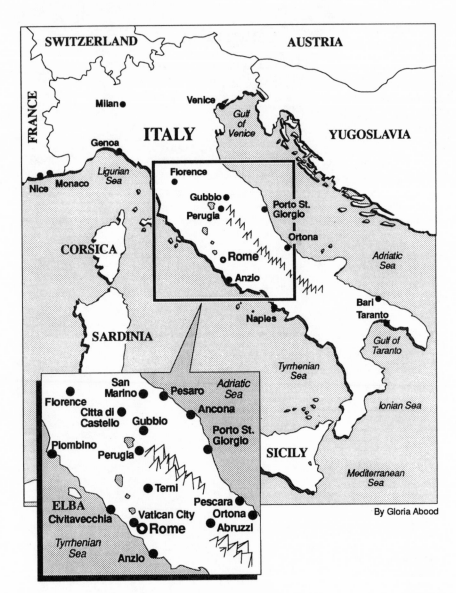

Map of Italy. Inset: Locale Pertinent to the Story.

Guerrilla in Striped Pants

A U.S. Diplomat Joins the Italian Resistance

WALTER W. OREBAUGH
with Carol Jose

Foreword by Ambassador Philip C. Habib

PRAEGER

New York
Westport, Connecticut
London

Copyright Acknowledgments

The author and publisher are grateful to the following for allowing use of their materials:

Francesco Bonucci. Photographs.

Nancy Charrier Burling. Photograph.

Raffaele Mancini. "Per riveder primavera."

Heliane Metzger. Photographs.

Library of Congress Cataloging-in-Publication Data

Orebaugh, Walter W.
　　Guerrilla in striped pants: A U.S. Diplomat Joins the Italian Resistance / Walter W. Orebaugh, with Carol Jose ; foreword by Philip C. Habib.
　　　　p.　cm.
　　Includes bibliographical references and index.
　　ISBN 0–275–94149–3 (alk. paper)
　　1. Orebaugh, Walter W.　2. World War, 1939–1945—Underground movements—Italy.　3. World War, 1939–1945—Personal narratives, American.　4. Guerrillas—Italy—Biography.　5. Diplomats—United States—Biography.　I. Title.
　　D802.I8074　　1992
　　940.53′45—dc20　　　91–32212

British Library Cataloguing in Publication Data is available.

Copyright © 1992 by Walter W. Orebaugh

Library of Congress Catalog Card Number: 91–32212
ISBN: 0–275–94149–3

First published in 1992

Praeger Publishers, One Madison Avenue, New York, NY 10010
An imprint of Greenwood Publishing Group, Inc.

Printed in the United States of America

The paper used in this book complies with the
Permanent Paper Standard issued by the National
Information Standards Organization (Z39.48–1984).

10 9 8 7 6 5 4 3 2 1

For my dear wife, Marguerite;
for Howard, Edith, and their families;
and for the wonderful "paesani" of Italy.

"To be courageous . . . requires no exceptional qualifications, no magic formula, no special combination of time, place and circumstance. Each man must decide for himself the course he will follow."

John F. Kennedy
Profiles in Courage

Contents

Maps follow page xv.
Photographs and illustrations follow page 116.

Foreword

Extraordinary feats by individuals have always been a feature of the American scene. Our history is full of stories of one man's efforts above and beyond the call of duty. Too often, such accounts are buried in dusty files, forgotten except by those whose lives were touched by the events. In more fortunate circumstances, the story is preserved as an inspiration for a new generation.

World War II has been called "the last good war." The United States knew what was at stake and citizens from all walks of life were proud to serve the nation. This book recounts the actions of one young American, caught up in the war in Europe, who braved danger and helped the cause in an unusual way. Born and raised in the heartland of the country, Walter Orebaugh dreamed the adventurous dreams of the youth of his day. Those dreams led eventually to a life in the diplomatic service and reached their height in the mountains of Italy.

Walter is a Foreign Service Officer, serving as Consul in Nice, France, when our story begins. Interned and kept prisoner, he escapes and joins the partisan forces in central Italy. From behind the lines, Walter and his Italian friends aid the Allied sweep north from the beaches of southern Italy. What they did, and how they did it, is at the heart of this gripping account of hardship and danger. Written more than forty years after the fact, it brings to life a remarkable adventure in the words of its principal participant.

For his actions, Walter received the Medal of Freedom, the nation's highest award for civilian service.

Walter now lives a quiet life with Marguerite, his childhood sweetheart, whom he married more than fifty years ago. Those who meet him at church services, or on the golf course, would find it hard to see the bold partisan leader, who is still remembered as "Il Console" (The Consul) in the mountains of Italy. But if you look closely, you will see the glint of past adventures in his eyes, as he recalls those days of struggle.

Ambassador Philip C. Habib

Acknowledgments

It is in tribute to the courage, the humanity, and the generosity of the Italian country people, and to the memory of the bravery of such people as Margherita Bonucci and her children, Vittoria Vechiet, my lifelong friend Manfred Metzger, Bonuccio Bonucci, the Bruschi family, Mario Bonfigli and Giovanni Marioli, the A Force, and all my comrades-in-arms of the guerrilla Band of San Faustino, that I set this story down.

Guerrilla in Striped Pants is based on a true story. The major characters, places, and events are actual; however, the names of some participants are of necessity fictitious, since during those years many families did not dare to use their real names. Some of the minor characters are composites of several people, and some latitude has been exercised in the narration, but only enough to add color to an authentic portrayal of this exciting chapter of history.

The story is my personal recollection of the events of that time, helped by some recently declassified State Department documents, reports filed by the partisan commanders, and my own extensive notes, clippings, correspondence, journals, and photographs.

I gratefully acknowledge the following assistance: use of the annals of the Band of San Faustino sent to me by Don Marino Ceccarelli, "il prete bandito," and of the memoirs provided by other surviving comrades of those times; the friendship and willing assistance of Nancy Charrier Burling, who shared the early part of the adventure; and of Signor Furio Benigni, the present Mayor of Pietralunga, Italy; the encouragement of author Herman Wouk; and the research help and assistance of my late friend and colleague, Dion K. Brown.

I wish to express my profound appreciation to Carol Lanza Jose for her patience and dedication, for helping me comprehend computers and word processors, and, most importantly, for her friendship, as we worked together the many months it took to write, edit, and rewrite this story. Thanks also to Michael Herman of Cocoa Beach, Florida, for his patient input of countless revisions, and to Dan Eades and Alda Trabucchi at Praeger for their confidence, guidance, and able criticism.

Above all, I am deeply grateful for the never-ending love, encouragement and understanding of my wife and life companion, Marguerite.

Preface

Even to this day, if you go to the town of Pietralunga, Italy, or to almost any one of the hundred or so farmhouses in that area and mention "Il Console" (The Consul) to any of the older folk there, you will in all likelihood have a glass of wine set before you, and your host will begin a fascinating story with the words, "aah, sì, mi ricordo . . ." (yes, I remember . . .).

In the annals of World War II, little if any recognition has been given to the staunch bravery of the Italian "paesani"—the country folk, or peasants—most of whom were tenant farmers. Many of them, in stubborn defiance of their own government and the German occupation forces, selflessly endangered themselves and their families to give aid to the hapless victims of that war. They unstintingly helped the "partigiani"—the partisans—and the thousands of refugees, evaders, and escaped Allied POWs who turned up, in desperate need, at their doorsteps during those turbulent times.

It is difficult for the mind to grasp what effect this aspect of war had on those largely uneducated, brutally impoverished rural folk, whose communication with the outside world had, up to then, been minimal at best. Nonetheless, when called upon they gave from the heart what little they had, often going hungry themselves so that another could be fed.

Too little, too, has been said about the fortitude of the partisan guerrilla forces in the hills and mountains of Italy. They were poorly armed, unprovisioned, and constantly on the run—yet they performed feats of outstanding valor. Using any means possible, they hampered and harassed the Germans, and the hated "Repubblichini"—the Fascists—to help the Allies win.

Many peasants and partisans paid with their lives, or suffered unspeakable torture at the hands of the neo-Fascists and the Germans. Their effort merits the highest niche in the cathedral of honor.

I know about their bravery and their selflessness firsthand, because I was one of the fortunate thousands they aided. I was the young American diplomat-turned-guerrilla-fighter they called "Il Console," who, through a bizarre combination of circumstances, came to live and fight among them in the mountains of central Italy from 1942 to 1944.

This, then, is their story as much as mine.

Per riveder primavera

Fuori
il bianco della neve
abbaglia
Nella tiepida stalla
con i buoi
che ora non sembrano piu
bianchi
restiamo chiusi
per giorni
à ruminare pensieri
angosciosi
che hanno ali brevi:
Forse
per reveder primavera
dovremo
macchiare di sangue
la candida neve

by Raffaele Mancini
(Translated by Walter W. Orebaugh)

To See Another Spring

Outside
the snow's whiteness
is blinding
In the pungent stall
with the oxen
who now no longer seem
white
we stay penned up
for days
to ponder
anguished thoughts
on shortened wings:
Perhaps
to see another spring
we will have to
drench with blood
the pristine snow

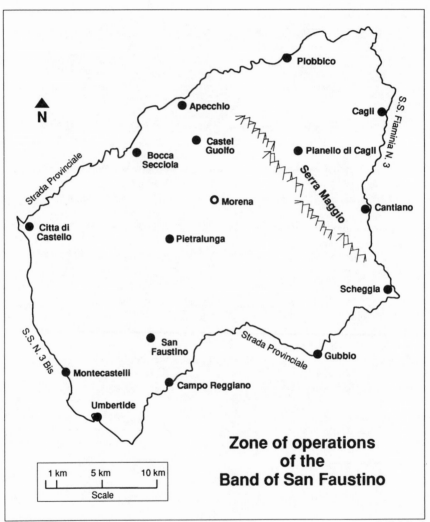

Zone of Operations of the Band of San Faustino.

Italy, with detail of Ancona Macerata area, showing Orebaugh–Marioli itinerary.

1

From Consul to Captive

The train clattered along on its aging rails, sounding as tired as I felt. Peering out the dirt-clouded window, I could see little in the gathering gloom of nightfall. It was a gray February day in 1942, and we were somewhere north of Barcelona, Spain, heading for the French border. That the seeming invincibility of the Germans was turning things topsy-turvy in Europe had been evident from the moment I'd stepped off the ship, in Portugal, barely a week ago. My four months of home leave up, I was returning to my post as American Consul in Nice, the small, fashionable hub city of the French Riviera. Mine was one of three Consular offices still functioning in the Unoccupied Zone, the area of central and southern France not yet under direct German control. The jam-packed train, and the morose expressions on the faces of its passengers, bore mute testimony to the effects of Hitler's relentless rampage across Europe. As ancient, rusty iron couplings shrieked in protest around every curve of the track, I couldn't help but wonder if this overburdened railway system would hold together long enough to even get me as far as the French border!

Just before my departure from Washington, I had been discreetly reminded by my superiors in the State Department that we were not at war with France. I knew I was expected to practice treading-on-eggs diplomacy with the despised Vichy government, while urging any remaining Americans to leave France and protecting American interests there as best I could. It wasn't going to be an easy assignment, nor a pleasant one. I glanced up at the baggage rack overhead, reassuring myself that my two canvas diplomatic pouches were still there. I relaxed a bit, dozing, and thought about my strange experience with the money changer in Lisbon.

Upon arrival in Portugal, I had found out that, by virtue of a special agreement between the American and Portuguese governments, my personal funds, which I had carried with me in a letter of credit for $2,200, could be exchanged at the pre-Pearl Harbor rate—unlike dollars on the open market, which were heavily devalued because of the war. That meant I could exchange my $2,200 into gold-backed Portuguese escudos without incurring any loss. I was pleased at such a stroke of fortune, but had no idea then what significance it would have in the future.

I had set out to find a currency exchange bureau to change half my escudos back into U.S. dollars and the rest into French francs to use in Nice. I didn't know that Lisbon had become a dump for all the French currency held by fleeing refugees and that there were few, if any, buyers for that money. I certainly hadn't been prepared for the reaction I got from the clerk at the exchange booth when I asked about the exchange rate for francs.

"WHAT?" he exclaimed.

"I would like to purchase French francs," I repeated patiently. "What is the exchange rate?"

He stared at me, as though he hadn't heard right. "But senhor, how will you ever use them?" he inquired.

"That is hardly your concern," I replied stiffly.

Quelled by my haughty remark, he quoted me an exchange rate. "How much would you like to exchange, senhor?"

The rate sounded pretty high; I figured I had probably misunderstood. I pushed the equivalent of $1,100 in escudos across the counter. "This much, please," I said.

The clerk looked at the bills, then at me, dumbfounded. "But, senhor, how can you possibly carry this amount in francs? You cannot carry it in your pockets!"

I was startled. "What do you mean? Is it dangerous?"

"No, senhor, it is not dangerous," he replied. "No one will steal French francs from you. They are worthless! I'm asking how will you carry all the notes that this exchange will give you? You will need two very large bags. You must go and get them. Then I will exchange your escudos to francs, if you insist." He shook his head as if to dismiss me for a crazy fool.

Returning to the exchange a little later with two large canvas bags I had gotten from the American Legation, I again plunked down my $1,100 in escudos.

"Francs?" he asked.

I nodded yes.

He snorted in disgust. Opening a large vault, he removed stacks of high-denomination franc notes from it. Calling for help from an assistant, they began counting them out. Soon one bag was crammed full, and they were shoving handfuls of 5,000 and 10,000 franc notes into the second bag. The numbers went into the millions. I had mentally calculated their final, somewhat haphazard count at the prewar exchange rate. At the very least, they put more than $100,000 in francs into the two bags! No wonder they thought I was nuts, if the franc was that devalued!

"Now I'd like to exchange this into American dollars, please."

The first clerk looked at his assistant, then threw his hands up in resignation, as if to say, "What can you do with these crazy Americans?" Even though the dollar had lost buying power, I'd had experiences in the Foreign Service in the past where dollars could accomplish things that no other currency could. I wanted some dollars with me. So I opted for the best exchange I could get and changed my remaining escudos for about $2,000 U.S. in large bills. My $2,200 emergency nest egg, which had taken Marguerite and me three years to save, had suddenly become so much money I needed a taxi to get it all back to my hotel.

Thinking about it now, with the bags of francs stowed up there across from me, where I could see them, I chuckled aloud, startling the other passengers in the compartment. Boarding the train in Lisbon had not been easy. In addition to my regular luggage, and the two bulging canvas diplomatic bags, there were three huge suitcases that my wife had filled with coffee, bars of face and laundry soap, candies, sugar, and canned goods— all of which I had been told were no longer available at any price. I had grumbled and objected, but now I wished she were here so I could share the story about the money with her. But I'd had to leave her, and little Howard, our two-year-old son, at home in Virginia.

The passenger across from me, a burly Frenchman in his late thirties, was watching me. He was probably my tail, from the Deuxième Bureau. So, not yet at my duty station, and already under round-the-clock surveillance! Well, at least it made life interesting. I knew I could lose him, or any of them, within five minutes if I needed to. My other assignments had given me experience in more than just "striped pants" diplomacy. My lifelong interest in, and study of, espionage and covert operations had been sharpened by my earlier four years in Trieste, in Fascist Italy, where even diplomats had to resort to ruses in order not to compromise friends or valuable sources of intelligence.

I leaned back and dozed again, but didn't allow myself to drop off the edge into deep sleep. By the time we pulled into Nice, nine hours later, I needed nothing so much as a hot shower, a shave, and about fourteen hours of uninterrupted sleep! I was happy to see Marino Sales, my driver, waiting for me.

"Benvenuto, Signor Console," he greeted me warmly, in his native Italian.

"Grazie, Marino," I replied, shaking his hand. "It's good to be back."

Signaling for the baggage handler to follow us, Marino took my pouches and led the way out of the station.

There at the curb stood my car, a gleaming black Studebaker. As its driver, Marino held an exalted position among the elite fraternity of chauffeurs along the Riviera, many of whom no longer had cars to drive. He stowed the canvas bags into the trunk and told another driver to follow us with the rest of my things. Swinging the right rear door of the Studebaker open with a flourish, he ushered me in. "Pleased you have returned, Signor Console," he said, closing the door. Relieved, I relaxed back into the soft depths of the leather seat, as Marino skillfully maneuvered us away from the curb and into the mainstream of what little traffic remained in Nice. I looked contentedly at the familiar landmarks as we passed. I had returned to duty and was eager to get back to work.

The months flew by. As the war progressed, the future of the U.S. Consulate in Nice became increasingly uncertain, but I was too busy to dwell on it. I was even too busy to worry about Marguerite and Howard, safe at home back in Virginia. Every day, letters and official despatches from the United States poured into my office by mail and diplomatic pouch. There were pleas by the hundreds for assistance in getting immigration visas for families and other individuals.

At that time, the general population of the world knew nothing about the existence of concentration camps in Poland and Germany, nor did I. But in the long line of refugees that snaked down the street in front of the Consulate every day there was fearful talk of relatives and friends who had been sent away and never heard from again. They brought these tales to me, beseeching me to help them. As soon as my car pulled up at the Consulate in the mornings, there would be a near stampede as people came to entreat me, "Please, please, one moment, only a moment, M'sieu le Consul!" "Please listen to us," they begged me tearfully; "please help us!"

Later, the crackdown began in earnest, and gendarmes were suddenly present, ready to hustle away anyone who might create a scene. Then, they just stood in mute appeal. The fear in the eyes that followed me as I passed, and the hushed silence, emphasized the enormity, the probable futility, and yet the need and worth, of my job. I would never be able to find a way, I knew—not even by bending the immigration laws and regulations—to get all of them out. For most, there was no hope. I knew it, and they knew it. We were racing against time, fighting an unseen menace to these people, most of whom were European Jews. With each passing day, the lines became longer and the outlook grew more forbidding. I worked nonstop.

I had also been tasked with establishing liaison with and rendering financial assistance to the French resistance movements operating in the south of France. Through them, we received a flow of information on movements of German military units into, or through, the Unoccupied Zone, on the plants producing military goods, and on proposals or plans to disrupt or sabotage rail lines and harbor installations. To maintain liaison with these groups took some doing. Since I was under constant surveillance, my ability to trick and lose my tails was constantly put to the test. I had to resort to innumerable ruses and disguises, back door and alley exits, trips on motorcycles and bicycles, quick transfers from car to car, dead-drops—secret places, known to the concerned parties, where messages could be safely dropped off and picked up—and "safe houses"— homes of French families where Jews were hiding out. Somehow I managed to meet my contacts and to gather and relay information. It was risky, but it kept me on my toes. Twice I was shadowed by the man from the train. So I had guessed correctly about him! I took a perverse pleasure in losing him quickly both times. After that, someone new replaced him, and I never saw him again.

In September of 1942, after night fell, I was taken by my resistance contacts to observe buses and vans, with police, out in the residential neighborhoods of Nice, rounding up people. Not just Jewish men, but entire families—even those with babies and small children. Before the outbreak of World War II, France was a favorite refuge for Jews from Germany, and all the countries of Eastern Europe. They were dropped off in an area of the main downtown park that was cordoned off with huge coils of barbed wire. Although I immediately reported this new and horrifying turn of events in despatches to Washington, I was powerless to do more than protest in outrage to the Prefect of Nice and to urge "Franc Tireur" and "Combat," the two most active and important resistance movements, to make life miserable for the French police doing the roundups, and any others engaged in this nefarious activity. Again always at night, the buses would load up the pitiful mass of people from the park and haul them off to the railway yards, where, we were informed, they were packed into freight and cattle cars.

After the testament of those nights, I finally realized what they themselves had known for months: that I, as the U.S. representative there, and that we, as a nation, effectively held the power of life or death over the poor souls who stood daily, in longer and longer lines, before the Consulate, with its emblazoned Great Seal of the United States. We were their last hope for escape from Hitler's control. It was a responsibility that weighed heavily on my conscience.

With Washington's concurrence, I had informally opened negotiations with Prince Louis of Monaco about establishing an American Consulate in that neutral principality. I felt we might soon need a fallback position from Vichy France, and Monaco seemed to represent our best hope. Like Switzerland, Monaco claimed neutrality and purportedly would provide the United States a safe ground for meetings and negotiations. Prince Louis had every reason for wanting to develop more favorable relations with us. One was the hope that it would serve to lift the U.S. Treasury decree that had frozen Monaco's assets in the United States along with those of France. With little or no industry, tourism at a standstill, and its small territory crammed with refugees, the tiny principality was desperately in need of access to its funds in American banks.

By October, conditions in Nice were severe. Food was in short supply. I was dipping into Marguerite's suitcases of foodstuffs to provision my household. Simple authorizations suddenly took longer and longer, or were ignored, with no reason given. Identity checks became more frequent. On November 5th, I had just gotten to my office, and was going through the mail, when my phone rang. It was Pinkney Tuck, U.S. Chargé d'Affaires in Vichy.

"Walt," he said tersely, "don't ask any questions. Just do what I am going to tell you. Take whatever staff you feel is necessary and go open a Consulate in Monaco today. Waste no time. Leave Nice as quickly as possible." He hung up.

I sat there, stunned, holding the dead receiver. Something big must be up. I mentally cataloged what needed to be done, then rang for Marino.

At precisely three-thirty that same afternoon, I presented myself at the Royal Palace in Monaco for a private audience with Prince Louis, of the House of Grimaldi. I was immediately ushered upstairs to the Prince's private study. Prince Louis was a corpulent man, showing his considerable age, but he was mentally alert, well-informed, and perceptive. He was dressed in an impeccably tailored dark gray double-breasted business suit. Close by his side sat Madame Ghislaine Marie Dommenge, his attendant and companion of many years. His Serene Highness rose to greet me, and when I explained the purpose of my visit, he was pleased.

"You have our personal assurances, Monsieur le Consul, that Monaco will extend to you, and the United States, the highest order of our help and cooperation."

"I am indeed honored, Your Serene Highness, to accept, on behalf of my government, your invitation to open the first American Consulate in Monaco. I am sure that the relationship between our governments will remain, as it always has been in the past, a long and cordial one."

"It is our sincere hope," said the Prince, "that the presence of the American Consulate will help to offset the intrusion and spread of German influence in both the economic and political spheres."

I knew that was an oblique reference to his desire for the release of Monacan funds. "Your Serene Highness can be assured that I will convey your strong pro-Allied sentiments to President Roosevelt in my very first despatch from the new Consulate," I responded.

As soon as my allotted half hour with the Prince ended, I hurried off to search for space for the new Consulate. By six o'clock that evening, I was thoroughly discouraged. Prince Louis might be the epitome of friendliness and cooperation, but what I needed at that point was a real estate agent with a couple of offices for rent! Space—any space—was virtually nonexistent in Monaco. I finally gave up and returned to my hotel. The Metropole remained a marvel of Swiss-run efficiency in the midst of general disarray. I needed to rest and to recoup from the events of this momentous day. As I was finishing my dinner, I saw Mr. Scheck, the manager of the Metropole, come in and look around, to be sure all was being handled well in the dining room. A light went on in my head. My God, I thought, if there's one thing better than a good real estate agent, it has to be a native Swiss hotel manager! They always make it their business to know about everything that's going on in their territory.

I beckoned to Mr. Scheck, and, over a brandy, I explained my problem. He sat and sipped for a moment, thinking. Then, "Would two large rooms suffice, if one of them opens onto a street?" he asked.

"That sounds like exactly what I need—do you know of such a place?" I replied.

Mr. Scheck took me to see the rooms he had in mind—a large suite of two rooms on the ground floor of the Hotel Metropole. One glance around and I knew I had struck gold. They were perfect. Shaking hands, we concluded the deal, and I phoned Nice and told the staff to get moving.

The following day, November 6, 1942, in the presence of British clerk Amy Houlden and American Nancy Charrier, the French office workers Mesdames Eme and Goff-Lowenstein, my Italian driver Marino, the Swiss-born Mr. Scheck, and two Monegasque workmen, I ran the Stars and Stripes up the flagpole at the corner of the building and supervised as one of the workmen hung the Consular coat of arms, bearing the Great Seal of the United States, over the door. I felt a small thrill of pride—the first American Consulate to be established in the Principality of Monaco was now a historical fact! Word spread through Monte Carlo like wildfire, and I was inundated with visitors offering congratulations and expressions of support and friendship.

Pleased to be in business again, I gave Marino a few days off, and he bicycled the 15 kilometers back to Nice, to visit family. On Thursday, I decided to drive back to Nice myself, to pick up some more things at the villa. After loading the Studebaker, I was exhausted, so I decided I'd stay in Nice overnight and drive back to Monte Carlo in the morning. It was about three A.M. when I woke suddenly, and, unable to sleep, reached out and snapped on my bedside radio. It was at that precise moment that the French radio network broadcast the news of Operation Torch—the landing of Allied forces in Algiers and in Morocco! The announcement staggered me as if I had been hit by a bolt of lightning. Now I knew why Tuck had told me to get out of Nice, and fast. I envisioned being cut off from Monaco by roadblocks. There was no telling what Vichy France, and the Germans, would do now. I jumped out of bed.

Dressing hastily, I threw my valise into the car. The Studebaker roared to life on the first try. As I backed out of the garage, the flags on the fender standards fluttered, catching my eye. I stopped briefly, yanked them loose, and stashed them on the front seat. I drove at a fast clip, staying alert, negotiating the hairpin turns at speeds that made the tires squeal. Not a soul was in sight at the border on the Lower Corniche and I sped across it and into Monaco. Having made it across the border without incident, I slowed down and took a deep breath, trying to slow the pace of my heart as well. Safely back in the garage at the Metropole, I breathed a sigh of relief, lit a cigar, and sat quietly smoking it, while my nerves settled down. The Allies have certainly put a new light on the direction of this war, I thought with satisfaction.

On November 12, 1942, I was in high spirits as I sent "Despatch No. 1" to the U.S. Department of State, making the new Consulate official. Events moved quickly after that—too quickly. That same day, a contingent of Italian troops raced through the tiny principality, ignoring its neutrality. They were hoping to capture the French fleet, before the French, desperately confused, made up their minds on how to react. An occupational force of Italians remained behind in Monte Carlo. The next day (appropriately enough Friday the 13th), the Monegasque Minister of State, Monsieur Roblot, notified me that the Italian military authorities had given Prince Louis a list of people they wanted expelled from Monaco. My name, of course, was at the very top of the list.

On Monday, November 16th, an Italian officer informed me that "henceforth no American or British subject can enter or leave the Principality without a military pass." I knew there was no way in hell they were going to give me one of those. I was already cut off from communicating outside Monaco, and that directive effectively placed me under informal house arrest. At about the same time, a cablegram went out from Washington, from Secretary of State Cordell Hull to the American Legation in Bern, Switzerland, inquiring about my whereabouts and safety. State wanted to know if I could still send and receive messages. The answer from Bern, which had been unsuccessful in its attempts to contact me, was a terse "No."

From the window of the front office, we could see Italian soldiers everywhere. I packed sensitive materials and a hammer and chisel into a large canvas valise, which I carried everywhere. I called in Amy, Nancy, and the two French clerks and briefed them on what to do to destroy the materials if a showdown came. They all nodded, solemn-faced. My driver Marino had gone back to Nice on an errand for me and had not returned, and there were no other men on my staff. Here I am, I thought grimly, representing one of the biggest, most powerful nations in the Western world, counting on the minuscule police force of one of the tiniest nations on earth to protect me, and four women, from an invading army!

On Friday morning, November 20th, I had gotten up from my desk and was walking toward the windows, to stretch my legs, when suddenly

I heard the heavy, rhythmic, "thump! thump!" cadence of hundreds of booted, marching feet. A cold chill ran down my spine. I dashed for the door between the two offices and yanked it open. "This is it!" I exclaimed. The four women stood frozen for a moment, staring at me. Then Nancy walked quickly across the room to the street doors and locked them. "Amy," I said, "go into my office and do the bag now. Lock the door behind you. I'll stay here and try to keep them out. Don't unlock the door for anyone but me." I turned to the others. "Quickly, burn any papers we don't want them to see. And remember, everybody, speak only English! Don't respond in anything but English if they speak to you. Let me do the talking, if possible. Don't be afraid." I don't know why I said that. Of course they were afraid! I was nervous and apprehensive myself. Amy and Mme. Eme had barely shut themselves into the inner office when there was a heavy rapping at the outer door. "Who is it?" I called.

The voice of Mr. Scheck came through the closed door. "You have visitors, M'sieu le Consul," he announced, emphasizing the word "visitors."

I turned to Nancy and Mme. Goff-Lowenstein, forced a smile, and whispered, "Be calm. Don't provoke them. They won't hurt us." Since the street was filled with hundreds of Italian troops, their weapons unslung, my reassurances sounded a bit hollow, even to my own ears. "Tell them the Consulate is closed," I called to Scheck. "We will open again tomorrow at nine."

I could hear talking outside. Scheck's voice came again, "Er, Monsieur Orebaugh, I think they must speak with you now. They say they will break down the door if you don't open it."

I quickly surveyed the room one last time. Then I shouted, loudly and indignantly, "That would be highly illegal! This is the Consulate of the United States of America! It is in a neutral country and is protected under international law! This is damned illegal!" I repeated, for emphasis.

I could hear a trace of wry humor in Scheck's voice as he replied, "Monsieur Orebaugh, I don't think these men are lawyers. I think you had better let them in." I heard a command shouted in Italian: "Break the door open!"

I unlocked the door and swung it open. Two Italian officers shouldered roughly past me. "Please DO come in," I said, sarcastically. Nancy and Mme. Goff-Lowenstein had seated themselves on the Louis XVI couch on one side of the room. I pulled the big, gilt antique armchair around and sat in it, in a deliberately relaxed attitude. I looked over at the women, to give them a reassuring glance. To my surprise, Nancy had begun fussing with her hair—flinging her mane of shoulder-length chestnut hair out— and crossing and uncrossing her legs. I was surprised at her. Nancy was a very attractive twenty one year old, usually very reserved. Then I realized she was deliberately distracting the young officers, so the girls in the other room could have time to do their destruction work. It was working, too. They were all staring at her.

Within minutes, at least twenty soldiers were milling around the outer office. The senior officer demanded, in Italian, "Where is the rest of your staff?" I pretended not to understand. A discussion between him and his men followed. They produced a young lieutenant who spoke a little English. He repeated the question, in halting English. I responded with another question, also in English. What staff did they mean? The one in Nice? This engendered more discussion among them. New questions were then passed, via the nervously sweating lieutenant's labored translation, to me. I was enjoying this verbal relay, glad for the extra time it was buying us, but I knew their patience would eventually run out. A couple of them had already jiggled the locked door to my office.

Suddenly, one raised his rifle butt to smash it open. Before he could hit it, the lock turned and the door opened. Amy stood framed in the doorway, a triumphant look on her face. I had seen that look before. It always reminded me of a librarian who had caught someone red-handed with an overdue book! For a few seconds everyone stood transfixed, staring at her as if a mirage had suddenly appeared in the desert. Then they rushed pell-mell past her, into the inner office. I got up and followed. I saw immediately that the women had done their job well. Nothing of any value remained for the enemy's hands.

The Italians in the outer office continued to gaze in wonder at Amy. They had apparently never seen anything like her. She stood nearly six feet tall without shoes, and her hair, above a narrow face, was a short-cropped cap of tightly curled ringlets. "Eh! Non finisce mai!"—"Wow, there's no end to her!" said one officer. Amy's blue eyes froze him with a look. I cleared my throat lightly and gave her a tiny negative shake of the head. I didn't want them to know she understood Italian, and she had almost given herself away.

The troops began discussing where they'd take us, the gist of their conversation being that with four women, we could not be housed in their military accommodations. As the discussion became more animated, I decided to speak up.

"We absolutely will not leave this hotel!" I announced clearly, in perfect Italian. At that, the entire assemblage was shocked into silence. My cool, assured manner, coupled with an unexpected command of their language, threw them off guard. "My staff and I are going to the dining room for dinner," I continued, with as much hauteur as I could muster. "We're hungry." The senior of the two officers spoke.

"No one leaves here!" He looked at me belligerently.

"All right then, we'll dine right here," I countered, with calm finality. "Mr. Scheck?" I said, turning to look at him.

Scheck had been standing quietly by, and he immediately took the cue. He began bustling around, pushing a small table to a spot in front of the windows, ordering the enlisted men around. "Bring those chairs over here. You! Bring me the flowers. Voilà!" The table arranged to his satisfaction, he left to order our meal, having adroitly set up our table where the troops on the street would see us dining, unperturbed, with flowers and silver, while their officers stood around in confusion, not knowing what to do next. Scheck was getting as much of a kick out of jerking them around as I was!

Our dinner arrived. Scheck saw to it that the reputation of the Metropole was upheld, even in these bizarre circumstances. He produced a five-course meal, with appropriate wines, all deferentially served by the hotel's white-jacketed waiters! The Italians stood by, discomfited, while we ate and chatted amiably among ourselves, completely ignoring their presence. I felt I was still in control of the situation and was determined not to back down.

Suddenly, the door burst open, and a colonel strode into the room. He was clearly not in the mood for the farce that was being played out right under his jurisdictional nose. Alternately questioning and berating his men, he stamped around, barking orders at everyone. They scurried to do his bidding. Then he whirled on me and shouted, "You! You are coming with me! Now! Immediately!"

I sat, fork and knife poised, and fixed him with a cold stare. "By forcing your way in here, you and your troops and your country have already committed international crimes and invaded United States territory! Are you prepared to add kidnapping of a U.S. diplomat to the list?" I inquired icily. "My staff and I will not leave here and go anywhere with you."

"You come with me!" he reiterated.

I resumed my meal with more outward calm than I felt. "We are on United States territory," I said. "You will have to carry us out, which I assure you will create an international scandal of the highest order."

The colonel hesitated. He hadn't anticipated this defiant reaction. Then his face flushed with rage, and as he opened his mouth to vent his spleen on me, Scheck adroitly stepped into the breach.

"Monsieur le Colonel, I think perhaps you could allow Monsieur le Consul and his staff to be housed right in the hotel, but in an area where you can keep them under surveillance. That would avoid the kind of incident Monsieur le Consul mentioned."

The Colonel grudgingly acceded. "Come!" he said, turning to me. "Enough of this! Your meal is finished! You will come with me, please!"

It was not a request. We were not armed, and there was no point in further resistance. "Let's go, ladies," I said, "stay close to me, and don't be frightened." They had been admirable, remaining calm although I knew they were terrified. But now, I didn't know what might lay ahead for us.

We were escorted out by way of the hotel's inner garden. The women and I followed the booted colonel, who strode haughtily ahead of us. The two officers and several troops, guns at the ready, brought up the rear. Entering an ingenious underground passage that had been hastily lined with Italian troops, shoulder to shoulder at attention, we followed along it until we reached the hotel annex. I looked around me. It was comfortable enough, even a bit luxurious. "Well," I thought, "at least Scheck managed to get us imprisoned in decent quarters."

The next day, our personal belongings were brought to our new lodgings. I was glad to see that my canned goods and my supply of coffee and soap were untouched, but most of all I was happy to have my hoard of American dollars and French francs again. Six days later, we sat down, in my room, to a very different sort of Thanksgiving dinner. I was determined to acknowledge the holiday as best I could, for Nancy's sake. We ate duck, for which I had bribed one of the waiters, and some canned ham and vegetables from my supplies. We tried hard to feel thankful for what we had, even though we were confined to our rooms and unable to communicate with the outside world. The following day, an Italian officer informed me that Mmes. Eme and Goff-Lowenstein, as French citizens, were being returned to France. We bid them a tearful goodbye.

It had been only ten days since the Italians took us prisoner, and the confinement was already gnawing on my nerves. For someone who had grown up on the great prairies of Kansas, and who had enjoyed his youth roaming free in the mountains of Colorado, my hotel room was like a cage. I wanted space and the freedom to be out in the fresh air. I hated being in, day and night. I had nothing useful to do. I longed for a change, to relieve the monotony. That evening, when our dinner arrived, there was a note from Scheck, hidden under Amy's bread. "Lester Maynard arrested," the note said, "being held incommunicado elsewhere in the hotel." Lester, a retired Foreign Service Officer, was the American Red Cross representative in Monaco. I wondered what would happen to him—and to all of us. I didn't have long to wait to find out—or for my foolish wish for a change to become reality.

December 2nd dawned unusually cold. I had built a fire in the fireplace, and was sitting close by it to stay warm, when the door opened to admit two Italian officers. Without preamble, the senior spoke. "You will be leaving for Italy today at one o'clock! Have your things packed and ready. You can take two bags. The rest will follow."

I could tell that any protest would be futile, but decided to try for one last concession. "I will not leave Monaco," I stated, "until I have met with the Swiss Consul!"

They went away, and, to my utter amazement, returned shortly with the Swiss Consul and Vice-Consul. Then, in an even more surprising move, they stepped into the hall, leaving us alone. To Vice-Consul Alex Manz I gave my diplomatic pouches, with my remaining French francs, and requested that they be sent to the Swiss Legation in Rome and kept there for me. "Please notify the American Legation in Bern, and ask them to notify my wife, of these latest developments," I said.

"Of course. Happy to do whatever we can. Have they said where in Italy they're taking you?"

"No, nothing yet. What's the latest war news? We've been kept isolated and have heard only what little was smuggled in on notes with our meals. How are things going for the Allies?"

"As well as could be hoped," replied Manz. "The Allies have met little resistance in North Africa so far." The explosions we'd heard a few nights before were the scuttling of the French fleet at Toulon, he informed me. That must have been a devastating blow to the Italians and Germans, who had hoped to get their hands on it. What good news! It must have been quite a show, I thought, if we could hear it from where we were—Toulon was about 100 kilometers away!

Manz also gave me the disquieting news of the arrest of my staff in Nice. My thoughts went to Marino, who had been so faithful, and to So, my houseboy, who had taken such good care of me for the time I was there, and to the Mmes. Eme and Goff-Lowenstein. I prayed that they would all be unharmed and liberated soon. Poor Mme. Goff-Lowenstein, being Jewish, was in the greatest danger of all. I scribbled a couple of messages for the State Department and for my family and gave them to Manz. The two Swiss shook my hand, and, with grave looks, wished us well. "We will do everything we can," they assured me. Before we knew it, it was ten after one, and the Italians had returned.

For the next two days, we journeyed interminably by foot, car, and train. Our four OVRA (secret police) guards ignored our requests for rest, warm clothes, or basic comfort. Exhausted, Amy, Nancy, Lester Maynard, and I were ordered off our fourth, and blessedly final, train, high in the convoluted hills and mountains of central Italy. "Gubbio" read the small sign at the station.

As the train pulled away we were left standing on the open platform in our lightweight clothing, suitable for the temperate climate of the Riviera, not winter in the mountains. We shivered uncontrollably as the fierce, biting December wind swept down and over us from snow-covered Mount Ubaldo. A far cry from my arrival in Nice in chauffeured comfort just nine months ago, I thought grimly. No amount of grumbling on my part brought any response from our warmly dressed armed guards. Nancy and Amy stamped up and down the platform, waving their arms. Both were blue with cold, and tears trembled at the corners of Nancy's young eyes. It had been a brutal trip. We were left there for two hours before the chief guard returned. "Your systemization is complete, and you have been transferred to the jurisdiction of the Fascist party secretary here," he announced.

We didn't care WHO had jurisdiction—"Just get us out of this damned cold!" I demanded. "We're freezing, we've been standing here for hours, and we need a restroom!"

He couldn't have been less interested. "You will follow me," he ordered. At his signal, we picked up our bags and trudged wearily up the slope, into the ancient town of Gubbio.

2

Internment in Gubbio

Reaching the town limits, a good quarter of a mile from the train platform, we finally came to a central piazza, or town square. There was a
large church at one end and some official looking buildings at the other.
On one corner of the square stood a small, dun-colored stone and stucco
building. Above it hung a weathered sign, "Albergo San Marco." The
guard walked us to the building and, signaling grandly for us to enter,
announced, with a trace of sarcasm, "Eccoci. Siete à casa, Signori" (your
new home, ladies and gentlemen.).

We were met in the tiny lobby by the local Fascist Party Secretary. He,
he informed us officiously, was charged with our "safekeeping." We would
not be kept totally confined, he went on, but there were rules and con-
straints we would have to live by. As he listed them, I translated for the
others: One, we were NOT, under any circumstances, to leave the con-
fines of the city of Gubbio; Two, we were NOT to attempt to use the
telephone or postal service; Three, we were NOT to speak to, or attempt
to fraternize with, any of the local people; Four, we were NOT to attempt
to engage in any political or military discussion or activity. As the Secretary enunciated each rule, Signorina Vera, the proprietress of the San Marco,
emitted an audible cluck every time he said "not." He then explained to
us that Signorina Vera had been entrusted with our care. "It is imperative," the Secretary continued, "that each of you shall, without fail, report
to me daily at the town hall."

I stepped forward.

"I have diplomatic status, and it is both improper and contrary to international law for me to do this. I must also inform you that we are entitled
to access to the protecting power, Switzerland, through communication
and contact with the Swiss Legation in Rome."

My pronouncement upset the Secretary but he didn't challenge it. Like most class-conscious Italians, he paid careful heed to rank and position, and nowhere in Italy did the word "Consul" carry more weight and meaning than in the ancient Roman towns of Umbria, particularly Gubbio. Was not their own most important and historic building named the Palazzo dei Consoli, the Palace of Consuls? He was also aware that I had come to Gubbio escorted by no less than four OVRA (secret police) agents, that his government considered my detainment of some importance, and that I spoke Italian fluently, a mark of education and high status. He turned all this over in his mind. Abruptly, he turned to the others and announced, "Signor Console need not report personally. The rest of you will report for him."

I decided to press my luck. "I must let the Swiss Legation know where we are. Where is there a telephone?"

"No, no telephone!" he exclaimed.

I adopted a slightly more aggressive tone. "I am asking nothing more than my right to communicate with the protecting power. Why do you deny my request?"

"Signor Console, please understand. We don't have a telephone," he said, almost ashamedly.

Noting the Secretary's discomfort, Signorina Vera stepped in. "Signore," she said acidly, "we have telephones here in the hotel. But because of the war, they are not working. Even the telephone at the carabiniere station is out of order," she added.

The Secretary then beat a hasty retreat, leaving us to Signorina Vera's ministrations. After informing us of the meal times, and that we were expected to report for meals punctually, she led us up the staircase to our rooms. Throwing open the door to a tiny, cell-like room, she indicated Nancy and Amy were to share it.

"Gawd!" said Amy, stepping in and glancing around. Finding no facility in the room, she said, "Walter, ask where the bathrooms are, for heaven's sake!" In response to my query, Signorina Vera pointed down the hallway, and the girls quickly headed that way. Then she took Lester into a slightly larger room. The last, and largest, of the three rooms was reserved for me alone, befitting my status and rank. The wardrobe in my room was massive and took up as much space as half the room allotted to Nancy and Amy.

As soon as Signorina Vera left us, I went back down to Lester's room. "Lester," I said, "I've got a huge room. Why don't you bunk in with me, and we'll let Amy have this room? That way, each of the girls will have her own space. My room is plenty big enough for the two of us." As he hesitated, I added, "This is awfully hard on them, you know."

"All right, Walter," he said, reluctantly, picking up his bags. We started unpacking, with great sighs from Lester, and I began to regret my generous gesture. Lester would be a gloomy roommate, I knew. He had done nothing but whine since we left Monaco. However, I couldn't deal with having this huge room all to myself, knowing the two girls were crammed into one tiny cubicle.

It was good to be out of that damned freezing wind, even though the room was damp and unheated and the chill penetrated to the bone. I wandered around, repeatedly stopping to lay my hand on the cold radiator, as if my touch might conjure some heat from its surface. Aside from the armàdio, the massive, free-standing wardrobe, the rest of the room's sparse furnishings consisted of a small dresser, a washstand with porcelain pitcher and washbasin, and a square wooden lamp table between two narrow iron bedsteads. A table with one straight-backed wooden chair stood in front of the single window overlooking the small, unkempt garden below. The brown ceramic tile floor was devoid of even a small bedside carpet to cushion the shock to bare feet on a cold morning. All in all, it was a dreary, uninviting haven.

There was no such thing as a private bathroom. The hotel's only bath was down the hall and around the corner from our rooms. I went to check it out. Its ancient cast iron tub, housed in an unheated room, was plumbed for cold water only. The toilet, installed in a separate little cubicle right next to the room with the tub, was in keeping with the medieval character of Gubbio. When the flush chain on the commode was pulled, the rush and roar of water, out of all proportion to its effectiveness at flushing, echoed around the chamber itself and could be heard throughout the hotel.

I took stock. Our clothing situation was pitiful. Lester didn't own a single garment suited for this rough winter climate, not even a pair of woolen socks. The girls and I had little better. We needed to buy or acquire warm clothing, and quickly. Winter in these mountains would be fierce. Soon it was dinnertime, and Signorina Vera's order that we be on time for meals was superfluous. We were famished.

Amy's eyes were red-rimmed, and I knew she had been crying, but she said nothing, and no one mentioned it to her. Nancy was hoarse, and she sneezed frequently. I, too, had the scratchy throat that signaled a cold was brewing. We filed quietly into the dining room. Signorina Vera pulled a wooden screen into place around our corner table, concealing us from view of the other patrons. We were served a cup of thin, bland, minestrone soup, then a plate of gray pasta, accompanied by broiled onions and chunks of coarse, hard bread. Ersatz coffee followed, and we were able to soften the bread somewhat, to make it edible, by dunking it in the murky brown liquid. As unappetizing as the meal was, we forced down as much as we could, to fill our stomachs. There was little conversation, and we wasted no time in returning directly to our rooms following "dinner." Sleep came quickly and heavily to all of us that first night.

The next morning, while Amy, Nancy, and Lester went out to make their first "report-in" to the Secretary, I drafted a letter to the Swiss delegation in Rome, appealing for assistance. "This location is unacceptable as a place of internment for civilians of diplomatic rank," I wrote. "Also, we are all sick with colds and in need of medical attention and warm clothing. We are not getting any of these things from the Italian authorities. Most of all, we need Italian lire to buy clothes and medicine." I had just finished when the others returned. "What's Gubbio like?" I asked.

"Grubbio, but interesting. You won't get lost," was Nancy's succinct reply.

I set out across the piazza to deliver my letter to the Secretary for forwarding to the Swiss, welcoming an opportunity to get out and stretch my legs. "How can I exchange some dollars or francs for lire, so that we can purchase necessities, like medicine and warm clothing?" I asked him.

The Secretary shook his head dubiously. "I do not think that will be possible, Signor Console," he said.

"Well, why don't you make every effort to make it possible!" I snapped. "We're all sick, and we don't have any warm clothes! You wouldn't want us to die while you're responsible for us, would you?"

"No, no, Signor Console!" he agreed nervously. "I will contact my superiors and see what can be done in this regard."

I walked out and went to explore the town.

An ancient, walled city, Gubbio was a cloistered mass of gray stone buildings, with orange clay tile roofs. It appeared to have stood still in time. During my walk, I saw fifteenth-century bronze tablets that placed activity at the site of Gubbio as far back as the second century B.C. As I wandered around and ascended the hill upon which the town sat, I came upon the street called "Via dei Consoli" (street of the consuls). Meandering along it, I noticed that some of the older houses had the "porta del morto" of ancient Italian culture—a secondary door above, or next to, the main door, which was purported to be used only for removing dead bodies. It was an ancient belief that it was a bad omen to take a dead body out through the main front door of a home.

Retracing my steps back to the main piazza, I saw that shops lined both sides of the square. Pausing in front of each, I peered in the window to see what kind of shop it was and what the merchandise was like, though I had no Italian lire with which to buy anything. I was pleased to find a "farmacia" (drugstore) among the many pottery shops, although it looked like it would offer little in the way of modern medicines. There were several smaller piazzas in lower Gubbio, down the slope from the Piazza della Signoria.

When I got back to the hotel, Isa, the chambermaid, was there cleaning my room. She was old, but how old was a matter of conjecture. Barely five feet tall, she was almost equally that in width, and garbed in the traditional head-to-foot black of the peasants, with her gray hair drawn back in the inevitable bun. She began chattering the minute I entered the room, and continued nonstop as she mopped, cleaned, and made the beds.

I learned her family history—that she was a widow, with two sons sent to war in Greece. They were reported missing, and feared dead. Every day I listened to Isa's tale sympathetically, asking a pertinent question now and then. By the third day, I decided she might be the local ally I needed. Going to the armàdio, I took out a bar of laundry soap and gave it to her. She was overwhelmed—and left, praising me to the heavens and imprecating the saints to bestow blessings on me. Thereafter I made it a point to be in my room every morning when she arrived, and every day I found some little thing to give her. She was always happy and grateful. After ten days, I asked, "Isa, could you possibly do me one small favor?"

"Certainly, Signor Console," she replied, "if I can, I will."

"I need two stamped postcards," I told her. "Can you get them for me? I want to write to an old friend, and I don't feel like sending it through that nosy Fascist Secretary." I didn't add that I wasn't allowed to use the postal system, but she had leaped ahead of me with peasant shrewdness.

"Not for Fascist bastards to read," she declared, with a fierce expression, turning her head and making a spitting sound. "Don't worry, I fix for you, Signor Console."

I got my first glimmer of how the peasantry hated and mistrusted the Fascists, and the government in general. Playing a trick on them was a pleasure for old Isa, and she smiled conspiratorially as she waddled away.

The next morning, she slyly pulled two stamped postcards out from under her voluminous black apron, raising her eyebrows and rolling her eyes theatrically. I thanked her profusely, and while she nattered on with her daily litany about her dead husband and missing sons, I quickly wrote a message in Italian on one of the cards and addressed it to my old friend Manfred Metzger in Trieste. "Here we are in Gubbio," I wrote. "We don't get out as much as before. The war is hard on our pocketbooks, and we must bundle up against the cold. Hope you are enjoying the ping-pong table. Regards, Felice." I gave the card to Isa, and she assured me she'd get it mailed. A few days later, I gave her the second card, with a similar message, again mentioning the ping-pong table. Before leaving Trieste in 1941, I had given an Abercrombie & Fitch table tennis set to Manfred. I knew that if anyone in Europe could help us, it would be Manfred Metzger. Scion of a wealthy family of Austrian merchants, he had been born in Trieste, which was then a part of Austria. Manfred already had everything anyone could want from life when I first met him in 1938. About three inches shorter than me, he had a stocky build, with a broad chest and powerful legs. He wore his straight sandy hair parted on the left and combed neatly over. It always looked well groomed, in contrast to my thick and unruly dark brown locks. Where my face was craggy and square-jawed, Manfred's was softer and rounded, punctuated by pale blue Nordic eyes and an aristocratic, aquiline nose. He had an air about him that demanded a second look. Wherever he was, and in whatever he did, Manfred never took a back seat to anyone. Gregarious and fun-loving, he liked nothing better than playing tricks or practical jokes on his friends.

We were both young, physically fit, and adventurous by nature, and on weekends in Trieste (where I had served as Vice-Consul from 1937 to 1941) we'd often hike out into the Carso, a vast, stony wasteland extending from the outskirts of the city. Manfred, always competitive, was also a daredevil, giving his utmost to anything he undertook. He was an accomplished horseman, a skilled skier, a fearless bobsledder, and an excellent yachtsman.

Once, when we were out hiking, he bet me that he could jump a deep, rocky chasm. I half-heartedly took the bet, and without hesitation he jumped, landing on his feet on the other side. "All right, Walt," he called, laughing, "now it's your turn—double or nothing!"

I looked down at the yawning chasm, which seemed a mile wide. "Are you nuts?" I said.

"Come on, don't be such an old woman!" he challenged.

Stung, I took a deep breath and jumped, falling to my knees as I landed, barely clearing the edge of the precipice. I scrambled forward on my hands and knees to keep from falling back into the chasm.

Manfred was laughing uproariously, already reaching for his wallet to pay me off.

"You bastard!" I said, laughing with relief, "I'll never bet you again—on anything! You're crazy as hell! It's a wonder you're still alive!"

Miraculously, Manfred managed to stay very much alive. He had been to visit me the previous spring, shopping for an apartment in Monaco. He looked dapper as always, and why not? He was outfitted by the finest tailors in Milan. We had a fine time together, and when he left he gave me a beautiful, solid gold Vacheron-Constantin watch, which I treasured and was still wearing. I knew I had no better or more faithful friend in all of Europe than Manfred Metzger.

Technically, with Austria now under German rule, he was on the other side, but I knew he would help me if he possibly could. I felt sure that in his heart he probably sided with the Allies. With the war effort on, I also felt confident that Manfred would have credentials, owing to the family tank-car business, that would permit him to travel widely and with few restrictions. He spoke French, German, and Italian so impeccably that one could only speculate about which of the three was actually his native tongue.

After Isa mailed the cards, we settled in and waited. We had no choice. Without help from Manfred or the Swiss Legation, we couldn't do much of anything. The weather was so cold we could rarely go outdoors in our lightweight clothing. Our luggage from Monaco, which the Italians promised was "on its way," had not arrived, so we had only the Spartan portions of food Signorina Vera served us in the hotel dining room. Amy summed up the daily menu in one succinct word—"hideous." There was little or no news of the war, or for that matter, of the world. There were no newspapers. Once in a while, an outdated copy of the Vatican newspaper, *L'Osservatore Romano,* would be left in the lobby, and I'd pounce on it, devouring every word. It was as if we were living in a dream, out of sight and out of touch with the real world.

Inevitably, boredom set in. Nancy decided to learn Italian and studied with me every day. An Italian version of the life of Winston Churchill, which I had discovered abandoned in a dark corner of the lobby, served as our training manual. We also played cards, mostly Hearts. Lester, who played mechanically and with little interest, was almost invariably the loser. He remained gloomy and depressed, always lamenting the fate that had befallen him. Amy barely tolerated him, calling him "very heavy weather." When she got fed up with his whining, she'd start cutting him to ribbons with her dry, sardonic wit. He seemed impervious to everything—even that.

About two weeks after I had given the first postcard to Isa, Lester and I were awakened early one morning by a gentle but insistent rapping on the door. I looked at my watch. It was barely five A.M. Even the Fascist Secretary wouldn't be out at this hour of the morning. It must be the girls. Shivering in the predawn cold, I pulled on my pants, scampered across the icy floor, and yanked the door open. A gaunt little man in a gray suit, carrying a valise, rushed past me into the room. I stood transfixed, my jaw dropping. Lester salt bolt upright in bed, his eyes wide with fright.

The man was struggling for breath, like a runner after a thousand-meter dash. Without a word, he hurried to the window and peered out, then scurried back to the door, looking up and down the corridor. Satisfied, he turned back into the room, and gasped out, "Mr. Metzger, he send me . . . he command me . . . he tell Signora Orbaw where you are . . . Mr. Metzger he keep in touch. . . ." Still stuttering and stammering, he turned his suitcase upside down about a foot over my bed, and scores of lire notes fluttered out of it. The valise empty, the little man turned, and without another word bolted out the door. I realized how terrified he must have been at the risk he was compelled to take, but I was of course relieved to know that Manfred had somehow managed to get word of my whereabouts to Marguerite. At least she'd know I was alive, and reasonably safe, so far.

As soon as the man was gone, Lester and I pounced on the money and began counting it. There was at least a thousand dollars worth of lire there! Lester ran up the hall to wake the girls. They immediately began devising shopping lists. "We'll have to be very careful," I warned them. "We can't do any wild spending when the market opens on Monday. Try to restrain yourselves, girls," I chided, chuckling at their enthusiasm. They wore the first smiles I had seen in weeks and were chattering together about what to buy. "Put your biggest necessities at the top of the list, and we'll try to get those taken care of," I said. In my own mind, I was determined to do something special for all of them for Christmas, which was drawing near.

To cover our windfall of lire, I asked the Secretary to arrange a meeting for me with a local banker to discuss a loan. I told him I was willing to put up American dollars as collateral. At the Monte Dei Paschi bank, I was ushered into the office of the short, swarthy Signor Meletti. I said, "I need to negotiate a loan." He waited politely for me to continue. "We are ill, and we need winter clothes and medicine. I expect that very soon we will be receiving funds on a regular basis through the Swiss." I took a hundred-dollar bill from my pocket and placed it on his desk. "I am willing to put this money up as collateral for whatever funds you are willing to loan me, Signor Meletti," I said.

He picked up the bill and fingered it for a moment, saying nothing. Then he went to the door and called for a clerk. "I will loan you 12,000 lire against this hundred-dollar note, Signor Console, at interest until you repay the loan."

I agreed, and we processed the loan in standard fashion. My transaction in Lisbon was again paying me dividends. I was glad I had insisted on some American dollars and that I had managed to keep them with me. As soon as we left the bank and rounded a corner, safely out of sight, we hugged each other, happy for our sudden stroke of good fortune. I gave everyone money, and they went off to shop. Fortunately, it was also market day. I headed for the farmacia to get some medicine for our colds, then to find woolen sweaters and socks. We all ran into each other again at the clothing store, and after making our purchases, we headed toward the hotel, in high spirits. Even Lester was smiling, for a change.

"Ooh! Look!" cried Nancy suddenly. She stopped and pointed at the window of the butcher shop, where a big turkey was on display. We moved closer and stared, pangs of homesickness knifing through us. It was holiday time, and we wanted that turkey. I made a mental note to use some of Manfred's money to bribe the hotel cook and buy that turkey for our Christmas dinner. Bless Manfred! Without him, life would be bleak indeed.

Back at the hotel, I pulled a chair up to the window and sat looking out at the small walled garden. I lit one of the two cigars I had treated myself to at the tobacconist, and puffed contentedly. I smoked quietly and thought about the day in Monaco when the Italians had first come through on their way to Toulon. Marino had come from Nice to bring some more things from the villa and to drive me to an appointment with Prince Louis. Dressed in my best business suit, I was seated in the rear of the Studebaker, with

Marino, in full chauffeur's uniform, at the wheel. The American flag fluttered from one standard at the front of the car, the consular flag from the other. Pulling out of the hotel garage, we encountered a solid line of Italian military vehicles moving at a slow crawl along the Lower Corniche. We had to get into this line of traffic to reach the Palace. After waiting more than five minutes for a break, I ordered Marino to move in on it. As a pair of Italian motorcyclists pulled abreast of us, he gunned the motor and wedged the car in between them. Then, instead of riding two abreast, one led and one followed the big black car flying the American flags. The enemy was unwittingly providing a motorcycle escort for us! I chuckled and remarked to Marino on the irony of it all, as the lead motorcyclist, throwing his arm in the air with his hand doubled into a fist, shouted something unintelligible.

The curious crowds of Monegasques, who had gathered to watch the procession of Italian invaders, smiled, cheered, and waved as our car came into view. Marino rolled down his window to wave back, and the cheering increased. The tension I had felt when we entered the line of traffic began to abate, and I felt a swell of pride in what my country represented to the world—freedom and happiness.

"Oh boy, Signor Console, will I have something to tell my grandchildren!" exclaimed the normally taciturn Marino.

"So will I, Marino," I had replied, "so will I."

The tables had certainly turned since that day. I was snapped back to the present as an old peasant woman suddenly appeared in the garden below. Without ceremony, she found a likely spot, hiked her skirts, and squatted. Apparently the hotel garden was the only facility available for the wives of the farmers come to market. The scene reminded me of a Brueghel painting. There was a peace and permanence about it, and about this place. How many centuries, I wondered, had seen this same scene? If it weren't for the homesickness, the deprivations, and the restrictions placed on us, one could almost forget we were prisoners, in the midst of a terrible war.

Before I knew it, it was Christmas Eve. The turkey had been sold, and there was nothing decent left in the shops. I made a feeble attempt to decorate our desolate little room with bits of colored paper. I was depressed and didn't want the company of the others. I wanted to be home with Marguerite and little Howard for Christmas. My spirits were at an all-time low. I was sitting slumped in a chair, staring into space, feeling sorry for myself, when there was a brusque knock at the door. I opened it to find Signorina Vera and two men, with our baggage from Monaco. Excitedly, we began to unpack the goods.

"Wow!" Nancy exclaimed, "look at this! Ham!" Triumphantly, she held up a canned ham that had not been purloined.

"That will be Christmas dinner," I declared, pleased.

"And look! Here's some cheese!" cried Amy, "and coffee, too!"

They were like children at a Christmas tree, and suddenly I found myself choking back tears. I gave each of the girls a bar of soap and told them to go pretty themselves up and come back that evening for a Christmas Eve celebration. What that would be, I wasn't sure, but I knew I had to pull one together for all of us.

I walked quickly along the streets of Gubbio, feeling frustrated and angry. Why in hell hadn't we heard from the Swiss? Why in hell hadn't they, or someone, done anything about getting us out of here? As I turned blindly into a small piazza, the tantalizing smell of bread assailed my nostrils. I looked into the window of the bakeshop, and there sat a big, beautiful pannetone, the traditional Italian Christmas bread. My mouth watered at the sight of it. It was high and golden, studded with jewels of citron and plump, crisp nuts, and capped with snowy sugar, and I knew this was the perfect treat for Christmas Eve. I splurged on two bottles of spumante at the wine shop. Then I searched out a hardware store and grabbed up the one hot plate in stock, along with a couple of pots and pans. My shopping was finished.

Exiting the hardware store, I found myself at the end of the piazza where the church was. I stepped inside. In the dim light, I could see the flickering votive candles and the festively decorated altar. Several old peasant women, swathed in black from head to toe, knelt in prayer, silently fingering their rosaries. They seemed impervious to the bone-penetrating cold that emanated from the stone walls and floor of the unheated church. On a step near the altar was a "precipio," a manger scene, made of beautifully detailed ceramic statues. I stood there, awkwardly holding my packages, looking down at the exquisite tableau of the little Family, and felt tears welling in my eyes. I thought of Marguerite and Howard, safe and warm at home in Virginia, and of the families in the barbed-wire enclosed park in Nice and the cattle cars that had taken them away to God only knew what fate. Suddenly I felt ashamed of my frustration. "Thank you, Lord," I whispered. Saying a silent prayer that we'd all survive and return to our loved ones soon, I turned and tiptoed out past the kneeling women. Their prayers, voiced in a different tongue, probably reflected the same fervent hope for peace as mine. With lighter heart, I headed back to the hotel, eager to surprise the others with a Christmas Eve treat.

They weren't around when I got back. Good! I unpacked my purchases and began setting up my "kitchen." I cleared off the washstand for the hot plate. A shelf in the armoire would serve as a pantry, and the window ledge would make a fine refrigerator. I opened the window and put the bottle of wine out to chill. Next, I dug into one of the trunks and found the little coffee mill I had bought years ago in Trieste. I didn't know how to use it—preparing and grinding coffee had always been our cook's job.

I carefully spread a layer of precious green coffee beans across the bottom of a pan and put the pan on the hot plate, over low heat. Soon the smell of roasted coffee beans filled the room. What a treat! I hoped I would know when the beans were roasted enough. I hummed a few bars of "Deck the Halls" as I draped a clean linen towel over the little table and set four plates out on it. If Marguerite and the servants could only see me now, I thought to myself—they'd never believe it!

When the coffee beans started oozing oil, I judged them to be roasted enough and took them off the stove to cool. Then I poured them into the mill, ground them, and stored all but two tablespoons of the ground coffee in an empty jar to use later. I filled my new pot with water, and after tying the fresh coffee grounds into one of my linen handkerchiefs, I heated the water and set the coffee in it to brew. That done, I wrapped the presents in some blue tissue I had found at the market and settled down in happy anticipation to await the others. I didn't have long to wait. Without a knock, the door burst open, and the girls hurried in.

"Walter, we smell something—what's going on?" cried Nancy.

They both stopped, astounded at the scene before them. Pinned to the curtains was a crudely lettered sign. "Welcome to Trattoria Gualtiero" (Walter's Cafe). The wrapped presents were stacked next to my chair. On each plate at the table was a thick slice of pannetone and a slab of butter, and each place had a cup for coffee and a glass for wine.

"Oh, Walter, how wonderful!" exclaimed Amy. "How did you ever do all this?"

"Coffee!" squealed Nancy, hanging over the pot and inhaling deeply. "I can't believe it! Real coffee! What a Christmas present!" She dashed over and hugged me. "Oh Walter! Thank you! Thank you!" Then, "Wait! We'll be right back," she said, and they both dashed out, returning a minute later with their own brightly wrapped presents. The room was cold as always, but the steam from the coffee, and the smell of it, gave us a feeling of warmth and coziness. When Lester arrived a few minutes later, he found us in a happy mood that even his usual depression could not dampen, and we soon had him laughing with us. I proudly poured a round of my freshly roasted and brewed coffee, and we all attacked the pannetone. Nothing ever tasted so good, before or since, as that one small cup of hot, real coffee and that first meltingly delicious mouthful of sweet, light, buttery pannetone. I retrieved the chilled spumante from the windowsill, uncorked it with a grand flourish, and we toasted one another and sipped it as we opened our gifts. We had all had the same thought—everyone gave something warm to wear. At midnight, the church bells rang out. We looked at each other silently, out thoughts inevitably turning to our loved ones far away, and our tenuous situation.

Nancy was the first to speak and break the spell. Jumping to her feet, she proclaimed, "I'm stuffed like a toad! I'm going to bed. 'Night everyone! Thanks for a wonderful Christmas, Walter." She hugged me warmly, and I hugged her back. The other two rose and gathered up their things.

"Pannetone for Christmas breakfast, and more coffee!" I promised. It wasn't such a bad Christmas after all, I reflected, as I turned off the lights and settled in to sleep. Lester was already snoring.

The year 1943 entered raging, spewing forth bitter cold and wind. Amy, though generally cheerful and helpful, seemed to have few hobbies or interests. She spent much of her time making observations about the local men, primping, and sniping at Lester. What she did otherwise, day in and day out, I had no idea. She declined to accompany Nancy and me when, on days when we could stand the cold, we'd venture out to walk. Every night, she painstakingly wound every strand of her hair onto metal curlers, and every day she appeared with the same immaculately coiffed head of light brown ringlets. She was extremely worldly, in a social sense. I knew that she was a friend of Somerset Maugham and had often frequented his villa on the Riviera. A rather cool, solitary person, Amy never revealed her age to anyone, but kept herself so well-groomed she seemed younger than she probably was. On most days she could easily pass for a woman in her late thirties.

One brisk morning in mid-January, when Nancy had begged off from our walk, pleading a cold, I set out alone. I decided to exercise by making the steep, two-kilometer climb from the cathedral up to the twelfth-century monastery of San Ubaldo, located near the summit of Monte Ingino. I had only gone a few steps, when I heard "Psst! Walter!" from somewhere nearby. My scalp prickled. There was no one within my range of vision. I turned carefully, quickly scanning the area around me as I did. I almost jumped with shock. There, at the hotel entrance, casually leaning against the wall, stood Manfred Metzger!

Dapper as ever, he was wearing a tan cashmere topcoat over his business suit. On his head was a fashionable brown fedora, and his expensive Italian leather shoes were polished to a high gloss. He stood out among the poor natives of Gubbio like a sore thumb.

"Go away!" I hissed. "Are you crazy?"

Manfred just looked at me. "Walter, dear friend . . . ," he began.

With as much urgency as I could muster, I cut him off. "Go away! You're crazy to come here! It's too dangerous!"

Manfred, shrugging, stepped to my side. "Walk along with me," he said in a low voice. I fell into step with him and we continued down the street. "Tell me what I can do for you—Felice." His tone was slightly mocking, and although I didn't dare turn my head to look, I knew there was probably a grin on his face. I didn't speak. Furious, frightened at the risk he was taking, I turned abruptly and began walking away from him toward the upper gate of the town. He quickly caught up with me.

"Metzger, you're mad," I whispered tersely. "I'm watched constantly! You run the risk of being arrested!"

"Hey, mon cher ami, relax! Talk normally. I'm just a stranger here, looking for directions."

"How did you get here?" I asked.

"Why, I'm here for perfectly legitimate reasons, Walter," he responded, grinning. "I'm here to buy wine. My papers allow me to go almost anywhere I want."

"How did you find me? How did you know where to look?" I asked.

"It was easy. You're quite a celebrity here. I just asked an old man where they keep the American prisoner. He told me all about you, and that you go for walks every morning in good weather."

"Were you able to contact Marguerite?" I inquired anxiously.

"Yes, dear friend, she knows where you are and that I am in touch with you."

I felt a wave of relief. "How can I ever thank you, or repay you, Manfred?" I exclaimed in a low whisper, "You don't know what the money you sent us has meant to us. We still haven't gotten any funds from the Swiss Legation."

"Don't worry about it, Walter," he replied. "I'll do everything I can. At the moment, it's too sticky to attempt anything official, but I wanted to see you myself and see how you are. Here. This will keep the wolves at bay." Thrusting a small packet into my coat pocket, he turned down a narrow side street and disappeared. I shook my head in wonder and disbelief. Only Metzger, I thought, could get away with something like this.

Several days later, I decided to go to the bank and redeem my hundred-dollar bill. In the packet Manfred had given me was more than enough to tide us all over until the Swiss Legation started sending us funds. Arriving at the bank, I was ushered into Meletti's office. "Buongiorno, Signor Meletti," I said cordially, shaking hands with him. "I'm here to pay back my loan and redeem my hundred-dollar bill." Meletti looked startled. Then he launched into a protracted monologue about Italian banking practices, the complex accounting procedures, and the terrible bureaucratic red tape that surrounded everything. I listened politely, then repeated why I had come. "So if you will get me my hundred-dollar bill, I'll be happy to have this note paid up," I concluded.

"Signore," Meletti replied, as if speaking to a simpleton, "you do not understand. This is now a new year."

"Excuse me," I said, "but what does it being a new year have to do with me paying off my loan? I insist you adhere to the terms of our written agreement."

Hearing this, Meletti flew into a rage. "You!" he screamed. "You are one to talk about violating agreements! You and your Jew-loving President Roosevelt! You Americans think you own the world! Hah! Now you are no longer masters of the world! It's high time you were humbled, and shown a thing or two! Agreements! Pah! You deserve whatever you get, filthy American!" He slammed his open palm down on the desk.

Infuriated, wanting nothing more than to reach across and strangle him, but knowing any move I made would be dangerous to all of us, I turned on my heel and stomped out, slamming the door as I went. I could hear Meletti still ranting and raving as I left the bank. I vowed that if ever the chance came, I'd show him a thing or two.

My mood lightened somewhat the next day, when we finally got a note from the Swiss Legation in Rome. They expressed surprise about our arrest and internment in Italy, making me wonder about the communication system, and said they were prepared to remit each of us up to 5,000 lire monthly (around $250) against signed receipts. The best news was "we are requesting permission from the Italian Ministry of Foreign Affairs to send a delegation to meet with you as soon as possible." We were convinced that now that the Swiss in Rome were involved, and knew our whereabouts, we would be released shortly. Amy started a betting pool on the date.

I wrote back immediately, requesting additional funds, informing them that conditions of our internment were primitive, and suggesting that we be moved to Rome as quickly as possible. The days and weeks dragged by, and we heard nothing more. Finally, in mid-February, we were visited by two members of the Swiss Legation. We were overjoyed. Just to talk to someone from the real world, the world outside this ancient, isolated hill town, was a treat beyond imagining, and we devoured every scrap of news they gave us.

"What about getting us exchanged or released?" I asked the senior representative, Mr. Antonini.

"That is a ticklish situation, at the moment, Mr. Orebaugh," he replied. "The Italians want the members of their Armistice Commission, who are prisoners of the Allies in North Africa, recognized as candidates for exchange with you. The Americans claim that as a diplomat serving in a neutral country, your seizure and arrest was illegal and a gross violation of international law. They want you released forthwith, with no terms, exchanges, or restrictions imposed. The Italian Armistice Commission numbers 120. Many of them are high-ranking members of the Italian government. You can see what a complex situation we have here. I'm afraid your release is not imminent, since your government adamantly refuses to negotiate on the basis of an exchange."

My spirits fell. We were in a far more precarious position than I had thought, now that I was of bargaining value to the enemy.

Fortunately, the Swiss agreed with me that Gubbio, and the Albergo San Marco, were far below minimum acceptable standards for our internment. "We shall certainly express our distress at the accommodations and treatment you are being accorded, and we will seek to get you transferred immediately to a more acceptable location," said Antonini, as he shook hands to take his leave.

"Please try to get us moved to Rome," I implored. "I think that that would be best in the event that an exchange is ever considered. The young women, especially, should be moved to a safer place."

"You have my assurance I will do all in my power," he replied.

When March arrived, with no further word, we were feeling more discouraged and depressed than ever. March 19th was my thirty-third birthday. Out of the blue, the two Swiss reappeared, accompanied by two uniformed Italians. We greeted Antonini and his companion effusively. "Please go and pack your things, Signori," said one of the Italians politely. "We will be moving you today."

"Today?" I was elated. "To Rome?" I asked.

"No. To Perugia," he replied. "I think you will find your accommodations there satisfactory."

Although I was disappointed we weren't going to Rome, where I'd have better channels to work on our release, I was happy to be leaving Gubbio. I hurried to find the others and give them the news. None of us had ever been to Perugia, but we all agreed that whatever it had to offer would probably be better than Gubbio, and the cold, sleazy rooms, the tasteless food, and the noisy, inadequate plumbing of the Albergo San Marco.

3

Transfer to Perugia

Our transfer by train to Perugia, about fifty kilometers to the south and westward, went smoothly enough. The two Swiss representatives stayed with us, and the uniformed Italians, municipal guards from Perugia, kept discreetly in the background. We were taken by police car from the train station to the "questura," or police headquarters. There, I was treated with deferential respect by the officer in charge. "Of course, Signor Console, you are excused from the requirement to sign in our register daily," he hastened to inform me. After a brief orientation about our restrictions and about the town, during which I learned that there were over 1,000 foreign internees being held there, the officer handed each of us a small brochure giving detailed descriptions of the major points of historical interest in the area.

This polite and cordial treatment, such a marked contrast to what we had experienced before, made us feel more like tourists than prisoners. The feeling was reinforced when we entered the Hotel Brufani, only a short walk from the questura. Its simple, mustard-color stone exterior belied the opulent expanse of white marble and gleaming mahogany, accented with shining brass, that struck our eyes upon entering the lobby. Nancy gasped as she glanced around, taking in the gilded, red velvet chairs, the sparkling chandeliers, the beautiful tables. Everything spoke of timeless luxury. It was a complete contrast to what we had just left in Gubbio. The five stories of the hotel, the registration clerk informed us, encompassed a ground floor of public rooms, including a bar and large dining room, three floors of guest rooms, and the top floor, which housed the hotel staff.

He apologized profusely for the limitations the war had placed on the quality of service the hotel was accustomed to offering its guests. "I am so sorry to tell you, Signore, that hot water is available only from eight o'clock in the morning until eight o'clock in the evening. From time to time, we must make substitutions in the items on the menu, due to shortages. Also, we have had to curtail the hours when the bar is open. It is open only from five o'clock in the evening until nine." Our registration completed, he rang for a porter to come and carry the luggage to our rooms. Nancy, Amy, Lester, and I looked at each other. Porters? Hot water? Bar? Menu?

"My God, if Signorina Vera could only see this," I whispered to Nancy, "she'd keel over!"

"Pinch me so I'll know I'm not dreaming!" she whispered back. She and Amy kept looking around, as if at any moment someone would come and say it was all a mistake.

We were shown to our rooms on the second floor. We each had our own room. Nancy's, Amy's, and mine were all to the back of the hotel, overlooking the well-tended garden. Lester's was to the front, overlooking the square. Best of all, there was actually heat coming out of the radiators! Not as much as we would have liked, but at least enough to take the worst of the chill out of the atmosphere. We wouldn't have to wear coats all day, as we had been forced to do at the unheated Albergo San Marco. We were grateful to find that each of our rooms boasted its own reasonably modern bathroom. What luxury! We decided that a hot bath was the one thing we all wanted first, even though it was already past lunchtime and we were pretty hungry.

I unpacked and surveyed my new home. My large, high-ceilinged quarters were partitioned into two rooms—a tastefully furnished bedroom and a small sitting room. The sitting room opened to the hotel corridor, and the bedroom had a small balcony overlooking the well-tended garden and the undulating Umbrian plain. I opened the doors and stepped onto the balcony for a look around. Like many of the ancient cities of Italy, Perugia was walled and built on the crest of a hill, for protection from invaders. From my vantage point on the balcony, I could see the city roofs and the monochromatic brown of barren hills, dotted here and there with sparse patches of green forest, stretching into the distance. It was a peaceful, pastoral scene that made it difficult to believe the circumstances that had transpired to land me there.

In the dining room, we were courteously and quickly ushered to a table, which, the maggiordomo (maitre d') informed us, would be our table throughout our stay. "You may order anything you like from the menu," he said, "and if you wish something special, it is possible to request it— for a consideration, of course."

"Of course," I echoed, trying not to laugh at the stunned looks on the faces of Lester and the girls.

"May I suggest a wine, Signore?" he continued.

I thought Amy's eyebrows would rise up into her hairline. "I don't believe this," said Nancy, incredulous. "Now I KNOW I'm asleep and dreaming!"

I ignored her and selected a wine for our lunch from the list. That evening, I invited the others to join me in the bar for an aperitif before dinner.

"But of course—how kind of you to ask us," responded Nancy, laughing gaily.

Then we adjourned to our table in the dining room, where we dined on an excellent antipasto, rich chicken soup, and roast squab. Cheese and fruit were offered for dessert, along with coffee. If it hadn't been for signs pointing the way to the air raid shelter, it would have been hard to tell that a war was going on. Only the coffee, which was thin and bitter, reflected any wartime shortages. The mushy gray pasta, hard coarse bread, and hostile atmosphere of the Albergo San Marco seemed worlds distant, instead of a mere fifty-nine kilometers away.

Life in Perugia settled into a comfortable routine. I ran into Jack Kutsukian, an old acquaintance from Trieste. He and his wife Florence were also interned in the Brufani. Jack, an expatriate metals and machinery dealer, knew the black market better than anyone and could get us almost anything but coffee. He kept the wardrobe in their room crammed with fresh eggs, cheeses, butter, honey, olive oil, and even fresh sausages and meat! There were things there we hadn't seen since leaving the States, and they often invited us for breakfast or dinner to share some of their bounty. Florence Kutsukian made us the world's best rice pudding, in an old coffeepot.

We also relished having more news, as well as more contact with the outside world. We attended the movie theater once, unsure of whether or not it was "allowed." The newsreel was so propagandistic, I snorted out loud in disgust, earning me a sharp jab in the ribs from Nancy. However, we could glean from what we saw that things were not going well for the Axis forces. A reference to "strategic withdrawal and regrouping" suggested that the Allies were at last gaining in North Africa. I was also able to initiate more frequent contact with the Swiss Legation in Rome. When I managed to get through the quirky Italian phone system to them in April, I was assured that a Mr. Riva would be coming to Perugia shortly to discuss our situation.

All in all, we agreed, this was the best way to sit out a war, if we couldn't be home. Manfred learned of our new location and sent one of his "clerks" with a large basket of food. Food, to someone of Manfred's tastes, unacquainted with deprivation of any kind, included such things as pâté with truffles, pickled quail eggs, tiny cocktail sausages, and chocolates. We laughed as we unpacked these treasures, the most precious being a store of Swiss coffee.

A few weeks later, stepping out of the Brufani for my morning walk, I spotted Manfred's distinctive green Willys, with its 1938 New York license plate, parked in front of the bank next to the hotel. Seated at the wheel, smiling and waving as though seeing me was the most ordinary of social occurrences, was Manfred himself! He beckoned me over. "Hello, old friend, good to see you've moved to something more civilized. Did you get my packages?"

"Manfred," I replied, "you know I'm always happy to see you, and yes I got your most welcome food package. But don't you realize how dangerous it is for you to be seen here, talking to me? How do you manage to get around like this? With a license plate that is four years out of date, to boot?"

"You worry too much about details, Walter, as always," he replied genially. "There is no law regulating foreign license plates in Italy. This plate is good for as long as it is on the car. Come on, we'll go to your hotel and have a drink together. I have to call some clients."

Manfred went on to tell me how he had managed to acquire the code words for getting through on the long distance military networks. "It only backfired on me once, a few months ago," he said. "They changed the code, or I had the wrong words. Anyway, I thought I was being put through to my associate in France, and instead I was connected with Hitler's staff headquarters in Berlin! That was a surprise!" He chuckled at the memory. "So, Walter, would you like me to call the Führer and tell him to send you home?" I couldn't help chuckling with him at that idea. His visit certainly perked me up and restored my flagging spirits. Our conditions were a thousand times better than they had been in Gubbio, but being a prisoner, restricted to one place, not knowing what the next day or the next week would bring, was not easy.

A few days later, I found Nancy in a foul mood, something I hadn't seen before. We all kept a small supply of food in our armàdios, the massive, freestanding clothes cabinets that served in lieu of built-in closets in most European homes and hotels. Nancy had stored a jar of honey, a precious commodity from one of Manfred's packages, on a shelf in hers. Somehow, it had tipped over and dripped honey all over her clothes. Amy and I couldn't help laughing as she described her reaction when she first opened the door and saw the mess. "I don't see what's so damned funny!" she huffed, "but I'm glad that you two are amused!" With that, she stalked into her room, slamming the door in our faces.

Amy and I stood in the hall, feeling sheepish. I was just about to knock on Nancy's door to apologize and invite her for a drink in the bar to try to cheer her up, when the earsplitting wail of air raid sirens shattered the silence. We froze. Nancy came bounding out of her room, wide-eyed with fright. She ran to me, and I put my arm around her shoulders reassuringly. We hurried to the stairs and looked down into the lobby. People were milling about, not knowing what to do. Some of the women started to cry. Men were shouting orders. "Here! This way! Quickly!" Everyone scrambled to the stairway that led down into a subterranean area. I had never been down there and was surprised and fascinated to find that it was an enormous cavern that dated back to Etruscan times. Here and there on the walls were remnants of ancient mosaics and murals. Huddled together, we could hear the drone of aircraft passing overhead. We tensed for the sound of bombs falling, but there were none, and after about an hour, the all-clear signal sounded and we filed upstairs again, shaken but relieved.

"Well," said Nancy with a tremulous little smile, "nothing like an air raid to make you forget a little honey on your clothes." We all laughed in nervous relief and headed for the bar.

During the next week, the air raid sirens sounded several times a day. It was nerve-wracking. It seemed like we were constantly on the run, dashing to shelter. One day, the sirens sounded while I was out on a walk. "Over here!" someone shouted. I was directed down an alleyway and through a gate, then underground. I found myself in a hidden underground city. Remnants of streets, houses, and shops from late Etruscan times were there, and Perugia was just built on top of them. It gave me an eerie feeling—a sense of the fleeting nature of time, and life. But although we were kept in a state of constant tension and nervousness, no bombs dropped on us, or near us. The Allied planes seemed headed for targets farther north.

In June, Amy heard from the Swiss Legation that she'd be leaving soon, with a group of British subjects. We were elated and rushed to help her pack. Then word came that it was all a mistake. Her spirits were crushed, and ours with hers. The air raid sirens resumed. We could see squadrons of Allied bombers passing overhead, flying north at high altitude. At night, from my balcony, we could make out the glow of fires far off in the distance, in the direction of Rome. By July, the bombings were coming closer every day. They were hitting only a few miles distant, on the trunk rail lines, or the air field.

On the Fourth of July, despite two air raids that sent us scurrying for shelter, Florence and Jack Kutsukian held a picnic. Florence somehow managed to come up with the essential dish—fried chicken. And Jack, to our eternal wonder, walked in with a watermelon!

As the months progressed, the four of us—Amy, Nancy, Lester, and I—developed more separate lives. We were no longer as confined, or combined, as we had been in Gubbio. We saw little of Lester. He had found a sympathetic group of American and British internees with whom he could enjoy commiserating. Amy had encountered a clutch of British and American expatriates whose interests were as mundane as hers. Nancy had become friends with a group of young people from the International University in Perugia and spent a lot of her time with them. I found myself feeling a little jealous. I missed the time we had spent together, studying Italian and talking.

But I, too, had developed new friends—including several young Italian professional men whose sympathies were with the Allied cause. We would gather on Saturday evenings and talk about art, music, theater, and a variety of other subjects. We were careful to avoid discussion of religion or politics. Enrico, a technician at one of the chocolate companies in Perugia, had given me a key to his apartment so that I could go and listen to his prized Zenith Transoceanic radio. Despite some jamming, it was usually possible to find the BBC broadcast or, failing that, to bring in one of the Swiss stations. On July 10th, I picked up the news that the Allies had landed in Sicily. I raced back to the hotel to tell Nancy, Amy, and the Kutsukians. The tempo of the bombing sorties increased. On July 19th, we heard the sobering news that Rome had been bombed, though later we learned it was the outskirts—the rail lines—and not the city itself.

A week later, Palmyra, a Greek woman who lived one floor below us and who had access to a radio through her boyfriend, knocked on the door while we were having evening coffee in my room. "Signore," she called out excitedly. "Such news! Such news!" In her agitated state, we could barely understand her English. She was jabbering in a combination of Greek, Italian, and English.

"Here, Palmyra, have some coffee and calm down," I said, handing her my coffee cup. "What news did you hear?" I tried not to show my anxiety.

"Mussolini!" she cried. "Il Duce, he go! Finish! Finito!"

"What?" I exclaimed. "Where? Where did he go?"

"Is over, finished for him!" she continued. "He is quit!"

We sat there, stunned. Did this mean what we thought it meant? That Mussolini was out of power? Throughout that night, tossing and turning on my bed, I could hear shouting and singing in the streets. I slept little. Jack Kutsukian and I were up bright and early, and as soon as we could safely go out on the street, we rushed over to Enrico's to listen to the early BBC news broadcast. My hands shook as I twirled the dials.

"Yesterday," came the voice of the announcer in clipped, British tones, "Benito Mussolini was expelled from power by the Grand Council of Italy. The King has asked Marshall Badoglio to form a new government." I was staggered. If the BBC was broadcasting it, it must be true. Mussolini out of power, after so long. That was difficult to imagine.

We went back to the hotel and roused Amy and Nancy to give them the news. They dressed hurriedly and we all went out into the streets. Crowds were already gathering. I tried to buy a newspaper, but they had all been snapped up. It was several days before I managed to get my hands on one. When I did, I was startled to find a full expose of Il Duce's long-time love affair with Clara Petacci. But not as startled as others. The Italians could hardly be classed as naive about such goings on, yet the people of Perugia were thunderstruck at this revelation of their leader's indiscretions. Two decades of a strictly controlled press had built Mussolini into a demigod, and now, like Humpty-Dumpty, he had fallen, and his image was shattered.

By that evening, Perugia was no longer a Fascist town. From our hotel balcony we could see the bonfires dotting the hills and plains, as the peasants heralded the news in the traditional way they always greeted a "great event." In the town, Fascist posters were torn down, along with street signs named after Fascist heroes. Windows were broken in shops owned by known Fascists, or paint was thrown at them, but there was little or no looting or rowdyism. We couldn't help laughing and cheering as a group of students passed below us, doing a snake dance to the tune of the "Beer Barrel Polka." After dinner that evening, I produced a bottle of champagne, and we all toasted the fall of Mussolini and his government. We were sure that with that momentous event, we could count on our liberation coming shortly—certainly within the next few weeks.

However, during the days that followed, demonstrations, reprisals, and air raids only increased in intensity. By August, the sirens were screaming almost continuously. Attacks on the rail lines, highways, and marshaling yards just outside Perugia could be seen clearly at night. Few people bothered running back and forth to the shelters anymore. The American bombers, flying almost always during the daylight, stayed high, while the British usually came over at night, at low level, striking at nearby targets and striving to put the local airfield, which served as a base for German and Italian pursuit fighters, out of business.

We felt the stepped-up pace immediately. Telephone communications became even more unreliable, and power outages were frequent. Food shortages increased. The Brufani cut its menu and services back drastically. Nancy and Amy, shocked at what they saw happening, looked to me for reassurance. "What do you think, Walter?" Nancy asked me almost daily.

"We'll be okay," I kept assuring her. However, in my own mind, I knew our situation would only get worse. The political situation in Italy was chaotic. There were rumors of a countermove by the Fascists to oust the Badoglio government and regain power. Already powerful and well organized as an underground movement, the Italian Communists were openly flexing their muscles. To make matters worse, the Germans had started tightening the screws on the Italians. More and more young Italian men, civilian as well as military, were being rounded up and sent away to Germany as prisoners, on involuntary "labor details." The general Italian populace found itself caught in the three-pronged trap of an oppressive ally, an aggressive liberator, and an unstable government.

At about that time, Jack Kutsukian fell ill and had to be hospitalized. Florence became one more person for whom I felt responsible. In late August, two delegates from the Swiss Legation arrived in Perugia, probably in response to my pleas for expedited action on getting us transferred to Rome. They did not bring good news. Monsieur Chauvet pointed out that we were safer in Perugia than we would be in Rome. "Monsieur Orebaugh, the situation in Rome is not pleasant," he said dolefully. "There are bombings almost daily, and food is in very short supply. The streets of Rome are full of German military. You would not be safe there." For the first time in a long time, I felt real despair about our situation.

A few days later, I was lying on my bed in a funk when Vittoria, the maid, arrived to give the room its weekly cleaning. I was curious about her. She didn't look Italian any more than I did. She looked more like a Viking. I exchanged pleasantries with her, and I could tell after a few words that her Italian was not the Umbrian dialect, nor the Roman one, but I was unable to identify its geographic womb. "Where were you born?" I asked her.

"I grew up in a small village near Gorizia, Signore, not far from Trieste," she replied respectfully. "I know who you are," she continued, smiling shyly. "For more than a year I was in service to a family in Trieste, and I heard your name mentioned many times. They liked you very much, said you were a very kind man." I was surprised and pleased to hear that.

"What brought you to Perugia?" I asked. Women like Vittoria rarely traveled to more than a few miles from their birthplace during their lifetime.

"I came here to be with my sister Margherita, Signore," she replied. "She married a Perugino, and he is in the Army and has not been heard from for months. We are very worried."

I really looked Vittoria over. She was unemotional, rather taciturn, and went about her business quietly, with great thoroughness. She might be someone we can trust, I thought, hopefully. For the next week, I continued to watch her carefully, turning options over in my mind, remembering my good luck with Isa in Gubbio.

By the end of August, German troops were tearing around the countryside below Perugia. The sound of their mechanized units being redeployed could be heard up and down the plain from early morning on. Judging from the volume of noise, it seemed like every German division in Italy was being shifted. The Allies responded by stepping up their strafing and bombing runs. We kept to our rooms a lot—it was unsafe to be out and about. I knew we needed to make some alternate plans. Just what they would be, I wasn't sure, but I knew that with the government as unstable as it was, and with Germans all around us, we were going to need escape plans, or hideout plans. I called Nancy and Amy to my room. "I hardly think I need to tell you," I began, "that our situation is getting more precarious every day." Amy nodded in agreement. Nancy looked a little frightened, but said nothing. "Being held by the Italians is one thing," I continued; "falling into the hands of the Germans is quite another. As soon as they realize who we are, or more specifically, who *I* am, they will probably pack us off to Germany as hostages, to exchange for some of their high-ranking prisoners. Conditions of imprisonment in Germany would be much worse than we can imagine." I didn't add that there could be worse than just imprisonment, under the Nazis.

"Well, what do you think we should do?" asked Nancy.

"What *can* we do?" Amy spoke up, in a more practical vein. "We haven't been able to get to Rome. We have no papers. The Swiss seem powerless to help us."

She turned to Nancy, "I agree with Walter; there is far more danger from the Germans than from the Fascists."

"So what do you suggest we do, Walter? Do you have any ideas?" said Nancy.

"Well," I said, "I think we'll need a place to go into hiding, if the need arises. Away from the hotel. Somewhere unknown to anyone else, including Lester and the Kutsukians. I think I can trust Vittoria Vechiet, the woman who cleans our rooms. I've been watching her carefully, and I intend to ask her tomorrow if she knows of a place we can go to safely, if we need to get away."

"Do you really trust her, Walter?" asked Nancy anxiously.

"Well," said Amy crisply, before I could answer, "we have to trust *someone*. She seems as likely a prospect as anyone. God knows we can't entrust our safety to the Germans. And if we wait much longer, it may be too late. I think you should approach her Walter, and see what she says."

"Nancy?" I looked at her. I could see she was shaken by this turn of events. "Do you agree?"

"I'm scared, and I don't know what we should do, but I've trusted you up to now to take care of us, Walter, and you've done the job, so I'll go along with whatever you decide."

The next day, Nancy, Amy, and I were all waiting in my room when Vittoria arrived. "Vittoria," I began, "we need to talk to someone about our situation here, and we all agree that you are someone we feel we can trust." Vittoria just looked at me and waited, saying nothing. I couldn't tell if that was a good sign, or a bad one. I decided to plunge on. "The Germans are coming closer, and we feel that it won't be long before they take over completely. This will put us in great danger, as I'm sure you know. We need your help. Do you know of any place where we could hide, if we have to leave here suddenly?"

Vittoria silently turned my request over in her mind. We held our breath and waited. Finally, she spoke. "Of course I will help you Signor Console," she said, as though it were the most simple request. "I will discuss the matter with my sister tonight. She will advise me what can be done. I will come tomorrow and let you know."

There was a collective sigh of relief from the three of us. I felt relieved that we had been right to trust her.

"Buongiorno, Vittoria," I greeted her the next day, and waited.

"Buongiorno, Signor Console," she replied. Then, wasting no time in small talk, she continued, "I have discussed the matter we spoke of with my sister, and she says she herself will shelter you if need be. She is very discreet. No one would know you are there. I would help you get away from here and go to her place."

I was elated. "Are you sure that would be all right?" I asked.

"Of course," she replied, simply. "However, I must tell you, Signore, that my sister's apartment is small and poor—nothing like the rooms you have here in the hotel. We hope you won't mind the plain and humble accommodations you would have there. But it will be safe, and you will not be betrayed."

I was so overcome by this act of faith, and her generosity to us, virtual strangers, that I jumped up from my chair, and went over and embraced her.

"Thank you, Vittoria, thank you. And please tell your sister how grateful we are to her. We don't want to be a burden, but we need help."

"Please don't worry about it, Signore," responded Vittoria, blushing with embarrassment. "What we have we will share. You and the two Signorine will be safe with my sister and her family. She lives not far from here. It will be easy to get there quickly. I will watch and warn you if I see any Germans coming."

"Thank you, Vittoria," I said sincerely.

She picked up her mop and began swabbing the floor as though no more than the weather had been discussed. I went to give the girls the good news.

The next day I received a letter from the Swiss. More bad news. On the subject of our exchange or transfer, the letter said, "negotiations with respect to the exchange between America and Germany and vice-versa seem to have come to a dead stop. This has probably caused the slackening, if not altogether the cessation, of the Italy–American negotiations." Up to that moment, I had not been aware that the Germans were involved in the negotiations. It was certainly a disquieting revelation. That evening, we heard that the Allies had managed to cross the Straits of Messina and had landed in Calabria, breaching the mainland of Italy. We were jubilant. Once again, rescue seemed near at hand.

"Don't be too optimistic," I cautioned the girls. "Before it was just planes and bombings. Now the war has come to land, and it's pretty sure to reach Perugia before long. We'll have to be very careful from now on, and be ready to move on a minute's notice. We need to stay in close touch with one another, and no one should go anywhere without letting the others know first."

They both nodded in agreement. "Gawd, I hope they get here soon," said Amy. "I'm ready to get out of the sticks and back to civilization!"

On Wednesday, September 8th, I was again at Enrico's listening to the news. I could hardly believe my ears. General Eisenhower himself came on to read the announcement. "Today," he said, "the Italians have agreed upon an Armistice. Italy and the United States are no longer at war." Without waiting for further details of this extraordinary turn of events, I rushed back to the hotel, grabbed Nancy and Amy, and danced around, hugging them both. Then I went to seek out Lester. "What do you think this means for our situation, Lester?"

"Well," he responded, "I would think it means we are no longer prisoners."

The fear of German reaction and retaliation still gnawed at me. We decided to go immediately to the questura. Upon our arrival there, we were saluted smartly by the two carabinieri on duty, and the chief of police seemed as excited about the news as we were. Pleased at his cordial manner, I said to him, "We realize how very busy you are, and we will not take any more of your time than is necessary. But we feel it is imperative that we be transported immediately to the Allied lines, before the Germans organize and take countermeasures." He kept nodding in assent as I spoke, so I decided to go for broke. Looking him squarely in the eye, I said, "Then will you see immediately about having us flown out of here, to an airfield behind the Allied lines? We would appreciate your assistance in that."

That made him nervous. He hesitated before answering. "Signor Console, I regret that I have no idea what might be arranged for you and your party. I do not have authority to make any decisions such as you request. However, I will be happy to send a telegram to Rome today for instructions. I will get in touch with you as soon as I have a reply. In the meantime, why don't you just go and enjoy the celebration in the piazza?" Realizing we would get no further with him, we left.

A celebration it certainly was! Just working our way back to the hotel was an experience. By the time we reached the front door of the Brufani, we had been kissed, hugged, danced with, and cried over by townspeople of every age and description. I handed the doorman the bottle of wine someone had pressed into my hands. More celebrating was going on inside. I saw Nancy and Amy, laughing and dancing with some of the other foreign internees. "Walter! Walter!" shouted Nancy, catching sight of me, "Isn't it wonderful? I'm so excited! It's going to be over soon!" She came running over to hug and kiss me. I hugged her tightly and held on to her. My instincts told me we still had a long way to go. Perhaps it's just as well they don't know, I decided. They need this interlude before harsh reality takes over. The Italians may have signed an armistice, I thought, grimly, but the countryside is still full of armed Germans, and THEY haven't signed anything!

The next day, having heard nothing further from the chief of police, Lester and I, accompanied by Colonel Rocke, a retired English officer, returned to the questura. The police chief wasn't there, but the senior officer on duty greeted us apologetically. "Everything is topsy-turvy in Rome right now, Signori, and we have had no answer yet to our telegram. Would you like us to send another one today?"

"No, not yet," I replied. "I'll check back with you again later."

Just then, the chief of police arrived. "I do not understand why our communications with Rome are not working," he said, "but I would suggest, Signor Console, that you go directly to the army with your request, since they have jurisdiction over all aircraft in this area at this time." He gave me the name of General Luigi Renzoni, Commander of the Military Zone of Perugia. I immediately called to request an appointment to see the general. Meanwhile, in Rome, unbeknownst to us, the telegram the questura had sent requesting air transportation for me, and for Colonel Rocke, by name, was intercepted by the Germans. They forwarded it to their intelligence unit, where it was compared against a list of names of enemies of the state. Of course our names turned up on that list.

The next morning, General Renzoni called me. "Signor Console," he began, "I understand your concern and your wish to get to Allied-held territory as quickly as possible. However, I have no capability to give you access to an airplane. Nor can I get you rail transport. All civilian transport has been curtailed."

"Tell me, General," I asked, "if the Germans decide to attack and occupy Perugia, can you defend it?"

"I will be honest with you, Signore. The answer is no. I do not have the troops, or the arms, to do so. Also, I am not clear on just what my position is. We are no longer at war with the Allies, and I understand that. But we are not at war with the Germans, either. So I have no orders to defend against them. It is all very confusing."

I felt the only reason the general had bothered to call me at all was to cover his own ass for all eventualities. After all, he didn't know who would be the victor, or where his future fortunes might lie. I sensed that he hoped it would be with the Allies, but he didn't dare take a chance, with the Germans all around us.

By that evening, rumors of every sort were flying. Lester came to me. "I've heard that the Germans are firmly in control in Rome, Walter," he said sadly. "So I think we can forget about getting there anytime soon." Later, Nancy informed me that her friends had heard the Pope himself had been taken captive and sent to Berlin. I reassured her that that was probably an exaggeration, but it made me uneasy, and I hurried to Enrico's to listen to the BBC. It was the only reliable source of news we had. The broadcast only confirmed what I feared—the Allies were managing to keep their toehold on the mainland of Italy, but the Germans, already there in force, were on the move and actively taking control in the vacuum of power that existed immediately following the Armistice. The Italians, not having declared war against the Germans, were caught in the middle. The Pope was not mentioned, so that must have been a wild rumor. As I returned from Enrico's, a motorcycle squadron of Germans roared into the Piazza Italia, pulling up in front of the questura. As they dismounted, every inch the imposing height and physique of the much-touted Aryans, one walked right past me, smiling coldly and disdainfully at the small clutch of civilians gathered in the street. Stopping, he unholstered his Luger and lifting it, snapped the chamber open and closed. The effect was electrifying. The faces of the people changed as though a switch had been thrown, from a mood of happy excitement to expressions of fear and dread. I quickly melted into the crowd and made my way quietly back to the hotel. I knew the time had come to make our move.

4

Hideout at the Casa Bonucci

I paced my room in agitation. I couldn't find Nancy or Amy anywhere. It wasn't like them to be gone at this time of day or to go anywhere without leaving me a note. Damn! I must not have gotten through to them how dangerous our situation was! I heard the rumble of armored columns from the highway on the plain below and stepped onto the balcony for a look. The Germans were approaching Perugia in force.

A sudden loud rap at the door startled me. I hastened to open it. There was no one there but a little Italian girl, about eleven years old. She stared up at me, wide-eyed, saying nothing. "What do you want?" I asked sharply, annoyed. The staff was usually careful not to let children from the street into the hotel. Yet, on second glance, it was obvious this child was no street urchin. She was neat, her hair was carefully combed and braided, and her worn cotton dress was clean and ironed. She continued to stare up at me in awe. I was probably the first foreigner she had ever seen, and I realized my gruff tone must have frightened her even more. "What is it?" I said more gently. "What do you want?"

She looked shyly down at her feet, nervously twisting one of her braids around her fingers, then, screwing up her courage, she blurted out, "Mi mandò la mamma" (my mother sent me).

"Your mother?" I asked in surprise. "Who are you?"

"I am Lucia Bonucci. Mamma sent me to tell you that your daughters are safe at our house. Zia Vittoria told me how to find you." With that, she made a small curtsy, turned, and bounded off down the hall.

I closed the door and paced the room, trying to collect my thoughts. The name Bonucci had not registered on me. That must be Vittoria's sister's married name, and the girls must have had a scare that caused them to go into hiding without waiting for me! I fretted over what might have happened, but it was too early in the evening, and still too light, for me to leave the hotel. I was relieved that they were safe. I began to get myself ready to go as soon as darkness fell. I put together my escape bag. Then I settled in as calmly as I could to wait for darkness. I checked my watch. Eight o'clock. With the wartime daylight saving in effect, darkness would not fall for at least another hour.

Once more, I carefully weighed my alternatives. I knew that whatever decision I made now would be final. Remaining in the hotel, exposing myself to certain capture by the Germans, I could still hope that my diplomatic status might afford the three of us some small margin of safety. But I didn't really trust that. On the other hand, I knew, better than the girls did, that the Germans would not treat us kindly if we escaped from under their noses into hiding and were eventually recaptured. By going into hiding at their house, we would be exposing Vittoria, her sister, and her family to possible severe consequences. With the political situation in disarray in Italy, we had at least a chance, however small, of reaching the Allied lines sometime in the near future, as long as we stayed out of the hands of the Germans. If we didn't go into hiding, we'd most certainly be taken by them, and then there would be little or no chance of escape. We would be truly imprisoned, and under the harshest of circumstances—of that I was convinced.

I thought of the child who had just left my door. What had she said her name was? Lucia. Lucia Bonucci. I had seen, in France, that the Nazis had no regard for women or children. How could I, in conscience, expose little Lucia and her family to some potentially awful fate if they were discovered harboring us? How much time would we have before they looked for me in earnest? Initially, I reasoned, the Germans will probably be more interested in getting the Italians under control than in rounding up foreigners. We might go unnoticed for some time. However, something had happened to make Amy and Nancy flee to the Bonuccis. Sending Lucia to me meant Vittoria and her sister had decided we should take cover immediately.

I worried about Lester and the Kutsukians. What would happen to them? A few weeks back, I had cautiously probed Lester and Jack about the idea of going into hiding, without revealing my own arrangements. The less anyone knew, I felt, the less the Germans would be able to pry out of them, should that occasion arise. Lester was adamantly against the idea. Jack had been cool to the idea of hiding out, and noncommittal. Now, of course, he was too ill to be moved, and I knew I could never convince Florence to leave him and go with us. No, I decided, Amy, Nancy, and I would have to go it alone, just the three of us. That was risky enough. Having thoroughly weighed everything, I decided that going into hiding, immediately, was my only option. That decided, I sprang into action.

I quickly changed into my oldest suit. My valise was not so large that it would be conspicuous. I surveyed myself in the mirror. I hoped I looked like any ordinary Italian businessman. Shortly after dark, I slipped quietly out the service entrance at the back of the hotel. Sticking to alleys and back streets, I made my way into the old section of town. I had checked out Vittoria's sister's place before, approaching it from different directions, until I knew I could find it easily, even in the dark. After about fifteen minutes of walking, I reached the cross street above the one on which the house was located, and glanced down the darkened street, to make sure no one was around. The houses in that area were all joined together, with common partitioning walls, so I didn't have to worry about anyone lurking between them. The buildings came almost to the edge of the street, with only a few inches of curbing between them and the actual street. I saw with relief that the street was deserted. Just to be safe, I circled around the block again and finally approached the house, keeping in the darkest shadows as much as I could. Slipping into the entryway, I glanced up the dimly lit stairway. Empty. Slowing, barely daring to breathe, I made my way soundlessly, step by careful step, up the stairs. The door to the apartment on the fourth floor stood slightly ajar. I drew a deep breath, and pushed it open just enough to slip inside, closing it swiftly behind me.

As I turned into the room, which appeared to be a kitchen, Nancy and Amy both rushed at me. Nancy threw herself into my arms, sobbing, "Oh, God, Walter, I'm so glad you're here!" she wailed. "You won't believe what happened! We were so scared!" Amy had grabbed my arm and was tugging on it, talking excitedly at the same time.

"Sssh. Sssh. Quiet! It's okay," I soothed them, hugging Nancy with one arm and patting Amy's shoulder with the other. "Now, calm down," I ordered. "One at a time. Tell me what happened." I could see that Nancy was too upset to be coherent. "You first, Amy," I commanded. "Tell me what happened and how you got here."

"Oh, Walter!" she burst out, "it was perfectly horrible! Those Fascist bastards were trying to shoot us!" From her tone, she clearly considered that a personal affront.

"Shoot you!" I exclaimed. "Why would the Fascists try to shoot you? What is all this?" I was alarmed. This was an unexpected turn of events! "Just take it from the beginning, and tell me everything exactly as it happened. Why would the Fascists try to shoot you?" I reached over and hugged the shaking Nancy. I was glad they were there within reach, safe and unharmed.

"Well," began Amy, "it was about two o'clock, and you weren't back, so we decided to go out and find a newspaper, to see what was happening. We were about three blocks from the hotel, not far from that newsstand you always go to, when we heard a gunshot just behind us." She paused to draw breath.

"It was really loud, Walter, and scared the hell out of us!" Nancy chimed in.

"Sssh, I know it did," I hushed her, stroking her hair, "let Amy finish."

"Right after we heard the first shot," Amy continued, "we dropped to the ground, crawled along close to the building to a doorway, and slid in there. There were more shots. We heard bullets hitting right above our heads as we crawled along. It was terrifying! We crouched there, not daring to make a sound. I don't think we even breathed. A minute later, more shots hit the street right in front of us. We thought we had been hit, but it was only flying splinters from bullets hitting the stones in the street. I poked Nancy and said, 'I've had enough of this—let's get out of here!' "

"You didn't go out into the street!" I exclaimed.

"No, there was an alleyway behind some shops. We scurried along it, trying each door. We found a door that would open and barged right in. It was the back room of a poultry shop, and the proprietor was sitting there finishing his lunch, drinking a glass of wine. I said 'scusi, scusi' and dodged the chickens and ran across to the front door of the shop. Poor man! He just sat there with his mouth open, thoroughly stunned. He never moved a muscle!" Amy smiled at the memory, and I was relieved to see her beginning to calm down. I patted Nancy's hand reassuringly.

"Then what happened?" I prompted.

Nancy took up the tale. "I poked my head out and looked up and down the street. There was no one there, so we dashed out and around the corner. Everything seemed quiet, so we tried to walk as slowly and casually as we could back to the hotel. We turned a corner, and suddenly there was a roar and here came a whole column of German soldiers on motorcycles! God! It scared us out of our wits! We jumped into another doorway. I said, 'We'll never make it back to the hotel, let's try for Vittoria's sister's!' And here we are," she concluded, smiling through her tears. I patted her hand again.

"You both did very well," I praised them. "You really kept your heads in a crisis."

"Margherita—that's Signora Bonucci—decided it was safer to send Lucia to let you know we were here than for us to go back ourselves," added Amy.

"Good! That was the smartest thing to do," I agreed. I sat back in my chair, mulling over what they had told me. Amy poured me a glass of watered wine. Gratefully, I downed it. She poured me another, and I sipped it slowly, thinking. My first impression was that it was doubtful that the Fascists had been shooting at the girls. More than likely, it was a skirmish between newly emboldened Italian factions, and the two girls had just happened to be in the wrong place at the wrong time. Also, from Nancy's description, I doubted that the German motorcycle unit was there to begin a roundup. There were not enough of them to do it . . . yet. It was probably just an advance party, for show, to instill the proper degree of fear into the populace. I was still sure the Germans were more interested in demobilizing Italian military units and rounding up partisans than they were in taking custody of a few stray enemy internees.

We've got to consider our next moves very carefully," I said. "We'd probably be safe for a few more days back at the hotel, if no one has missed us and started looking for us. Life in hiding here won't be pleasant, or easy. There will be severe consequences if we're caught, not only for all of us, but for Vittoria and the Bonucci family too." Our hostess had not as yet appeared. Apparently she was giving us privacy to talk, and I appreciated her tact and understanding. "What do you have with you?" I asked.

"Just our handbags," replied Amy. "Everything we own is back at the hotel. What about you?"

"I just brought what I could get into a small valise. It's enough for me to make out with, for a short period, but if we're going into hiding for good, we'll need some of our stuff from the hotel. I don't dare risk going back. I know the Germans want me. I am definitely going into hiding. Whether you want to or not is up to you. If you decide you want to join me, I think it's still safe for you two to go back to the hotel and get some of your things."

Soberly, they thought it over. We sat in silence for a few minutes. "I've decided," said Amy suddenly. "I'm coming with you, Walter."

"What about you, Nancy?"

Nancy nodded her assent.

"Let's go and get our things, then," said Amy briskly, rising and heading for the door of the apartment. "We'll be back here tomorrow, bag and baggage," she declared.

"Are you sure? We can't turn back," I warned.

"We know that, Walter," said Nancy quietly, "but we'd rather take our chances here with you than sit at the hotel waiting for the Germans to come get us." With that, they left.

Concerned for their safety, I got up to follow, when Margherita Bonucci suddenly appeared, detaining me with one hand on my arm, the other to her lips to signal for silence. "It is better for you to stay here, Signore," she said quietly. "The Signorine will be watched, and guarded, until they are safely back here." I returned to my seat at the table and looked my hostess over. Margherita Bonucci was not as tall as Vittoria, or as blonde, but I could see that her bloodlines were more northern Italian than Mediterranean. "You are most welcome in our home, Signore," she informed me graciously. "We are honored to have such a distinguished guest as you to share our poor home." She was a quick, vigorous woman, slender, and almost monochromatic in coloring. She had pale gray eyes, and a pale, narrow, sharp-featured face. Her gray-blonde hair was tied back with a strip of ribbon, and she wore an old, shapeless gray cardigan over her simple dark brown woolen dress. A gold wedding band and a string of inexpensive beads around her neck were her only adornments.

"It is I who am honored, Signora," I replied, in Italian, "and I am grateful to have such friends as you to help me in this time of need."

She smiled, showing large, slightly crooked teeth. "I am glad you speak our language so well. You have no worry, Signore," she assured me, "we will see to your safety and comfort, and that of the Signorine when they return." Putting her finger once again to her lips to signal that I must be careful not to wake the others, she led me to my room.

Because this was the only other bedroom in the apartment, I knew it would turn into *our* room when the girls returned. Fleetingly, I wondered how we would handle that but realized there was no sense worrying about it. We were committed, come what may. Margherita must have moved her children into the other bedroom with her. It was going to be a very cramped household, with no privacy for anyone. I hoped our stay would be brief—that we would be liberated before the month was out. I stretched out on the bed and was soon sound asleep. It seemed only minutes later that I woke suddenly, completely disoriented. Dawn was breaking. For a moment I couldn't remember where I was. Then it came back to me—the Bonucci apartment. As I looked around the bedroom, I realized what Margherita had meant. It was definitely a humble abode. The dim light that filtered in from the single shuttered window of the room revealed my bed to be a cast iron affair, which rose nearly four feet from the bare, red tile floor. Two ancient, overstuffed armchairs crouched disconsolately on either side of a doorway, which, upon investigation, led to the bathroom. The coldness of the tile on my bare feet made me wince and brought memories of Gubbio flooding back. If it was this cold in September, I didn't want to think of what winter would be like! Hopefully, we'd be safely behind Allied lines long before November. In the bathroom, I found an old bidet, a toilet that looked to be of the same vintage and noise production capability as the one in the Albergo San Marco in Gubbio, and a small sink. I tried both spigots, but only one worked—the cold. Hot water would have to be heated on the stove, and carried in from the kitchen. It was probably a luxury reserved for a weekly bath. Shivering, I washed and shaved in cold water, and got myself dressed. I hoped the girls had made out all right for the night. I was hungry, and worried, and suddenly not sure I had made the right decision. I already missed the amenities of the Hotel Brufani.

When I stepped into the kitchen, which was the only other room of the apartment besides the two bedrooms, I found Margherita already there, preparing breakfast. The kitchen was about fifteen feet wide by twenty feet long. There was a black cast iron cooking stove against one wall. The smell of burning wood, and a tiny amount of heat, drifted from it. Across from it was a sink. Against another wall was a plain wooden cupboard, with a drawer and two doors on the lower half, and open shelves on the top. In it, Margherita stored and displayed her meager store of kitchen utensils—one or two pots, a few dishes, some glasses and tableware. Above the sink was a window, with a line and pulley arrangement for hanging out laundry extended from it. A couple of sagging shelves served as a makeshift pantry, and there was a battered old icebox. Lucia and a young boy of about eight were seated at the well-scrubbed wooden table, finishing their morning meal. Above the table hung a framed and faded print of Christ on the cross.

Margherita motioned me to sit, and I took one of the empty chairs. Lucia jumped up to get me coffee. "Franco! This is Signor Orebaugh. Say hello!" commanded Margherita.

Franco gave me a cursory stare, mumbled "buongiorno," and darted out the door before his mother could demand anything further of him. Lucia set a large mug of coffee before me, then stood close, smiling shyly. I smiled back at her.

"Lucia! Sit down and finish your breakfast! Don't stare at Signor Orebaugh, it's not polite," remonstrated her mother. I winked at Lucia, then caught my breath as a stunningly beautiful girl appeared, like a vision, in the doorway.

"Buongiorno, Signore, I am Valentina," she said in a soft, husky voice, as she advanced into the kitchen.

I rose to greet her. "Buongiorno, Valentina, I am Walter Orebaugh," I replied. "I'm pleased to meet you and to be here in your home. Your mother is most gracious to help us."

She gave me a warm, open smile, revealing even white teeth. "It is nothing, Signore, as my mother has told you. We are happy to be of help."

She went over to the stove and poured herself coffee, giving me a chance to regain my senses and observe her. She was about five feet eight inches tall, with a slim, full-breasted figure, and she radiated youth and energy. I was impressed with her poise and maturity, which were both well beyond her seventeen years. Thick chestnut hair fell to her waist, curling at the ends. It was held back from her face by a ribbon headband. And what a face it was. In Valentina, the strong Vechiet features of her mother had been softened and refined. Her dark brown eyes appeared even larger, set in a delicate oval face. It was hard to believe that the stolid Margherita and her as yet unseen husband, Gregorio, had produced this beauty! Finishing her coffee quickly, she departed to do the morning errands. Without her presence, the kitchen somehow seemed dingier. Her casual departure, like Franco's, alarmed me.

"Margherita, I'm worried that the children will leak information about us being here. Can we trust them to keep our secret?"

Margherita was unperturbed. "Don't worry, Signore, they understand," she reassured me, refilling my cup. "I have given them orders. They will obey."

Just as I finished my coffee, Amy and Nancy arrived, breathless from the four-story climb. "Here we are, for better or for worse, as they say," said Amy bravely, hugging me. They'd had to slip past two German guards who had taken up stations close by the entrance to the hotel, so had managed to bring only a few essentials along in a shopping bag, in order to get out without attracting the guards' attention. "Not to worry, though," said Amy, "Vittoria arranged for the rest of our stuff to be hidden and brought here after dark."

We sat down at the kitchen table with Margherita while she outlined the new household rules and arrangements. As I had expected, the three of us were to share the bedroom, and all seven of us would share the only bathroom—the one off our room.

The children had been ordered to respect our privacy, Margherita assured us. She would serve us our meals first, then her family's. I protested that, but she was insistent. "It is best that way, Signore, so that if anyone comes, there will not be too many places set at the table. Also, there are only four chairs," she concluded, on a practical note. "Valentina and I will do the shopping and the cooking." I handed her what ration coupons we had. They would provide little, but she was happy to get them. I also insisted I would pay her a sum every month for our board. She protested, but I was adamant. Over the next couple of days, our baggage came, brought in on separate trips, a piece or two at a time, by Vittoria, Valentina, and Margherita. They somehow managed to cover the telltale expensive leather of my luggage, to conceal it from curious eyes. I turned the foodstuffs—flour, sugar, coffee, and canned goods—over to Margherita, with the exception of some bars of soap, which I stored in our room. They were as good as money and might help us some day. Margherita was thrilled. Much of what I gave her hadn't been seen on the markets in months.

The first night, I tried to sleep on the floor and let the girls have the bed, but I only lasted an hour lying on the icy tile floor. We had only one sheet and two blankets, and needed all of them to keep even minimally warm. After a few nights of sleeplessness and nervous adjustments—Amy's curlers jabbed whoever slept next to her, and her snoring kept both Nancy and me awake; I was a restless sleeper and kicked both girls; Nancy was a light sleeper, who woke in a start at every noise and turn—we finally became accustomed to sleeping three to a bed. Although it might seem hard to believe, sex was never a consideration. Our crowded living conditions precluded intimacy, and we were too tired, too cold, too hungry, and too frightened to even think about it. Moreover, we had to sleep fully dressed in layers of clothes—for warmth, and also to be able to make a quick escape if we had to. As winter arrived, and the temperature dropped further, we were grateful for our enforced physical closeness—it made for shared body heat. Warmth, like food, had suddenly become paramount in our lives.

We nearly cried for joy when Naples was liberated in mid-October.

However, we knew the Germans were firmly in control in Perugia. Vittoria reported that Jack Kutsukian had been arrested. All foreign detainees were confined totally to the hotel and could only leave if they had a letter of authorization. Later, Vittoria brought worse news. "Today there were German officers in black uniforms, not the gray ones like the others, asking about you at the registration desk." Hearing that, fear snaked through me. Black uniforms meant the Gestapo, the most dreaded force of the German military. They would not abandon the search easily.

At about that same time, Margherita received the first news of her husband. His returning army unit had been surrounded by Germans, forced into cattle cars, and shipped off to Germany. As the train passed through the area of Lake Tresimeno, Gregorio Bonucci, and others whose families lived nearby, had tossed notes out, hoping they'd be found by sympathetic Italians who would relay the information to their families. Which is exactly what happened. The usually stoic Margherita lost her composure on hearing of her husband's fate. We were all distressed to see her so upset. After a few minutes, she resolutely dried her tears and began preparations for dinner.

"Sit and rest, Margherita," I urged her. "You've had a bad shock. We can make our own dinner."

But she would have none of it. "No, no, Signore, I am all right now," she assured me. "Life goes on, and the children will be home soon, and hungry." She was an amazing woman. Almost fearless, endlessly resourceful, and a well of emotional strength for the whole household.

Not everything in our lives was glum. The closeness, and the family atmosphere, kept our spirits up. "At least I don't have to worry about how to lose weight anymore," remarked Amy one morning, showing us several inches of gap in her skirt waistband. She and Nancy helped Margherita as much as possible with the household chores. I kept Lucia and Franco mesmerized for hours with "cowboys and Indians" tales about America, which they loved. Lucia became my shadow. She doted on me and waited on me personally at every opportunity. When I came into the kitchen in the morning, she was there, dressed and waiting to pour my coffee. Then she would sit close and watch me solemnly as I drank it. One morning I overheard her admonishing Valentina, "Remember! I saw him first! You already have too many boyfriends." I chuckled over that, but was surprised to feel a slight twinge of jealousy at the thought of the beauteous Valentina having "too many boyfriends."

One evening, Vittoria appeared with an envelope from Manfred containing more money. She repeated the message that the messenger had passed verbally when he handed her the envelope: "Keep you chins up, we're working on getting you to Rome." Although part of me was skeptical of how successful Manfred would be in that, the other half hoped against hope it would happen, and soon. The Allies would take Rome

long before Perugia, and our chances of eluding capture might be better
there than here. We knew the Germans were fighting bitterly before giving up an inch of Italian soil. Also, they had rescued Mussolini and rein-
stalled him in a puppet government in north Italy, dubbed the "Republic
of Salò." Neo-Fascists, worse than any of the heyday of Mussolini, had
come to Perugia. They began arresting people, requistioning their homes,
and simply taking whatever suited their fancy. They were, for the most
part, the dregs of Italian society, recruited from the bowels of Naples,
Palermo, and other urban cesspools. They were a blend of scum, ruffian,
and ruthless cutthroat—hoodlums to be feared more than the Germans.
These neo-Fascists began periodic searches of the houses in Perugia, arresting Jews and any foreigners they found. We now had a real fear to live
with every day. Up to then, I had tried to make light of our plight, but
now I had to face the ominous danger we were in, and worse, make the
women and the children live with it, too.

Margherita and I carefully rearranged the kitchen, putting the table directly under the trapdoor to the attic. We put a large wooden crate beside
it, to boost us up to reach the trapdoor. I made Nancy and Amy practice
pulling the crate to the table top, getting on it, pushing open the trap, and
boosting each other into the attic. Then I climbed up into the attic as fast
as I could, and practiced pulling them up after me. We spent most of two
afternoons practicing getting into the attic under every possible condition
and combination. When those afternoon sessions ended, we were all exhausted, and every bone and muscle in our bodies hurt, but we had cut
the time to less than two minutes from first warning to being in the attic,
with the trapdoor shut and the crate being taken down off the table by
Margherita.

As we lay in bed that night, trying to get to sleep, there was a noise on
the roof, and Nancy gasped aloud and jumped a foot off the bed. "Ssh,"
I soothed her, "it's nothing. Probably just a roof tile falling. Try to go to
sleep. You're just jumpy after this afternoon."

"Oh, Walter," she cried, and though I couldn't see her in the dark, I
could hear the fear in her voice, "do you think we'll ever get out of here
alive?"

"Gawd, I hope so," Amy piped up out of the shadows. "With all that
bloody climbing about, I've ruined my last pair of leggings. I need to get
out of here alive, and soon, to go shopping." We all managed a laugh at
that, and the tension was relieved.

The next morning, for no real reason, I decided I wouldn't shave again
until we were liberated. Although at that time I didn't think about dis-
guising myself by growing a beard, it later tuned out to be a fortunate
decision. At first, no one commented on my budding beard. A few nights
after I had stopped shaving, Margherita and I were the last ones up, sitting

at the table, quietly discussing the latest big news—Italy had now declared war on Germany—when there was a light tap at the door. I dived for the bedroom, waking the girls, and we huddled there, not daring to breathe, fearing this was it, we had been betrayed. After all our practicing, there hadn't even been time to try for the attic. I hugged the trembling girls close to me. Suddenly, the bedroom door flew open, and we jumped in fright.

A man stood there, laughing. "Come out here, all of you!"

I couldn't see in the dark, but I recognized that laugh. It was Manfred! I leaped at him, laughing and cursing in relief, and pounded him on the back. "You bastard! You scared the hell out of us! How did you find us? What are you doing here?"

Amy and Nancy threw themselves into his arms, hugging him. Margherita stood by silently, a stunned look on her face.

We all crowded into the kitchen. Margherita cautioned us to be quiet, to whisper, not to wake the children or arouse any neighbors. I tried to explain Manfred to her. Then Valentina appeared. The commotion had awakened her. Framed in the doorway, in a tattered old robe, hair tousled, she was still breathtakingly lovely, and from the look on Manfred's face, I knew he was feeling the same reaction I'd had on first seeing her. After the introductions, he reluctantly tore his eyes from her and turned back to me. Valentina disappeared, reappearing a few minutes later in more presentable garb. Manfred again appeared dumbstruck by her. By that time, Margherita had made coffee for everyone.

Manfred turned and suddenly peered closely at me. "You look funny Walter," he said. "What's the matter with your face? Here, I brought some oranges." He reached into the sack he had dropped on the floor and pulled out an orange for each of us. The three younger women immediately began tearing the peels off theirs. Margherita just held hers, turning it around and around in her hands, gazing at it in delight. I wondered how long it had been since she, or any of her family, had seen an orange. Manfred turned to the women. "Doesn't he look funny, ladies?" he demanded.

"Yes, as a matter of fact you do, Walter," whispered Amy, finally taking a good look at me. "What on earth have you done to your face?"

"I'm growing a beard," I replied sullenly, shooting Manfred a scathing look, which only started him snickering again. "I'm not shaving again until we're liberated!"

"Oho!" said Manfred, who couldn't resist a jibe, "at the rate this liberation is progressing, you'll look like Methuselah. You'll have time to grow a beard down to your feet!" With that, he and the girls went off in a gale of laughter.

Although it was a pleasure to see them happy for a change, Margherita shot me a look of consternation. "Ssh! Hey! Quiet down!" I commanded in as stern a whisper as I could muster. "You'll have the Germans and the Fascists down on our necks if you keep that up. Shush! Whispers only! How did you find us, Manfred?"

He picked up the sack from which he had pulled the oranges and placed it on the table. Then he beckoned to Margherita, who cautiously approached him, curiosity overcoming her normal reserve. "I have my ways," he replied, "but so far they haven't been good enough to get you to Rome. I'm still working on it, though. Just wanted to see for myself that you're all right."

As he spoke, he was pulling foodstuffs out of the bag. Margherita exclaimed softly as each miraculous new item appeared. Once she realized they were for us, she hustled to stow everything away, thanking Manfred profusely, and imprecating various saints to bless him for his generosity. He had brought sugar, Swiss coffee, and there were more oranges—enough so that each of the children could have one in the morning. There were tins of pâté, canned vegetables, and other delicacies. We sat there, slowly and carefully eating our oranges, savoring every morsel, as Manfred gave us news of the outside world. Never had an orange tasted so good to me!

Manfred noticed our obvious hunger. He turned serious. "Walter, I know it is difficult to find enough food to keep all of you fed, but you must be very careful about making purchases on the black market from here on," he cautioned. "Everyone and everything is being watched now, and if Margherita spends too much, or too freely, for the size of her family, it will arouse suspicion." He turned to look at Margherita. "You must be very careful," he reiterated, in Italian. She nodded her understanding of what he had said.

Then, turning back to me he said, "The Allies are not making headway. It looks like you'll be here for a while, so take every precaution. Stay alert!" With that, he pressed a wad of folded bills into my hand, and, opening the door he peered cautiously down the stairwell. With a casual wave, he was gone.

Our excitement kept us awake and whispering for another quarter of an hour, then we turned off the single kerosene lamp and filed quietly to bed, each of us lost in our thoughts. Manfred's news had put a big damper on our optimism. The longer we spent there, the greater our chances of being discovered, or betrayed, became.

Weeks passed, and just finding food to feed all of us became Margherita's main occupation. She had a battered bicycle, which she used for her long forays into the countryside in search of food. As the winter progressed, her trips lengthened, sometimes reaching thirty to forty kilometers—almost twenty miles—every day. She was lucky if these grueling trips produced a few carrots, or a cabbage, or a few handfuls of Brussels sprouts. With those, she'd concoct a thin minestrone, or a broth, more

warming than filling. On the rare occasions she lucked into getting a rabbit or a chicken, there was general elation and celebration.

Never before in my life had food occupied such a place in my thoughts.
Never before had I known real hunger, either. I gained a new respect for
cooks, and for the overwhelming responsibility placed on women like
Margherita. The small can of condensed milk, from the few that remained
in the supplies I had given her, held a place of honor in the kitchen. We
were each allotted one teaspoonful of the thick, sweet milk a day, and we
all looked forward to that treat. I had repeatedly tried to give my portion
over to the children, as had Nancy and Amy, but Margherita would not
hear of it. "We need this to keep our strength," she had said, with finality.
"If we fall sick, who will take care of the children? No, everyone must
take their share, adults as well as children, to keep well."

Oddly enough, it was real coffee that I yearned for, almost as much as
food. Our morning "coffee" was a roasted barley concoction. The coffee
Manfred occasionally brought was drunk only on Sunday, and treated with
great reverence. Margherita saved the used grounds, dried them out, and
mixed them in with the roasted barley, a spoonful at a time, all through
the week. Breakfast was a mug of barley "coffee" and a couple of chunks
of coarse bread, which we called bread only from force of habit. I didn't
want to know what it was made of. Lunch was always a bowl of soup,
or broth, carefully crafted by Margherita out of ingredients held back from
the previous evening's dinner supplies. In it we dunked stale bread. Anything to fill our growling stomachs. There was no such thing as a "left-
over" or a "snack." Ceci (chick-peas) were standard at every meal. Sometimes ceci were the entire meal. There was no salt, and few other seasonings
were available, so everything was bland and tasteless. We ate simply to
keep ourselves alive. The evening meal was pasta—now a uniformly gray
mush that was almost inedible. "Sauce" consisted of a thinned tomato
paste, or a ladle of broth from the lunch soup, unless it was one of those
rare red-letter days when Margherita had found a bit of sausage, or some
other meat, somewhere in her travels.

Manfred's occasional bags of goodies were our lifeline. He always brought
a little food, but his visits were weeks apart, and we were seven people
who needed to keep functioning. Margherita had to produce at least fourteen, and usually twenty-one, servings of some kind of sustenance each
and every day! It was a phenomenal task, and it was her constant worry.
She did better than most, but I could see the weight dropping off everyone
in the household. My own face, in spite of the bushy beard I now sported,
reflected a gaunt image when I looked in the mirror.

Vittoria kept us informed of happenings in Perugia. Jack Kutsukian had
been sent to a concentration camp somewhere. Florence was at the Italia,
the third-class hotel to which the internees had been moved when the

Germans arrived. The Germans now occupied the Brufani. "Eh, it is terrible out there now," Vittoria lamented, during one of her evening visits. "They take everyone, every man under sixty—Jews, foreigners, Italians, no matter, and send them off to Germany to labor camps. All our men are being taken. Who will save us?"

Although it was of little comfort to us, we knew there were thousands of Italians and other foreigners in hiding, just like we were. "Macchia" is the Italian word for bush, and the phrase "darsi alla macchia" (go into the bush) was the expression that described hiding out—whether it was in the hills, in the woods, in a barn—anywhere other than in one's own home.

As with the Bonucci family, this wholesale arrest of Italian men by the Germans and the neo-Fascists, or their only alternative to arrest, which was to go into the "macchia," was having its inevitable effect on local families. For Italians, nothing is as important as the integrity of the family unit. What may be lacking in them in the way of patriotism, civil loyalty, or religious ardor is more than compensated for by the deep and abiding devotion they manifest toward the family as an institution. The degree to which the integrity of the family was threatened by the acts of the Germans and the puppet Italian regime generated a hatred in the general populace that knew no limits.

The tenant farmers' families of the area around Perugia (and in other areas of Italy as well, we later learned) united to feed and shelter these refugees hiding out from the Germans and the Fascists. Valentina, like Vittoria, told of the hills being full of refugees—youths evading internment, British ex-prisoners of war, civilians of all ages and all walks of life—including, it was rumored, many aristocrats and some members of the deposed royal family, as well as police and carabinieri who had deserted their duty posts. All were labeled "brigands" by the neo-Fascists. Valentina heard through her friends that they were organizing themselves into guerrilla bands (partigiani) up in the hills, to take resistance action against the enemy. That interested me. I was determined to learn more.

"Valentina," I said one Saturday, as we slowly consumed our scant cups of soup, "I need you to find out as much as you possibly can about these guerrilla bands."

She looked at me seriously for a few moments, her dark eyes now huge in her thin face. Then she nodded. "I will find out what I can for you Signore," she replied. "I will talk with my friend Renzo. He knows the leader of one of the bands."

I leaned toward her and placed a hand on her shoulder. "Thank you, Valentina," I said. "Please do it soon, but be careful, be VERY careful," I cautioned. "We don't want anyone to have a clue that you are harboring refugees."

"Do not worry, Gualtiero," she assured me, smiling, "I will be very discreet."

The slothlike advance of the Allied forces gnawed at us as much as hunger did. We were deeply worried about how long we could continue to impose on Margherita. Never by word or act did she indicate that she was tired of having us there, but we had come in September for "a few weeks," and it was November, and we were no closer to being rescued, moved, or liberated. I knew Manfred was trying to get us false identity papers, so we could try to escape, but so far he had come up empty-handed.

It was the ever-watchful Amy who spotted the Fascists conducting a house-to-house search on our street late one afternoon. "Oh, God, Walter," she cried frantically, "here they come!"

"Quick, to the attic! Hurry!" I commanded. We all dashed for the kitchen table. I threw the crate up on it, and Margherita steadied it as I jumped up on it and pushed open the trapdoor to our "hell hole," as we had dubbed it.

Before I was in and fully turned around, Nancy was up on the crate, reaching to be pulled up. "Here, grab me, Walter, hurry!" she begged. Amy was already clambering onto the table behind her. We could hear the Fascisti pounding on the door to the apartment on the first floor. Our hearts were pounding almost as loud. I got Nancy in, and together we hauled Amy up and into the attic with us. As I was slamming the trapdoor shut, I could see that Margherita had already moved the crate, and Valentina was calmly and quietly seating the two children at the table with cups of soup in front of them. They were the picture of a poor family at their meager supper. In the blackness of the attic, working quickly and quietly, we pushed some big pieces of junk and some boxes close to the trapdoor opening, to block the view of anyone sticking their head up through the opening for a look around. Then we waved our arms to fan the dust, to resettle it where we had made marks in it.

We crept to the farthest, darkest corner and crouched there, barely breathing. We were sweating from fear, despite the attic's icy temperature. The urge to sneeze or cough was unbearable, but we didn't dare even clear our throats. We strained to hear sounds from below. Nancy had hold of my hand and clutched it in a grip so tight I thought the bones would be crushed. There wasn't a sound from our corner, except for our shallow breathing. After what seemed like an eternity, we heard the welcome sound of a broom being banged against the ceiling—it was the "all clear" signal! We let our breath out in a whoosh and scrambled for the trapdoor. Back down in the kitchen, we broke into a spasm of coughing and sneezing. I couldn't help laughing when Amy's face reappeared in the light—she was as black and as filthy as any chimney sweep! The attic had built up its thick layer of dirt and dust for over a century.

Amy, ever the coquette, did not find her condition amusing and burst into a storm of tears when she saw herself in the mirror. After that, it was difficult to get her to go into the attic. "Oh, Walter, I can't stand another minute of this!" she would wail. "I'd rather take my chances with the Germans. God only knows what's up there crawling around in that filth!"

We cleaned up every trace of dirt, then wolfed down our sparse supper and turned in. Undernourished, weakened from months of forced inactivity, the experience had exhausted us, and we fell asleep almost instantly. For once, Amy's snoring didn't keep us awake. The winter became one of the most severe any of the natives could remember. Perhaps, with sufficient food, the cold would have been more endurable. I prayed daily for a return visit from Manfred. We had no fuel for heat, and our breath made frosty puffs when we talked. Dressed in all the warm clothing we owned, we huddled together in bed day and night, trying to keep warm. We were miserable. Several weeks had passed since Manfred's last visit, and our small hoard of food had vanished. Margherita gleaned little from her long bicycle trips. She was weakening to the point that soon she would no longer be able to pedal such distances. I knew she secretly stinted on her own rations to give more to us and the children, but she never complained.

One evening, Vittoria came, and out of the lining of her coat, like a magician, she pulled two hard-crusted rolls, a pat of real butter, and about a third of a bottle of brandy. We were overjoyed. "I stole these from those pigs of German officers," she declared proudly. "They had stuffed their bellies and weren't paying attention."

We froze in horror. "Vittoria!" I scolded. "You mustn't ever take a chance like that again! If you had been caught, the punishment would have been out of all proportion to what you did! They would probably have executed you!"

She was impervious to my outburst. "Never mind," she said, stolidly. "Here, Franco, eat your bread." She broke a good-sized chunk from one of the rolls, dabbed it with butter, and handed it to the child, who immediately wolfed it down. She gave me a look that spoke volumes. Seeing the children hungry was unbearable torture, and the women would take any risks to get food for them.

I wished I had something useful to do besides sit around and watch my beard grow, which it did with a slowness as agonizing as the stalled Allied advance.

"That beard is the ugliest thing I've ever seen, Walter," remarked Amy, snidely, one day. "It rivals Joseph's coat of many colors!"

That was certainly true enough. Sandy in some places, black in others, salt and pepper gray in others, the beard was hardly an enhancement to my looks. But I was glad I had given up the torment of daily shaves in cold water, and I had no desire to go back to them, no matter how mottled and ugly the result was. Besides, I had vowed not to shave until we were liberated, and I wasn't about to break that vow.

From our table conversations, half in English, half in Italian, Lucia was fast learning English. When Amy made her unflattering remark about my beard, Lucia came to my defense with an outburst that was totally out of character. "The Signore looks good with his beard," she snapped. "You should not be so quick to criticize him, for you are not that good to look at yourself!" Bursting into tears, she fled the room. Amy sat there, stunned. Later, I asked Nancy what had provoked Lucia.

"Walter, you are hopeless," she chuckled. "Can't you see that Lucia has a major crush on you?"

I was startled, and protested that it was Nancy's imagination. It didn't help matters when, that same evening, I asked for a few minutes alone with Valentina. Nancy, Amy, and Margherita knew I wanted to discuss news of the macchia with Valentina, and they left the room without question. Lucia, however, flew into a rage. "First Signor Metzger, and now Il Console," she spat at her sister, hands on hips. "Do you have to have them all?" She turned and flounced out of the room.

Valentina flushed slightly, but said nothing back to her little sister. I was shocked by Lucia's temper tantrum, not only because it convinced me of the truth of what Nancy had said, or because of its vehemence, but because of the mention of Manfred and Valentina. I knew that Manfred had given Valentina some gold coins as a gift, in appreciation of her and her family being so good to us. Or at least I hoped that's what they were! Later, I couldn't help wondering, with a stab of resentment, if Manfred had an ulterior motive where Valentina was concerned. Lucia's sharp comment had no real substance, I was sure. It was just provoked by the cloying closeness of our confinement. Besides, it was natural for sisters to fight and be jealous of one another. Dismissing it from my mind, I turned my attention back to Valentina.

"Have you been able to find anything out?" I asked her. "Yes," she replied. "I think I know someone you can contact. His name is Bonuccio Bonucci. He is no relation to us, or to our family. He is well known in these parts, and it is rumored that he is head of a band of partigiani in the hills. I'm trying to arrange for you to make contact with him."

"Wonderful!" I exclaimed. "When?"

My eagerness startled her. "You must be patient, Gualtiero," she said seriously, "it may take a while."

"Valentina, as casually and discreetly as you can, check this Bonuccio Bonucci out with one or two of your other friends, no more than that," I instructed her. "Again, take no risks."

I called Margherita in and shared Valentina's news with her. "It is possible that I may need to go to the macchia soon, if things continue to get worse," I informed her gently. "Valentina has the name of one Bonuccio Bonucci, an agriculturist. During the next few days, as far from the city as possible, please make inquiries about him among the farmers, and see what you can learn."

"I don't know, Signore Console," she said dubiously, "it will be difficult to get anyone to talk about him. We do not talk to anyone about our people, and especially not to strangers, ever! The farmers are even more close-mouthed than we are. But I will try, Signore."

"Thank you, Margherita, thank you both," I said sincerely. "Please, don't take any chances."

Valentina reached across the table and covered my hand with both of hers. Looking directly into my eyes, she said, with uncharacteristic intensity, "Better to be in danger and hope to live, than to be safe and pray to die." With that, she got up and left the room. Her statement, wise beyond her years, hung in the air. It gave me plenty of food for thought.

Three days later, we again met in the kitchen. Amy and Nancy were telling improvisations of Grimm's fairy tales to Franco and Lucia in our bedroom. They were all bundled up together on the bed. I was amazed at how well Nancy had progressed in Italian since our lessons in Gubbio. With daily practice, she had become quite fluent, and her accent was perfect. Amy was adding theatrics by providing sound effects. The children were hugely amused.

Settling ourselves at the table, we each sipped from the thimbleful of brandy Margherita had poured into a glass. It was amazing how, with little or nothing in the cupboards, traditional customs, like sharing of food or drink, still prevailed at any meeting or occasion.

Valentina spoke first. "Gualtiero, I have found out more about Signor Bonuccio Bonucci," she began. I leaned forward, holding my breath. "At first, no one would talk of him at all. Then two of my friends took me aside to ask why I was interested in knowing about him. 'Valentina,' they said, 'why do you want to know about such an old man? Aren't we good enough for you?' It was Renzo who asked me, while Pietro watched me closely to see what I would say. 'Well,' I said, 'I've heard well of this Bonucci so far, but I want to make absolutely sure. I want to join the partisans.' You should have seen their faces, Walter! They laughed at me. I pretended to be angry. 'Damn you both!' I said. 'I can do as much as you can! I can help. You're the ones who want to sit here, and look good.' That really got them mad. 'Well, you can forget it, little girl,' Pietro said sarcastically, 'he only wants men—real men!' And that was the end of it. I turned and left. Really, men are so simple, so easy to manipulate." She smiled triumphantly at her success in finding out for me that Bonucci was okay and was recruiting for a partisan band. Then she casually dropped her bombshell. "Oh, and I also learned he occasionally comes to town on Sundays and will be at the north corner of the Piazza Italia this Sunday afternoon." Bonanza! That set my mind buzzing.

Margherita's news was also positive. "I could not get anyone to admit they knew Bonuccio Bonucci," she began, "but I could tell from what was said, and from what was NOT said, Signore Console, that this Bonucci is widely known and respected, and is a person of importance."

So far so good. There was one major concern, however. "Did either of you find out anything about his political affiliations?"

Valentina shook her head no. Then Margherita spoke up. "We know he is not in the Fascist camp," she said. "Beyond that, the peasants would say nothing."

I was elated. This Bonucci sounded like the contact I was hoping for. I didn't want to risk the women further, but I needed someone else to contact him directly before I did. I took a deep breath, and, not looking at Margherita, I addressed Valentina. "Valentina, is it possible that you could find a way to encounter this Bonucci on Sunday afternoon?"

Margherita's eyes widened slightly, but she said nothing, and waited for her daughter to speak. Valentina sat in thought for a minute. "I think I could try to do that, Signor Console," she said slowly, "but what should I say to him?"

"You'll have to use your own judgment on how much to tell him," I said, "but let him know there is an important American who wants to make contact. Above all, don't let him know who I am, or where I'm staying."

She nodded assent. "I will talk to Renzo again tomorrow morning."

I raised the glass, with its few drops of brandy. "Buona fortuna," I said, and sipped, passing the glass to Valentina.

She took it and raised it without drinking. 'Buona fortuna," she said softly, handing it to Margherita. "Mamma, you drink the rest," she urged; "it will warm your bones a little."

Margherita took the glass and ceremoniously tipped it toward me. "Buona fortuna," she echoed, and drained the glass.

I felt an excitement I hadn't felt since Monaco. Although I was concerned for Valentina's safety, and hated for her to take such risks, I could hardly wait for Sunday. That Sunday afternoon, December 14th, Valentina skirted the piazza carefully. As planned, Vittoria followed her, at a discreet distance, then stood in the shadow of a doorway and watched, to be sure that nothing happened to her niece. When Valentina spotted the man she thought was Bonucci, she walked toward him, and, as artfully as any practiced spy, contrived to let her purse fall to the ground in front of him, as though the strap had just broken. She had, in fact, undone the strap moments before. As they both bent to retrieve her purse, she acted appropriately flustered. "Oh, how clumsy of me, scusi, scusi," she murmured. "Bonucci," she said as she picked up the identity card that had fallen out of her purse.

The man unconsciously patted his own coat pocket. Then he realized she was reading the name Bonucci from her own card. "Why, that's my name too," he said, surprised.

"I know," Valentina smiled her radiant smile up at him, and in the same tone of voice, as though thanking him for his assistance said, "I know an important American, who wants to meet you. He cannot come out on the street himself."

Bonucci quickly countered, "Perhaps you and I should meet again first. A lot of important men would like to meet me. Some of them are not my friends."

"This one is," Valentina replied, turning to leave.

Bonucci quickly slid his hand under her elbow, gripping it tightly. "Walk along as though we're friends," he said, continuing along with her. "Why would an important American want to meet me?" he asked, with just an edge of menace in his voice.

"To talk about joining your partisan band," replied Valentina quietly.

They were silent for several moments while Bonucci digested this information. Then he named a street corner about three blocks from the apartment. "Eight o'clock Friday. I will wear a red scarf. The American, white scarf." Giving her a slight push of dismissal, he let go of her elbow. As she walked away, Bonucci stood and stared at her back for a few moments, before turning away down a side street. Vittoria waited until both were safely out of sight, then rushed back to her job at the Brufani.

When Valentina recounted the story, I nearly jumped for joy. Then came a moment of concern—the white scarf! I didn't have a white scarf. Without a word, Margherita disappeared into her bedroom and came back with a white linen dresser scarf. "Washed and folded, no one will know the difference," she stated matter-of-factly. I hugged her in gratitude, then demanded that Valentina recount her adventure again, leaving out no detail. I made her describe Bonucci to me three or four times, until I had him fixed in my mind. Valentina glowed. She was the center of attention, reveling in it, and rightfully so, I thought. To be naturally devious, while basically honest, was a quality to be valued in times like this. And, most importantly, she had succeeded admirably in her mission.

"You did a wonderful job, Valentina," I praised her warmly, "I will always be in your debt for the risk you took for me today."

She flashed me a warm conspiratorial look—so she had enjoyed the adventure too!—then dropped her eyes demurely. "I was pleased to be able to be of help, Signore," she said modestly, grinning.

The icing on the cake came that same night when, just after nine o'clock, Manfred appeared. We all gathered around hungrily as he unpacked the two bags of food he had brought. Each article was passed along from one to the other and examined in exquisite detail, with ooh's and aah's of pleasure. Lucia hugged the tin of powdered chocolate to her thin little bosom in delight. "Mamma! Can we have some now?" she begged.

"Later, after the Signori have talked," decreed Margherita. Franco and Lucia were shooed from the kitchen, and while Margherita busied herself putting the food away and making the chocolate, Manfred brought the rest of us up to date.

"The news is not good for either side right how, I'm afraid," he began.

"The weather is keeping the Allies from mounting an offensive. Bombings are giving the Germans hell in the north of Italy. Rail lines are a mess, and the Germans are shipping tremendous amounts of materiel, so travel is impossible for most, and is becoming difficult and a little dangerous even for me. I don't know when I'll be able to come back here again." That was a frightening prospect. What will we do without Manfred and his connections, I wondered? How will we survive?

"Walter, your plan for heading south is totally impractical now," he said, completely dashing my hopes in that direction. "But if you're worried about the exposure to the family here, we might take a chance on getting you out of here and holed up somewhere near Rome."

I decided not to mention my upcoming meeting with Bonucci to him, or my thoughts about going to join the partisans. It was not that I didn't trust Manfred; it was because I had always considered it a sound operating principle not to give anyone information that could be pried out of them during interrogation, or worse, under torture. "I agree with you, Manfred, but we can't try anything at all without Italian identity papers. With identity cards, we'd stand a better chance if we had to leave here suddenly. We could pass normal checkpoints, if we weren't questioned too closely. Nancy and I could probably pass as Italians. Amy would have to play a deaf mute."

At that last, Amy looked insulted, and Manfred chuckled appreciatively. I could see he was once again snared by the idea of intrigue and adventure. "I'll do my best to get cards for all three of you as quickly as possible, my friend," he assured me.

We called the children in again, and Margherita served us all a cup of chocolate. We sipped it blissfully. I saved the last third of mine for Lucia, Manfred gave half of his to Valentina, and Amy and Nancy each poured some from their cup into Franco's. Margherita clucked in feigned annoyance at this, claiming we were "spoiling" the children, but she flashed me a look of gratitude. Warmed by the unexpected good fortune of hot chocolate, and the thought of real food on the morrow, we were in high spirits when Manfred took his leave. "I'll be back again as soon as I can," he promised me quietly, at the door. "I know you need food, with all these mouths to be fed every day, and I'll work on the identity cards, so you can get the hell out of this mess as soon as possible."

On Wednesday, Vittoria came with two large bags from Manfred. One contained the special gifts I had asked him to buy for me for Christmas. I hurried to hide those before anyone saw them. The other was crammed with food. With some of it carefully hoarded, as I knew Margherita would do, and a few presents for everyone, Christmas would not be as bleak as I had feared. I was more deeply indebted to Manfred Metzger than ever; to a point that could never be repaid, I realized. He was certainly showing me the true meaning of friendship.

Thursday dragged by. I mentally rehearsed, over and over, what I would say to Bonucci when we met. My nervous tension was transmitted to the others. I had told Nancy and Amy I felt I had to consider going into the hills and throwing my lot in with the partisans. They were not keen on the idea. "Really, Walter," said Amy, "in theory it sounds logical, and even a bit exciting. I can't blame you for not wanting to stay holed up here indefinitely. But it's so dangerous! You'll give up any diplomatic immunity you still have if you do it."

"Yes, and you'll be abandoning us, all of us. You're the only man we have to count on!" added Nancy, accusingly.

"I know, I know, and I don't want to leave you, either," I protested. "But if we're caught, and I'm with you, it will go much harder on you, and on the Bonuccis, than it would without me. I'm one of their prime targets. Harboring and aiding an enemy agent is no joking matter to the Germans. I'm putting you all in danger of torture, imprisonment, even execution if I stay. I can't do that. I have to go. Manfred will look after you. He has promised to stay in touch and to do everything possible to get you out of here to the Allied lines. We have to trust him."

"Have you told him what you're up to?" demanded Amy.

"No," I replied curtly. "I really don't want him, or anyone, to know my plans. I don't like it that you and the Bonuccis and Vittoria know. That knowledge is dangerous. I don't want Manfred, or any of you, at risk any more than we are now."

Tears quivered in Nancy's eyes. "We don't want you to go, Walter," she said plaintively. "We're afraid for you. And we need you." She burst into harsh sobs, burying her face in her hands. I felt terrible. For over four months, they had depended on me to give shape, form, and reason to our crazy situation and to afford them some protection, though what I could do to save them was a mystery, given my present state of weakness.

Margherita shared their feelings of despair at the idea of my departure. That evening she remarked, "It is good to have a man in the house, even if he is too young, and too Inglese." I was in an impossible position and began to have second thoughts about my upcoming meeting with Bonucci. All the next night and morning I turned it over in my mind, but always came up with the same inescapable conclusion—it was best for us all for me to go. I knew Manfred wouldn't abandon the women. I knew the Germans were looking for me. I knew that rescue, in the form of the Allies, would be a long time coming. I knew I would be giving up all diplomatic immunity, and all United States protection, if I joined the partisans. I also knew, without any doubt, that I couldn't sit the war out hiding in the Bonucci's bedroom and attic. Above all, I could not continue to depend on Margherita to find food to feed me, and all the others too.

I will keep my rendezvous with this Bonuccio Bonucci tonight, I decided. I'll see what the situation looks like. Maybe he won't want me. Maybe he won't take me. But if he does, I'm going. That evening, I dressed warmly, putting a heavy woolen sweater on under my old business suit. I was startled at how the suit, snug when I left the Brufani, now hung slack on my body, even with the thick sweater beneath the jacket! Well, I thought philosophically, at least I've lost the twenty or so pounds I've always promised myself I'd lose! I knotted the white dresser scarf loosely around my neck and pulled on one of Margherita's husband's dark, shapeless felt hats. I looked in the mirror. In the semi-darkness, the white scarf stood out like a beacon. Bonuccio Bonucci will have no problem spotting me, I thought. I just hope no one else spots me too. My heart was already pounding. In the kitchen, the women hugged me tightly, and Nancy and Amy clung to me in a kind of quiet desperation, which only served to heighten my already frazzled nerves. I hoped that Valentina's assurance that the curfew was never strictly enforced would apply to this evening. I slipped out the door and moved stealthily down the stairs. It felt strange to be out in the cold. I hadn't set foot outdoors in almost three months.

Emerging from the darkness of the stairway onto the street, I quickly glanced both ways. The street was deserted. I turned the corner, and, feeling conspicuous and vulnerable, tried to walk at a normal gait. The rendezvous point was only a few blocks away, but I dreaded having to go even that short distance. Worse, I had to pass the barracks of the local Fascists, which was in the next block. I had absolutely no identification on me. I made up my mind to break and run at the first hint of being stopped or challenged for my papers. The few townsfolk I passed seemed shrouded in a cloak of wariness and weariness. None of the usual cordial greetings were exchanged when people passed each other. I crossed to the opposite side of the street to pass the barracks—I wanted as much space as possible between me and the young thug who, rifle unslung, guarded the entrance. I forced myself to count, to maintain an even gait, and not hurry. I was relieved to turn the corner, and in a few minutes I reached the rendezvous point.

As I slackened my pace slightly, a tall, slender, middle-aged man swung in beside me, matching my stride. I noted his red scarf. Bonuccio Bonucci. "Keep walking," he murmured in greeting. "Just act like we are going someplace, Signore Console." At the realization that he knew who I was, my stride faltered. He touched my elbow lightly to urge me onward. I was jarred inside. If *he* knew, how many others did, I wondered? I glanced sideways at him. There was a half-smile on his face. "You are surprised that I know who you are?" he said. "Don't be. When a pretty young girl tells me an important American wants to meet me—well—I, too, make inquiries. It was not difficult to find out which important American has not been seen for a while. I was glad to get your message, Signore—I have wanted to meet you almost as much as our German guests have." He flashed me an open, boyish smile.

For whatever reason, I felt an instant trust and like for this man. He seemed self-assured without being cocky, and he was able to communicate without braggadocio. He quickly and quietly outlined his operation. He had the rare gift for revealing just enough, and yet concealing enough, that made for a valuable leader in a clandestine operation. His goal for the immediate future, given enough food and arms, he said, was to raise a force of 150–200 men, commanded by no more than 10 officers. From there a force of several thousand could easily be recruited—all depending on arms and food. His terse summary had been completed by the time we reached the next corner. He stopped and turned directly to face me. "Well," he said in heavily accented English, startling me, "that's it. Do you want in?"

"Definitely," I replied, without a moment's hesitation.

He reverted to Italian. "Think it over a bit more. We'll meet again Christmas Eve. Two blocks north of here, northeast corner. Eight o'clock. There will be many people out that evening, and we will not be noticed. Carry a package, as though you are going to deliver a Christmas gift to a relative." He turned down the next street and vanished into the gloom.

I doubled back to the apartment, going a few blocks out of my way in order to avoid the Fascist barracks, reaching the apartment from the opposite direction. I had to restrain myself from bounding up the stairs two at a time. I felt a great sense of relief and exhilaration. I had gotten a taste of being outside and moving about again, and I was finally doing something. The exercise of walking those few blocks was sorely needed. It was not much of a walk, but, even so, as I reached the third-floor landing I was winded, gasping for breath. Poor diet and restriction to the tiny flat for so long had taken their toll. As I stopped to catch my breath before taking the final flight of stairs, I thought about Nancy telling me I was their only protection. Hah! In my present condition, I'd be pretty useless as a protector of anything, I reflected wryly—even a kitten.

Everyone greeted me happily when I entered the apartment. Margherita pressed a mug of hot broth into my hand, insisting I sit and drink it before telling my story. I recounted our meeting, omitting that I had agreed to join Bonucci's band of partisans. Nor did I tell them how close I had come to asking Bonucci for help with our desperate food situation. Margherita had come up empty on two successive days of searching. Empty cupboards stared back at us. For the first time, driven by hunger and frustration, Margherita lamented having so many mouths dependent on her. Tears slipped down her cheeks as she looked around at all of us. "I don't know what I am going to do! I don't know where I can find food! I'm so tired!" she cried despairingly. We rushed to comfort her and assure her that somehow, some way, we'd find some food, we'd manage. I was determined to ask Valentina to find Bonuccio Bonucci again the next day, if need be, to beg for assistance.

However, miracle of miracles, the following morning Manfred the Magician appeared! He brought a large basket of canned goods and other delicacies. "Well, in the 'nick' of time comes Saint Nick, I see," he greeted us jovially, trying to cheer us up. "I wish I could have brought more, and I can't stay long this time, but I will be back soon, don't worry." After a cup of coffee and some socializing, he drew me aside. "I haven't been able to come up with identity cards for you yet, but I'm going to Trieste soon, and I feel sure I'll be able to get them taken care of there."

"Good," I replied, "we must have them, and soon. We can't stay here much longer."

As Christmas drew near, we tried to get into a holiday mood for the sake of the children, and for our own drooping morale as well. Amy and Nancy helped Lucia construct little garlands, out of bits of colored paper and cloth, to hang on the mirrors in the bedrooms and kitchen. Lucia disappeared for hours into her bedroom. She would reappear with a secret, knowing smile on her lips. I was alarmed at how she looked—she had become little more than a thinly padded skeleton.

The Thursday before Christmas, Franco came bursting through the door after school, gasping for breath. "Mamma! mamma!" he cried to a startled Margherita, "Hurry! Hurry! They have birds in the poultry shop! Big ones!" Hearing this, I grabbed for my wallet and thrust a thick wad of banknotes into Margherita's hand. Without pausing for coat or shawl, she dashed down the stairs and out into the freezing twilight on a run, headed for the poultry shop.

Less than ten minutes later she was back, triumphantly holding aloft her prize. "Look! A goose!" she cried, eyes shining. We sat, staring at it. We couldn't believe it. Then we all rushed at her at once, hugging her and the goose and Franco, praising them for being so quick-thinking. Valentina and Amy reverently carried the bird to the sink, while Margherita sat and sipped a well-earned cup of hot broth, laced with a splash from the carefully hoarded brandy Vittoria has swiped from the Germans at the Brufani.

"No, no, Signore," she protested, catching her breath, "It is you we must thank for this blessing. We could never have afforded this, no matter how hungry we were."

She clasped my hand gratefully. The price, of course, had been astronomical. The goose was one of perhaps only a dozen in all of Perugia. Paying such a price posed a risk, but risk be damned! We'd have a Christmas Eve feast with that goose, and a Christmas dinner, and more. Margherita called us all to her side and insisted we kneel then and there to say a prayer of thanks for our good fortune, adding a prayer for the health and safety of her husband. Only then did she rise and begin preparations for dinner—a soup in which she used the feet and a piece of the neck of the goose.

The next day was Christmas Eve, and it really took on a festive air as the slowly roasting goose warmed and scented the kitchen. We all waited hungrily for it to finish cooking. Margherita hummed as she moved about the kitchen, preparing small dishes from some of the canned goods Manfred had brought, to go along with the goose. From time to time she would open the oven, releasing a mouth-watering aroma into the room, and carefully spoon grease from the roasting pan into a jar, an act that required her utmost concentration, so as not to spill or waste any of the drippings. In Margherita's thrifty hands, I knew that goose would be paying dividends for weeks, just from the fat it provided.

The apartment door opened, and Valentina came in, rosy-cheeked from the cold. "Hello everyone! Look what I got!" She beamed as she held aloft her prize—a current issue of *L'Osservatore Romano*! I grabbed it up, and read the key articles aloud, adding my own editorial comments as I went along. The Swiss had been right about the situation in Rome. Food shortages were critical there. On hearing that, every eye swung gratefully toward our well-charged oven. Milan, however, was by far the worst off. The industrial belt around the city had received repeated bombings. There were vague references to "citizen unrest" in that area, but no details on how the Germans were reacting to control the problem. Once we had digested every scrap of news, I took Franco and Lucia aside and did my best to tell them Dickens' *A Christmas Story*.

At one point, Franco interrupted to inquire seriously, "Is Scrooge a Blackshirt (a neo-Fascist), Signore?" That he wasn't did not dim their enthusiasm for the story, and I could see that they identified with the joy of Tiny Tim's family over the Christmas goose. Flushed with success, I launched into a fractured version of "Twas the Night Before Christmas." Of course it didn't rhyme, and I took literary license here and there— especially since I didn't know the Italian word for reindeer. I had horses pull the sleigh. Lucia giggled at the idea of someone coming down a chimney. By the time I reached the end of the tale, Valentina and Margherita had joined the audience and were sitting there enthralled, dinner all but forgotten.

When Vittoria arrived, her chores at the hotel finished, we were ready to sit down to our Christmas Eve dinner. We decided we'd risk eating together just this once. Nancy, with help from Valentina and Franco, had hauled the two old armchairs from our bedroom into the kitchen. I was ushered ceremoniously to the seat of honor at the head of the table. I felt a lump rise in my throat as I said grace, asking a special blessing on Manfred, and on all our distant loved ones. It was indeed a feast. We savored every morsel of our allotted portions, which were especially generous, although by no means as much as we *could* have eaten. After the dishes were cleared away, Valentina set Manfred's "tórta" of dried and candied fruit on the table, and the adults lingered over a half cup of Swiss coffee, while the children had a bit of hot chocolate. We wondered if we would ever enjoy such a meal again in our lives. Margherita brought out the last of the bottle of brandy and poured each of us a sip. I raised a glass, the others followed suit, and we drank a misty-eyed toast.

Then it was time for presents. Although they had been cautioned not to expect much, the children were on tiptoe with excitement, and if the truth be told, so were the adults. Amy, Nancy, and I had had to do our shopping by way of Manfred, Vittoria, and Valentina. There was little of any interest or worth available in the shops, so our gifts to one another were practical items like scarves, gloves, and woolen socks. I gave little Franco the book on the life of Winston Churchill that I had found in the hotel in Gubbio. He hugged me gratefully, then sat down to turn the pages of the book—his first. For me there was a diary from Nancy and Amy, which served as a sharp and painful reminder of just how long I had been away from my own family.

We gave Margherita and Vittoria sweaters. Valentina tore the tissue from her gift, and gasped in delight. It was a brown leather purse, to replace the badly worn one she had feigned to drop when approaching Bonucci in the piazza. "Oh, Signore Orebaugh," she exclaimed, "it is much too beautiful and too expensive! I will be the envy of all my friends! Thank you!"

"Look inside," I urged her, smiling. Inside, she found a thin gold chain with a medallion of the Virgin—from Manfred. She sat back in her chair, stunned, a soft blush suffusing her cheeks. "Now for Lucia," I said, whose eyes were glowing in anticipation. I produced a huge box. How I had managed to smuggle it past them all had them baffled. Lucia squealed with delight, and threw Valentina a triumphant look before turning to tear off the wrapping. She drew forth a forest green wool coat and a woolen head scarf to match. She threw herself into my arms, hugging me, and tears streamed down Margherita's and Vittoria's cheeks at the sight of the coat.

"Oh, Signore, Signore," said Margherita, as Lucia danced around the room, showing off, "there is no finer coat on anyone in Perugia this winter! How can we ever thank you?"

"It is I who can never thank you, and your family, Margherita," I replied, embarrassed by the display of emotion I had aroused. I hastily excused myself to get ready for my second rendezvous with Bonuccio Bonucci.

I donned my sweater and coat, but couldn't find the white dresser scarf anywhere. Strange. There wasn't time to search for it. I couldn't leave Bonuccio waiting, thinking I had changed my mind. I returned to the kitchen, ready to leave. Vittoria was waiting. She would be walking with me. A man and a woman taking a Christmas Eve stroll together were less likely to arouse suspicion. Lucia stood by the door, her new coat on, a package in hand. Wordlessly, she held it out to me. The missing dresser scarf! It had been transformed into a real scarf, the ends carefully fringed and knotted. Near the corner, on one end, was a painstakingly hand-embroidered representation of an American eagle. Tears filled my eyes. I handed the scarf to Lucia, and ceremoniously bent down so she could place it around my neck. As she did, she shyly gave me a kiss on the cheek. "Thank you, Lucia," I said, "I will treasure this all my life." I hugged her and hurried out the door. I didn't want them to see my tears. Some day, I vowed, I will find a way to repay this family for all the love and care they have given me.

Vittoria and I walked quickly, without speaking, toward the corner where I had agreed to meet Bonucci. She split off a block before. When Bonuccio fell into step with me, I said quickly, "I want in. How do we arrange it?" After turning the matter over in my mind for days, my initial decision held.

"Good," he said, as we walked along together. "We'll be glad to have you with us. I'll be back here Sunday, January 16th. We'll meet in the Piazza Italia, where I first met your young lady friend, at four P.M. sharp."

"Okay," I replied, "I'll be there—the 16th, Piazza Italia, four o'clock."

"Be sure you know what you're doing," he cautioned me again. "If you change your mind, I'll understand. But once you're with us, there's no going back."

"Don't worry," I assured him tersely as we parted, "I understand. I'll be there."

Now that there was a promise of action, time passed more slowly than ever. I had not informed the others, yet. If action was what I needed, it came sooner than expected. The afternoon of December 28th, Margherita spotted a search squad of Repubblichini (neo-Fascist militia) working our street. The girls and I scrambled up into the attic. I had barely finished pushing the discarded furniture and old crates between us and the trapdoor when we heard pounding at the door of the apartment. We huddled in our freezing corner, not daring to breathe. We could hear loud, male voices below. Nancy was shaking. I patted her to reassure her, feeling no assurance myself. The voices grew louder, and in one I detected a decidedly German accent. Clammy sweat broke out all over my body. None of us moved a muscle. Not that we could have—we were paralyzed with fear.

Suddenly, the trapdoor popped open, and the peaked cap of a Fascist militiaman came into view. His eyes barely cleared the sill of the trapdoor. From our dark corner, we could see him silhouetted from the kitchen light below. Fortunately for us, his eyes weren't adjusted to the darkness. They raked the heaped-up articles obstructing his view of us, then his head disappeared, and we heard the trapdoor pulled closed with a bang. Amy jumped. I moved only enough to pry loose the fingers painfully digging into my arm. We didn't dare speak. We could hear voices, and some shouts, below us. I was terrified for Margherita and the children. We heard the apartment door slam, and boots clumping down the stairs. I tried to count how many of them there were by the sound of their feet, but realized that was useless, since I hadn't counted them coming up! We waited for the "all clear," growing more frightened with each passing second. After what seemed like an eternity, we heard the "thump! thump!" of the broom, and Nancy immediately burst into sobs, followed quickly by Amy.

"Sssh!" I hushed them. "We're okay. Easy, now. We'll be out of here in a minute." I scrambled to move the obstacles blocking our exit. We climbed down on shaky legs and washed the filth and grime off, then collapsed around the table to hear details from Margherita.

"There was one German, Signore, and three militiamen," she said.

"Were they looking for us?" I asked. She shook her head no. "Did they mention me, or Americans?" I pressed.

"No, Signore, they didn't seem to be looking for anyone in particular. At least they didn't mention, or ask about, anyone in particular."

"What did they want?" I wanted to know.

"I don't know," she said, "I think it was just a routine search. They took our radio." We laughed with her at the idea of the four men carrying her virtually worthless radio down the stairs—the big result of their raid, when the real prizes were right under their noses, or, rather, right above their noses!

However, this was an added worry. We might not be lucky the next time they decided to do "a routine search." I didn't like that there were Germans along with them on their searches. I was relieved when Manfred showed up again that very night. I swiftly filled him in on what had happened that afternoon.

"Good thing, then, that I have this for you," he remarked casually, and, reaching into a pocket, he produced a blank identity card, with an excise stamp to be affixed to the reverse side of it. I grabbed it excitedly. At last! This was like a ticket to freedom! "I didn't have a picture of you, so I couldn't complete it," Manfred said, as I carefully turned the document over and over in my hands.

"God, how much did you have to pay in bribes to get this?" I asked in wonder.

"Not too much," he replied, chuckling at the memory. "I just said to the guy, 'what the hell, the Germans are going to lose anyway. You better start getting on the right side now, while you still can. I'll get you a note you can show to the Allies, to protect you.' So a few lire, and he gave it to me."

Awhile back, I had written out a tiny note on a slip of paper not more than a half inch wide by an inch and a half long. It stated that Manfred had provided valuable assistance to the Allied cause, and I had signed it, added my title, and given it to Manfred. "Okay, I'll do one for the guy who gave you the blank card. Who was it?"

"Criminal lawyer," replied Manfred. "Big-shot Fascist. Has been pro-Nazi, all that crap. Wants to cover his ass now. You can fix me a note for him?"

My mind raced. "I will, but only if he gets documents for Nancy and Amy too. If he produces those, he'll get his piece of paper. Either we all get out, or he gets nothing from me." I tried again to explain to Manfred why it was so important that we all get out, and soon. Without giving specifics, I alluded to the possibility of my joining a resistance band somewhere in the Umbrian hills and told him he would have to see to getting the girls out.

He grunted at hearing that news, then said quietly, "If you go, how can I contact you?"

"Valentina will keep you in touch with me. You should enjoy that, you dirty old goat," I said, teasing him. "She knows who to contact. And you can always get to Valentina through Vittoria at the Brufani."

"Well," he sighed in resignation, "it's your neck! I'll get the cards for the girls, don't worry. You be careful. I'll take care of things here, I promise."

Wordlessly, I embraced him, and he slipped quietly out into the night.

When he was gone, I turned to the women. "Margherita, bring me your card so I can make this look official," I said. I was disappointed to find that the raised seal, necessary to validate the card, was missing from the one Manfred had provided. Damn! I'd have to think of a way to fake it. I worried that I had asked too much of Manfred and put too much responsibility on him. I didn't want to alienate my best friend and ally. But then, who understood better than Manfred the danger we were in? He'd put the screws to his lawyer friend, if need be. If anyone knew how to do that, Manfred did.

The year 1944 arrived dressed in a cloak of ice. We spent New Year's Day huddled in bed. The temperature inside the apartment was barely above thirty degrees. When Margherita cooked, we all crowded around the stove, absorbing any feeble heat seeping from the weak cooking fire. The news was even more chilling. Vittoria reported that several units of the German army had moved into and around Perugia. That meant we'd now be an Allied bombing target.

Our "two-to-three-week" stay was into its fifth month. Manfred's supplies, even with the careful stretching of the Christmas goose, were almost at an end. The cold, the constant gnawing hunger, and seven people crammed into those three rooms finally began to tax our nerves and our personal relations. Everyone was civil, but the atmosphere became even more tense when searches came two days in a row. On one of those times, Margherita had our newly washed, obviously foreign underwear strung across the kitchen to dry. Stripping it down in a panic, we dragged it with us into the attic. Afterward, it all had to be rewashed, along with us.

Two more weeks passed, and Manfred had not returned. I worked on my identity card. I had found an old passport picture among my belongings, and I doctored it up and put it on the card. Valentina named me Michele Franciosi, son of Luigi Franciosi and Anna Maria Spada. We described my features, as the card required. For occupation, I decided on "clerk." Valentina wrote " 'SFOLLATO" in large script diagonally across the card. This marked me as a bombed-out refugee from Naples. She signed the card as an official in Naples. I made up a Neapolitan address— Piazza Villa Fiorelli 8, Napoli. Who would check? Naples had been extensively bombed and was now occupied by the Allies. For hours, using the point of one of Margherita's fine knitting needles, I worked at duplicating the raised seal. The finished product gave me a strong surge of pride in my counterfeiting craftsmanship. Even on close inspection, it was difficult to tell my homemade seal from the genuine one. My identity card looked as authentic as Margherita's in every respect.

Sunday, January 16th, finally arrived. I took the card with me to my meeting with Bonucci. He was suitably impressed. "Well, Signor Bonucci," I said, as we strolled in the late afternoon shadows of the piazza, "I am definite about joining you and ready to leave whenever you say."

"If you are certain about this, Signor Console, and understand that I can offer you no assurance of protection because of who you are, then I am happy to have you join us."

"I understand," I assured him, "and I'm ready to accept the risks. I'd rather do something to help the Allied cause than sit and wait to be captured. Besides, I am too great a burden to place on Signora Bonucci and her family."

"Then it is decided," said Bonucci with finality. "Four days from now, on January 20th, be at the railway station at six-fifteen sharp. You will take the six-thirty train for Ponte San Giovanni. You'll get off there and transfer to the train to Monte Corona, then take the local train to Campo Reggiano. At the station at Campo Reggiano, you will cross the tracks after the train leaves, and begin to walk northward. My man Giuseppe will approach you and give you whispered instructions and continue on. You must be quick and catch his instructions the first time. He will take the same trains you do and will be in the same cars, but away from you. Should anything go wrong, he will do whatever he can to create a diversion, so that you can escape, if possible."

"All right," I replied, and repeated his instructions back, to be sure I had them perfectly clear in my mind. Reaching the opposite side of the Piazza, we went our separate ways.

The plan was a tightly scheduled one, which had only one chance to work. Since it was my hide at risk, I was determined to see that nothing went wrong on my part. Back at the apartment, I gathered everyone together. "I'll be leaving you for good in several days," I announced. As I gazed around at their stunned faces, a pang of guilt lanced through me, and I tried once more to assure them, and myself, that my decision was in everyone's best interest. No one said anything negative, but I sensed their deep hurt.

"And when is this all to happen, Walter?" inquired Amy, in chilling, if not icy, tones.

"January 20th," I replied.

Margherita said nothing, but from the noise she made with dishes and pans as she set about preparing supper, I could tell she was deeply affected. After throwing me a look of anguish, Nancy got up to help Margherita with supper preparations. The vacuum of silence that ensued was depressing.

After dinner, I carefully went over with the girls everything Manfred and I had discussed about getting them identity cards and getting them to Allied lines. "I'm trusting you to do whatever Manfred tells you to do. He is your ticket to freedom." They both assured me they would follow any instructions from him to the letter.

The next morning, over coffee, I went over details again with Valentina and told her I expected Manfred to get in touch with her through Vittoria and that he would continue to provide food for them whenever he could. I told her that she would be Manfred's contact with me, through Bonuccio Bonucci, and it would be her responsibility to get messages to me through him and to assist Manfred in making arrangements to get Amy and Nancy to freedom.

She nodded from time to time, saying little, but I could see she was pleased and proud to be given such important responsibilities. "Don't worry, Signore," she said, briefly touching my shoulder as she got up to leave, "we will look after the Signorine, and I will get messages to you somehow. I am proud that you are joining Bonucci. I wish I could go with you." With a fiercely loyal, partisan Valentina in my corner, I felt immensely reassured. Despite her youth, I knew that she'd see to it that all went well here without me.

Vittoria joined us for supper the 19th. I had packed and re-packed the battered suitcase I borrowed from Margherita. I had made room for the white dresser scarf so carefully reworked by Lucia. The mealtime mood was somber. I tried to lighten things up with joking remarks, which sounded corny even to myself. I felt like I was participating in my own wake. Everyone just sat there and stared at me, wide-eyed and wordless. I escaped to our room as soon after dinner as possible, using the excuse that I had last-minute details to handle. Whether the others pretended to sleep well that night, or actually did, I don't know. I wondered if I would miss our closeness. I worried about my family. I worried about Manfred, the girls, and the Bonucci family.

I had so much on my mind, dawn broke without me once closing my eyes. As soon as I heard Margherita in the kitchen, I dressed quietly and joined her. Lucia was there, too, and for the last time she brought me my cup of coffee. Soon everyone gathered in the kitchen. "Don't worry about us, Walter, we'll be just fine," Nancy assured me seriously, then burst into tears. Lucia followed suit, and soon they were all crying. I was astounded to see tears sliding down even the stolid Amy's cheeks. Lucia again waited alone by the door. I picked her up and hugged her long and hard.

"Bye, little Lucia," I said, "keep safe and keep smiling, and take care of your mother."

"Oh, Signore," she cried, "please come back! Please be safe. God be with you and protect you. I love you."

Gently, I set her back down and untangled her arms from around my neck. "I love you too, Lucia," I said, and hurried out the door. I didn't want any of them to see that tears were coursing down my cheeks.

5

Michele Franciosi, "Il Console"

As I walked the twenty-minute distance from the apartment to the train station, my head cleared and my emotions calmed. The predawn cold was invigorating, and the few people who were out gave me no more than a passing glance. Over and over I rehearsed my new name. Michele Franciosi. Michele Franciosi. I knew I needed the sound of that name implanted in my brain so well that I would react instantly to it. I certainly looked the part. Bearded, thin, dressed in a frayed coat and battered felt hat, carrying a scruffy cardboard suitcase—no one could possibly associate me with the dapper, clean-shaven American Consul who had strolled the streets of Perugia a few months back. Would my own mother recognize me now? Probably not! I chuckled to myself at the thought of what her reaction would be if she could see me.

The tension that always crawled just below the surface of my skin nowadays rose and rippled in waves as I neared the railroad station. Stepping into the station house, I was relieved to see quite a few people gathered there, waiting for the train. That would make it easy for me to blend in. I purchased a third-class ticket to Monte Corona—the agent barely looked up as he shoved my ticket and change across the counter to me. Then I joined the line of people waiting to have their documents checked by the "questorino" (police agent). He was seated behind a small table, hunched down in his chair, bundled against the early morning cold. This would be the acid test of whether or not my homemade identity card would pass inspection. When my turn came, I proffered my card, open to the photograph, and kept shuffling slowly ahead, as I had seen the others before me do. The agent's eyes flicked up at me briefly, then back at my card. There was no cry of "Alt!" as I shuffled on. Then I was out on the platform. I had made it! Taking my handkerchief from my pocket, I faked blowing my nose in order to wipe the nervous sweat from my face.

The train came chugging in and I slipped into the third-class car among a group of workingmen. The run to the junction at Ponte San Giovanni, my transfer point, took less than fifteen minutes. We had to walk the final half mile to the junction station, since the railroad bridge leading to the town had been bombed out. As I walked, I tried to spot Giuseppe, whom Bonuccio had handpicked to shadow me for the journey. If he was tailing me, as I assumed he was, he was extremely good at it and was being careful not to show his hand. The wait for the connecting train was agonizing. I felt exposed and vulnerable, standing alone on the platform. The restaurant was shuttered closed, there were no newspapers, and all I could do was pace up and down.

When the northbound train pulled in, I scrambled aboard with the others. Searching for empty seats in the crowded car, I was shocked to see that twenty or so passengers were German military officers and enlisted men. I proceeded, outwardly calm, down the aisle. The only available seat was next to two young German soldiers. Screwing up my courage, I sat down, bracing my suitcase between my knees. Neither of them took any notice of me. We rode along for a few minutes, and they talked together in German and pointed at things they saw from the window.

Suddenly, one of them turned to me and said, "Scusi, à che serve?" pointing to a row of mulberry trees pruned down to stump length.

Praying they would not detect any foreign flavor to my Italian, I replied that I thought that grapevines were secured to the cut off trunks and strung from tree to tree. That seemed to satisfy them, and they continued asking polite questions from time to time, when passing scenes caught their attention. "Scusi, Signori," I apologized at one point, "I'm not a farmer, so I don't know much about these things."

As the train slowed to a stop in Monte Corona, I rose to leave. The one called Christian reached across and shook my hand, thanking me for the company and the conversation. I jumped off the train as soon as it stopped, and crossed over to the odd-looking, midget-sized train already waiting on the narrow gauge line. I jumped aboard, and almost immediately the little locomotive tooted its whistle, and chugged upgrade toward Campo Reggiano. I scanned the carriage, hoping to spot Bonuccio's elusive Giuseppe. No luck.

The Campo Reggiano station was a small, weatherbeaten masonry building, whose unpainted concrete interior offered a couple of wooden benches. Outside, next to it, was a small, open-sided shed, stacked with boxes waiting to be loaded onto the single baggage-freight-livestock car. I ducked into the tiny waiting room, to shelter from the biting wind, while the freight car was loaded. After about ten minutes, the little two-car train went on its way. Then, carefully following the instructions Bonuccio had given me, I crossed the tracks, turned north, and paused at the beginning of a slope. From this height, I could see the cluster of buildings below that made up the village of Campo Reggiano. Just beyond me, on my side of the tracks, was a dirt footpath that led over the brow of the hill.

The sun was shining, and it felt good on my back. I watched the few poorly dressed farmers head off in various directions. Some went toward the town, others set off on the narrow, overgrown footpath. Coming up behind me, a nondescript, middle-aged man muttered "follow me," and, without pausing, added, "not too close." Turning onto the footpath, he took off at a fairly brisk pace. My heavy suitcase slowed me down, so there was no possibility I would follow "too close." In fact, I was afraid I would lose my escort. The path led uphill, and footing was treacherous. After only a few minutes, I was panting. Months of inactivity had taken their toll on my endurance. Twenty minutes later, we reached a level clearing.

Giuseppe paused, motioning for me to catch up with him. There were fields all around us, and in the distance I saw a couple of dilapidated stone farmhouses. "Benvenuto Signore," he said respectfully. "From here we can go together. It is safe. Any stranger walking alone here might arouse suspicion. With me, you will be taken as one of us—Bonucci's band—and therefore to be trusted." With that, he picked up my suitcase and set off again. I quickly caught up to him and tried to match his stride. He said nothing, but I was aware of his intense scrutiny of me. Just trying to keep up with him commanded my full attention. Since he was older than me by at least a decade, and carrying my suitcase to boot, I was determined that I would, by God, keep up. After about an hour, when I thought I couldn't continue no matter what, we arrived at a small cluster of weathered stone houses scattered along a narrow, cart-rutted dirt road, and we paused briefly. In their midst stood an old stone church, its square bell tower topped with a flat roof of red clay tiles. The simple utilitarian buildings, and the church, looked as though they had sprung from the rocky soil that surrounded them. Giuseppe stopped in front of the church and made the sign of the cross. Then he turned to me. "This is San Faustino," he informed me. This gaggle of old stone buildings could hardly be classed as a town, let alone a strategically important one. We continued on. The path resumed its gradual climb. About five minutes later, we came upon a villa—a rambling, sturdy edifice planted foursquare on the crest of the hill, commanding a panoramic view of the countryside below it.

Constructed around the turn of the century out of native rock and tile, the villa did not compare in size or elegance to other villas I had known, but it was impressive enough to suggest substance and importance, especially in relation to the other buildings in the surrounding area. It boasted a square bell tower like the one on the church in the village, and its window frames, painted a bright azure blue, injected a jaunty touch of color into the otherwise drab winter landscape. We turned into the entrance path and went through the old iron gates; as we stepped onto the terrace, the front door was thrown open and Bonuccio Bonucci himself appeared, smiling broadly, his arms wide in greeting. "Benvenuto, Signor Console!" he exclaimed warmly. "I am happy you made it without incident. I see you have met Giuseppe—my right arm." He walked up to me and clasped my hand in both of his. "You are welcome to my home," he declared. Putting an arm around my shoulder and signaling with a jerk of his head for Giuseppe to follow, he walked me into the main living room of the villa.

The Bonucci villa showed signs that a woman had a hand in its interior appointments. The feminine touch was evident in the dining room, with its henna-colored drapes and lace curtains. In the living room, next to the massive fireplace, was a dainty, Empire-style French desk, with a mottled tan marble top and crenellated bronze railing. Beside it was a chaise longue. Evidently that corner was feminine turf, because the rest of the room's furniture was solid, dark, heavy, and masculine.

Seated in a comfortable armchair, with a glass of wine in my hand, I was at last able to take a measure of this man who had so dominated my thoughts, and my life, in recent weeks. Tall for an Italian, slim yet powerfully built, he exuded a boyish charm that was infectious and disarming. He moved with the natural grace of a well-trained athlete. The effect of the strong, masculine features of his face was heightened by his ability to impale his listener, and hold him mesmerized, with a steady look from those deep, liquid brown eyes. "Occhi parlanti," the Sicilians call them—"talking eyes." They were the most notable feature of his fair-complexioned face, which was framed by a thick mass of dark curls that belied his age. I judged him at around forty. He paced the room, speaking in a rapid-fire staccato, his voice sparked with fervor and enthusiasm. His naturally gregarious nature reached out and, like a strong ocean current, pulled those around him into, and along with, whatever activity he was pursuing. The dread I had felt over having to adjust to a new way of life, a new set of associates, dissolved into insignificance as he spoke with pride about the "Band of San Faustino." After just a few moments, I could hardly wait to meet the others and start taking action against the Germans. No wonder this man was so well liked and respected! No wonder his name was a household word to the peasantry of the region. Bonuccio Bonucci was a real charmer—a born charismatic leader of men. I was glad he was on our side.

He left me for a few moments while he said good night to "Gigi," as he called Giuseppe, then escorted me upstairs to the bedroom he had set aside for me. After the crowded apartment in Perugia, the spacious, light and airy room he ushered me into was a sight for sore eyes. It was high-ceilinged, with tall double windows on two sides. Its antique furnishings were dark mahogany, heavy and solid, with a large, comfortable bed, a

huge carved armoire, a dresser, and a washstand. Bonucci dropped into
the comfortable armchair that sat in a corner of the room with a low,
square wood table at its side, and continued his briefing, while I stowed
my gear. "You have come at a good time, my American friend," he said.
"Your presence will give everyone a boost, and will lend a lot of credibility to our efforts. And, your assistance in getting word of our existence
to the Allies will be invaluable. We are just getting started as an organization, and there are many problems to be confronted and resolved. We
are fortunate to have you join us at this stage."

"How can I be the most help to you right away?" I asked him.

"By getting word out to the Allies somehow that we are here and ready
to begin operations, that we are badly in need of arms and of some means
to communicate with them, but that we will begin operations anyway,
hoping they can get help to us soon," he replied.

"What is your manpower?" I inquired, retrieving my comb and soap
from among the sweaters in my suitcase. "What numbers are we talking
about?"

Bonucci got up and stood looking out at the fields that stretched to
woods at the back of the villa. "Signore," he answered quietly, as if speaking to himself, "numbers have little relevance in our situation. In this area
there are hundreds, probably thousands, of people who have taken to the
macchia for various reasons. With little effort, we could recruit a force of
a thousand good and able men in a week, if we were so minded. But we
are unable to feed a force of such a size. And we must also require that
each man we take on have a weapon, that he be physically strong and
hardened, which most peasants of this area already are, that he have previous military experience or training, that he be able to face the danger
and hardship of guerrilla life, and that he be motivated to support our
cause against the Germans and the Fascists. That is not an easy order to
fill, by any means." He turned and flashed me a sardonic smile. "As you
yourself have learned, we recruit slowly and carefully, Signore, to be sure
that every man among us is fully with us, and fully trustworthy. It is the
only way."

"D'accordo," I agreed. I closed my suitcase and slid it under the bed.
"That's the only way it could possibly work."

Bonucci went on to clarify his own role. "I am not the military commander of this movement," he said, pacing back and forth at the foot of
the bed. "That is in the hands of Colonel Mario Guerrizzi, a seasoned
professional. You will meet him soon. I represent the CLN, the Committee for National Liberation, which is the organization responsible for planning and coordination of resistance at the national level. The Band of San
Faustino, which you are joining, is a nonpolitical, partisan group that is
ready to undertake aggressive military operations in our range."

"And what is our range?" I asked, deliberately using "our," to reinforce my intent to join with the Band in their partisan activities.

Bonucci didn't miss it, and he smiled in acknowledgment. "Roughly 200 square kilometers," he said proudly.

I whistled. "That's quite an area. Where?"

He turned, and with his finger drew an imaginary map on the wall. "The zone of our operations lies between the Parish of Morena on the north," he said, punching a dot with his index finger to indicate Morena, "to Città di Castello on the west," a line and another finger jab, "and Gubbio on the southeast."

"I know Gubbio well," I told him, giving him a brief rundown on the time I had spent in the Albergo San Marco.

Resuming his pacing, Bonucci explained how the military presidios of the partisan movement were organized. "We have already recruited several seasoned Italian officers for our organization," he said. "Colonel Guerizzi's second-in-command is Captain Stelio Pierangeli, who is also responsible for the presidio in the Città di Castello sector. Other sectors are under the command of other Italian officers. Lieutenant Mario Bonfigli is in command of our sector here in the Pietralunga area, and he is the one you will be working with."

"Where are the partisans billeted?" I wanted to know.

He hesitated only a fraction of a second before replying, but it was enough to show me the inherent caution in the man. "Well, we keep them scattered in local farmhouses, two to three to a farmhouse, in an irregular pattern. That prevents detection, but it allows us to round everyone up on short notice. Each cadre has twenty to twenty-five men."

I told Bonucci I had heard there were some British and American officers connected with the partisan movement in this area—was that true?

"Your information is partly correct, Signore," he replied. "There are several British and American officers sheltered in this area who have offered us their services. We hope to avail ourselves of those services soon. But there are problems. One, they don't speak Italian, and, two, they don't know the terrain, so their usefulness is rather limited."

"Well," I rejoined, "there must be some way we can use them to our advantage, even if they don't speak the language. Are any of them trained in explosives or demolition? Or bridge engineering?"

He thought a moment. "There is one," he said, "a fellow named Ramsay—he's British. I heard only two days ago that he has a good working knowledge of explosives. Now that you are here to ease the difficulty of communicating with them, we can certainly make use of all their experience and abilities." Suddenly he stopped and smiled his engaging smile at me. "But I am being a poor host, Signore—it has been a very long and tiring day for you. I will not keep you longer if you wish to rest."

I was tired, and it *had* been a long and eventful day, but I was much too keyed up to sleep. "No, Signor Bonucci, I am not ready to sleep. I want to continue our talk."

"Well, then, we'll go back down and share a glass of wine. And we'll talk no more of business! I want to hear about you—about your home and your family and your background." We adjourned back downstairs to the parlor and sat in armchairs in front of the fire, which he kindled into a warming blaze. Over a glass of wine, we exchanged sketchy information about our families, our backgrounds, and our respective careers—mine in the Foreign Service, his as an agriculturist. It was easy to talk to him, and with each passing moment, I felt more relaxed about my decision to join him.

"You know, Bonuccio," I said finally, "I'm curious about the paesani— the peasants—I guess we'd call them tenant farmers. I'm particularly interested in them, in their way of life, and their attitude and role in this war. So far I've found them difficult to get to know, and more difficult to understand. Can you enlighten me any?"

Bonucci sipped the dregs of his wine, stared at the fire for a few seconds, then shrugged. "I wish I could, Signor Console," he replied thoughtfully. "I have lived among them all my life, and as an agriculturist, I have been as closely associated with them as any nontenant farmer can be. I believe I have their trust and respect. I am engaged in business dealings with them almost daily. I often eat with them and, occasionally, sleep in their beds. I am invited to their baptisms, their confirmations, their weddings, and their funerals, yet I cannot say that I really understand them, either." He set his glass down on the small table next to his chair and leaned forward, hands clasped between his knees, looking at me intently. "The paesani are, and always have been, an enigma, a mosaic of contradictions, of conflicting values and desires. Yet today, beyond a doubt, there is a solidarity among them that has never before been seen in this country. One could almost believe that a magic wand has been waved over the countryside, brushing aside and covering all their previous political ideology." I was surprised at the depth of this man's intelligence and perceptiveness.

"So what will happen now?" I asked.

"Ah, that is anyone's guess, Signore," he said, leaning back and tapping the tips of his fingers together thoughtfully. "Relative to what they want, no one is sure. We know that the Communists are at work, spreading their dogma among them. The only thing we know for sure is that they want no more of Fascism or any of its trappings. And they hate the Germans."

"What do they think of the partisan movement hereabouts, and of you, personally, as a key organizer?" I asked.

He smiled at the directness of my question, but did not hesitate to answer. "Surprisingly, though they usually avoid affiliation of any sort, their attitude is very favorable to us," he said. "We have never been refused by any family when we've requested billets and board for our men. Even when their houses are full to overflowing with their own families they take in 'sfollati (bombed-out refugees) and invariably offer to put our men up as well, even if they only have stalls or outbuildings available. It is truly amazing. And now, Signore," he said, rising and stretching tiredly, "we must stop this and get some rest. We will talk more tomorrow."

I thanked him again for giving me the opportunity to join him. Back in my room, I fell gratefully into the big bed. Giving only a brief thought to Nancy, Amy, and the other Bonuccis, I dropped into deep, dreamless sleep. When I woke, the sun was already up. Looking about me, I knew without a doubt I had turned a page in my life. All that had gone before now receded from concern or concentration. I was irrevocably committed to Bonuccio Bonucci and his partisan Band of San Faustino, for better or worse. I bounded out of bed. After hastily washing and dressing, I headed downstairs, toward the enticing smell of something like coffee brewing.

Bonucci and Gigi had already breakfasted and were just coming in from a morning meeting somewhere. Gigi put on a fresh pot of the inevitable barley coffee, and there was a loaf of good bread and some real butter, no doubt from one of the neighboring farms. "Good morning, Michele," Bonuccio greeted me heartily.

I stopped for an instant, confused, then realized that he was using my new identity. Michele. Michael. I'll have to get used to using it, and hearing it, and certainly to answering to it better than I just did, I thought, chagrined. "Morning, Bonuccio, Giuseppe," I said, pouring myself a cup, and breaking off a chunk of bread. "Sorry I slept so late—I guess I was more tired than I thought. I haven't had so much exercise in months."

"You'll get back in shape fast around here," laughed Bonucci. "Gigi will see to that." He poured himself some barley brew and motioned for me to join him on the terrace, which was in a sunny corner just outside the kitchen. The warm sun was welcome on my face. I was glad I had put on my heavy sweater; it was just enough covering in this sheltered spot. What a pleasure to breathe fresh mountain air again, I thought gratefully, inhaling deeply. "So, my friend, you are glad to be out and free again, eh?" commented Bonucci, with a knowing smile.

"You don't know how glad," I said. "I hate being confined and helpless, the way I've been for the past five months!"

"Well, you don't have to worry about that any more—as long as you don't get captured again," he said. He then began bringing me up to date on activities of the Band of San Faustino. Shortly after the Armistice in September, they had hit a German convoy and had managed to destroy several trucks. They salvaged one for themselves, which was hidden under hay in a barn near the village of Pietralunga. The Germans had retaliated with ferocity, executing several dozen innocent villagers—including old folks, women, and children. Bonucci's eyes clouded with pain at the memory, and his face twisted in hatred. "Pigs! Animals! They have no soul, no conscience!" he spat out, in fury. Then he continued, "After that raid, and the reprisals, we went through a period of fear and were pretty disorganized. To keep everyone frightened and demoralized, the Germans and the Fascists stepped up the "rastrellamenti"—the roundups. They took the young people away, and confiscated all weapons. Then, feigning to enforce the ammasso—that's the tax in crops the tenant farmers pay to the government—they requisitioned most of our wheat. With their sons gone, and no wheat to even put bread on their tables, people were not willing to be active, let alone openly resist."

"So how did you get going again?" I asked.

Just then, Gigi appeared in the doorway with two visitors and another pot of coffee. The two middle-aged men, neighboring tenant farmers, were also members of Bonucci's resistance group. Both were dressed in the drab work pants and shirts and the frayed woolen jackets and caps typical of the farmers of the area. As they approached the table to be seated, Bonucci spoke quickly and quietly in an aside to me. "Signore, forgive me, but I think that when you meet others who are in our Band, I need to tell them your real identity." I nodded assent. He introduced me to the two men.

Their eyebrows rose in surprise when Bonucci told them I was the American "Il Console." Both men immediately pulled off their caps in a gesture of respect, holding them against their chests as they leaned forward to shake my proferred hand. "Benvenuto, Signor Console," they welcomed me gravely.

"As I was telling Il Console," Bonucci said, bringing them into where our conversation stood, "we were inactive for a while after the raid on the convoy and then the reprisals." The two men made a low guttural sound, either of hatred or acknowledgment, but neither spoke. "Oh, there were some individual and small group actions here and there," Bonucci went on, "like sabotaging of telephone and telegraph lines—we did that so often that they gave up trying to repair them—and we removed or redirected road signs, so they'd get confused or lost. We've disarmed, and stolen arms from, a dozen or more of the Fascists—that helped us with our need for weapons. But although it is useful to do those things, I consider it child's play. We haven't done anything really big. Certainly nothing on the order of our September raid on the convoy." As Bonucci spoke, my mind was racing. I could see that an organized guerrilla group's destructive actions would require the German Wehrmacht to devote some time and attention to protecting itself from the small dogs nipping at its flanks. Yes, we needed to get word to the Allies as quickly as possible that there were organized and professionally directed partisan groups in this area, anxious to help our cause.

By the time the visitors left it was lunchtime, and, although Bonucci continued to fill me in on operations, I found the offering of fresh meat, fairly decent pasta, and good local red wine a strong distraction from the business at hand. Bonucci smiled as he watched me. "Mangia, mangia" (eat, eat), he urged, putting more meat on my plate. It was an expression I was to hear often from the Italians, no matter how scarce food was. "Some meat and some good red wine in your belly will get your blood going and your strength up. You need to be strong, Signor Console. This is not an easy game. It is not for children, or weaklings."

After months of subsisting on starvation rations, I needed no urging to eat, but was careful not to overeat. As soon as I was reasonably sated, I pushed my plate back, got up, and stretched. "If it's okay with you, I think I'll take a walk around," I remarked to Bonucci, smiling. "I need some more fresh air, and some exercise, after all that good food. I won't go far," I assured him. "I just want to wander around the villa property a bit." Undoubtedly, Gigi would be ordered to guard me from a distance.

"Fine, Signore, enjoy your stroll on such a beautiful day, then maybe you should have a little nap," replied Bonucci, rising and heading back into the house. "Oh, and Gualtiero," he said, startling me with his first use of my given name, "there will be a major organizational meeting after dinner tonight. Please be so good as to prepare a draft of a brief message to the Allies about our need for recognition and assistance."

I nodded and set off on my walk. As I walked briskly around the property on which the villa stood, I thought over all that Bonucci had told me. That there was serious risk in what I was about to undertake, I had no doubt. But I was excited and exhilarated, too. I thought of Nancy, and Amy, and Margherita and the children, and I hoped they were over the depression of my departure. I was confident that Manfred would come through for them. I had to think positively on that. This new venture would require all my concentration, and all my attention, for me to succeed and stay alive. The rest would have to be pushed into the background, like it or not. I looked up. I was about the length of two football fields from the villa. I decided to test my strength by jogging back. The sharp, clear air hurt my lungs as I chugged along, and after only a couple of minutes I realized just how out of shape I was, but I stubbornly stuck it out, and, arriving back in my room, threw myself on the bed, gasping for breath, my heart pounding. God, I felt good! I felt alive again—ready to face whatever challenges lay ahead.

I looked at my watch. It was four-fifty. Time to get going and draft that message. I saw that Bonucci had provided pen and paper—it was lying on the table next to the armchair. I sat down and picked up the pen.

I'm Orebaugh, American Consul, arrested by Italian 6th Army, Monaco, Nov. 1942, detained Perugia, evaded capture by Germans. Am now with Bonuccio Bonucci, CLN partisan leader, have joined organized resistance group, Pietralunga area. Resistance force here estimated 100–150, led by Col. Guerrizzi and Capt. Pierangeli, Italian army. Ready to assist Allies by ops to harass and distract enemy forces, provide G2, in area bounded by Morena, Città di Castello, Gubbio. Need funds, immediate airdrop arms, ammunition, medical supplies, grenades, radio transmitter & receiver. Locations for airdrops: Morena Valley: field directly across from church; or further up valley. Code words for signaling airdrops: "Puoi Gioire" (you can rejoice) and "Abbia Fede" (have faith). Six bonfires to mark drop area. Suggest message via BBC signal at 2:37 A.M., repeat 4:12 A.M. Anxious to begin ops. Await acknowledgment and further instructions. W. Orebaugh.

When I finished it was dinnertime. For the first time since opening the consulate in Monaco, I felt as if I were being useful again and doing something positive. It was a great feeling. I headed down the stairs, whistling tunelessly. Giuseppe intercepted me at the bottom.

"Scusi Signor Console," he said deferentially, "Signor Bonucci would like you to join him for a glass of wine before dinner." He pointed to direct me.

Bonucci greeted me and poured me a glass, and we raised our glasses in a toast. "Saluti," he said.

"Saluti," I replied.

"To our successful joint enterprise." I handed him the draft of my message. He sat down and read it through.

When he finished, he stood up and shook my hand. "You have been here less than a day, and already you have made a valuable contribution to our effort. I can see that you will be very important to us. I am grateful to you and honored to have you with us," he said, sincerely.

"I'm glad to be of some help. We are working for the same goal, Signor Bonucci," I replied simply and turned the talk to another subject. I continued to be impressed by the man. His manner was straightforward, but warm and sincere. He was genuinely interested in me and wanted to know more about my recent experiences. I was flattered by his open admiration of how I had handled things at the time of my arrest in Monaco—he especially enjoyed the story of our impromptu dinner party. Bonuccio Bonucci was also a realist. He entertained no exaggerated illusions about the Band and what it could and could not accomplish. Nonetheless, he was determined to have a go at showing the Germans, and the world at large, that the Italians were tough and ready fighters, and not the feckless cowards that the British and foreign press often accused them of being.

We continued sharing "war stories" throughout dinner. Giuseppe's wife served us a tasty minestrone, which had a few vegetables in it, in addition to the inevitable ceci. After the soup came a bowl of fairly decent pasta, dressed with garlic, olive oil, cheese, and a little red pepper. With it, we each had a slice of some kind of local dried sausage, and bread. There was a flask of the villa's red wine on the table. It was an excellent supper. We had just adjourned from the table to the living room, when the first person arrived for the meeting. I was elated to find he was an American! The tall, slender young man who came forward to shake my hand introduced himself as Lieutenant Joseph Withers, of the Army Air Corps. He had been shot down in June of 1943, he told me, on a mission over northern Italy and was detained for a while in a prisoner of war camp near Brescia. Like many other Allied POWs, he had been turned loose to fend for himself when the Armistice was signed in September 1943. He and some British officers had slowly worked their way south, keeping to the hills and woods, aided by the Italian peasant farmers. He had finally arrived in this area, glad to be alive. Friendly peasant farmers had put him in touch with Bonucci.

Shortly before eight o'clock, several others arrived. One in particular, Captain Bice Pucci, both amused and annoyed me. Assuming I was the "man of the hour," and the star to be seen with, he hovered close, trying to say things that would impress me and emphasize his pro-American stance. Somehow having gotten the notion that Americans and Scotch whiskey are inextricably intertwined, he repeatedly assured me of his liking for scotch and declared with utmost seriousness, "I like my whiskey straight, and my women crooked." I tried not to laugh and managed eventually to sidle away and introduce myself to Captain R. D. G. Ramsay of the Royal Tank Regiment, who had just arrived. I was particularly anxious to meet him, since he was the one Bonucci had mentioned was a possible demolitions expert. I liked Ramsay on sight. He was an affable sort, with a deep respect and affection for the Italian people, unlike most Britishers I'd met who, like Amy, tended to denigrate everyone and everything not British. "I'm really happy to meet you," I said. "Bonucci has spoken very highly of you." He flushed with pleasure at hearing that. "I look forward to seeing a lot more of you," I added, shaking his hand. Looking around, I saw another face, which was familiar, but escaped the edge of my memory. I pointed him out to Bonucci. "Who is that?" I asked.

"Eh, Gualtiero, you've been gone from America so long you don't recognize another American?" Bonucci teased me, smiling. "His name is Mills."

That brought the flash of recall. Leonard Mills was a young American graduate student whom I had met briefly, almost a year ago, at the Hotel Brufani. He was one of Nancy's group of friends from the university. I walked over and greeted him warmly. By this time there were over twenty people in the room, and Bonucci decided to call the meeting to order.

He began with a recap of previous accomplishments of the Band of San Faustino, praising the men highly for their successes, then pointed out that now, more than ever before, the Germans were exposed and vulnerable to the kinds of harassment that we, and other partisan bands, were in a position to inflict on the enemy's lines of communication. He acknowledged my presence, and said, "Il Console is to be protected at all times against any exposure to risk. His well-being and safety are the guarantee we have that we will be heard, and listened to, by the Allies." Heads turned toward me, and I felt, rather than saw, the frank stares of the assembled men. "He has already taken steps to establish a communication channel and to request arms, ammunition, and other material by airdrops," he continued. There were murmurs of approval. "His very presence here will bolster our credibility and will be of incalculable help in getting assistance from local tenant farmers, other partisan groups, and the CLN. It is imperative," he paused briefly for the effect of the word to wash over them, "that he be safeguarded and delivered unharmed to the Allies when the great day of the liberation of Italy comes." All eyes swung toward me. I felt awkward and embarrassed. On the one hand, I couldn't blame Bonucci for making the most of me as an asset. On the other, I wasn't about to accept the role of a bird in a cage. I was determined to play an active part in the Band, to be with them on their raids, to share their life. I needed to make that known to them immediately. However, I would have to do it discreetly. I couldn't in any way offend Bonucci, or nullify his protective posture toward me. At that point, Bonucci formally presented me to the assemblage: "I give you now Signor Console, Gualtiero Orebaugh, our esteemed friend, and the man who can convince the Allies of our extreme need."

He extended an arm toward me, and I stepped forward and faced the group. I drew a deep breath, and began, in Italian, "I am happy to be here, and to join the Band of San Faustino." Eyebrows went up in surprise at my command of Italian. I smiled at them. A few, like Ramsay, Withers, Mills, and Pucci, smiled back. The rest just watched, solemn-faced, waiting to hear what else I had to say. I held up the papers in my hand. "I have here a draft of a communiqué to the Allies, which I want to read to you. But first, I would like to say a few words." I knew I would have to walk a tightrope to avoid offending Bonucci. I genuinely admired him, but I did not want to be nothing but the "show wafer" on their altar of liberation. "I would like to start off with an English epithet—Bull!" The sharpness of my voice quickened their attention. "By that I mean I don't want you to treat me like some sort of magician or demigod. I am here to be with you, to be one of you, and to do what I can to hasten the victory of the Allies over the Germans. Whatever I can do because of my position, I will do. But I also intend to help in other ways, because I am a man—a man who cannot endure watching the rape of a country that I have come to love." I concluded firmly: "Senz'altro potete contare su di me!" (you can damn well count on me!) The Italians broke into whoops and applauded wildly. The Americans and British looked puzzled. Seizing the advantage I had gained, I immediately translated the message I had prepared for the Allies into Italian, reading from the English text.

When I finished, any concern I had for Bonucci's reaction was dispelled. He strode up to me and grabbed me in a bear hug. Then he turned to his men. "Tonight we have added an important officer to our ranks," he declared. "I propose Signor Console as Communications Officer with command responsibility." The Italians shouted approval of that and applauded again. The Americans and British still looked puzzled. I sent Ramsay a look that said "I'll explain later," which he acknowledged with a nod.

We decided a special messenger would go north to Florence, to send our message to the Allies via the CLN's clandestine transmitter there. Then Colonel Guerizzi got up to address us, briefing us on the activities of the Florence partisan group, then saying, "I welcome Signor Console to our midst, and wish to commend and recognize Signor Bonucci. Because of his organizational efforts, his contributions to our liberation effort, and his connections to the CLN, he is hereby declared the overall leader of the Band of San Faustino, with Captain Pierangeli as his second-in-command." At this, there was more shouting and applause. Men went to Bonucci to shake his hand and to hug him. Then the meeting was over. The men slipped quietly, in ones and twos, into the cold January night.

When everyone had gone, Bonucci took me aside and poured out two brandies from the bottle sitting on the little desk. "To our success," he toasted, raising his glass to me, "not just yours and mine, but the success of our countries."

"And to our health, and perseverance," I rejoined, raising my glass. "Not just yours and mine, but all our comrades in this endeavor." We drained our glasses and said good night. I had time for only fleeting thoughts of the outside world before dropping again into a deep, dreamless chasm.

The next morning, entering the dining room, I was startled to find two rough-looking strangers there, calmly drinking coffee. The local help, I had noticed, ate in the kitchen. Even Bonucci's most trusted aide, Gigi, took his meals in the kitchen when on duty. The two men ignored me. I decided my best move was to ignore them, too. Then Bonucci entered, and both men immediately stood up, and exchanged hearty greetings with him. "Eh, Gualtiero, what did I tell you?" exclaimed Bonucci, turning to me with a broad smile on his face. "You bring us good fortune already! See? These men will take your message to Florence for transmission!" Noting my raised eyebrows, he went on to explain, "These are Special Service officers attached to "A Force" in Bari. After going to Florence, they will head back to Bari. I have given them a second copy of the message to send from there. This will double our chances of getting it through to the Allies!" He poured himself coffee, obviously pleased and happy. I knew where Bari was—far south, on the Adriatic, but knew nothing about

A Force. However, I trusted Bonucci implicitly. I gave them the message, and they left almost immediately.

By the afternoon of my third day with Bonucci, I was nervous. Far too many people openly came and went at the villa. Surely all this must be a matter of common knowledge by now. How and why he had been left free to continue his activities for this long was puzzling and amazing. Over lunch, I expressed my concern. "I also hate being unarmed," I told him.

"I know you must be worried, Gualtiero," he said seriously. "And I'm sure you're right, some of my activities must certainly be known to the Fascist authorities. But don't forget, there are always a few of the Band, and Gigi, around here to protect me. And the farmers in the area will warn us if anyone strange appears."

"Well, I still don't like it," I insisted, stubbornly.

"We're very careful, Gualtiero, I assure you," he smiled at me, "but to make you feel better, I will see that you have a weapon tomorrow, for your own protection. Just remember, I want your role to be more passive than active, for the time being." He twirled some pasta around his fork and ate it, chewing thoughtfully. Then he took a sip of wine. Setting the glass down, he wiped his mouth on the rough linen napkin, sat back in his chair, and, looking directly at me, said, "You're right, Gualtiero, my friend—there *are* a lot of people around. Maybe too many. It is probably not safe to keep you here with me any longer. You are much too important to us." He sat for a moment, idly crumbling a bit of bread between his thumb and forefinger. Then he sat forward and said, "For your security and safety, Gualtiero, Gigi will take you tonight to a farmhouse, where you will stay for a while. The conditions there are primitive, but the family is completely trustworthy and will look after you. You'll be safe there. I will stay in touch with you through Gigi." Abruptly, he got up. "Meet me back here at four o'clock," he said, and left.

I spent the rest of the afternoon poring over the maps of the countryside Gigi brought me. Painstakingly, I began committing to memory the routes from the farmhouse where I was to stay to each of the partisan presidios in the district, as well as all possible ambush areas and escape routes, as Gigi pointed them out to me. By the time Bonucci returned, I was well versed in the terrain of the area. He showed me where the farmhouse was, in relation to the villa. "But that's only a stone's throw from here!" I said, surprised.

"Ah, my friend," Bonucci replied, "it looks only a little way on the map but to reach it you will have to travel eight kilometers, over very rough country." I looked at where he was pointing again. "See here—the farmhouse looks to be located on the main route to Pietralunga, but it is actually well off to one side. Anyone seen heading that way has to have a reason for doing so. There, you will have plenty of warning if anyone comes looking for you." He got up, clasped my hand in both of his, then embraced me warmly. "Godspeed, my friend," he said in farewell. "Gigi will see you safely to your new home. We will meet again soon."

"Keep safe, Bonuccio," I responded, giving him a firm handshake. "Thank you for all you've done, and for making me one of you. I have found a new friend in a strange land. Watch your back. See you soon." He waved and left.

That evening, Gigi and I ate in the kitchen together. We packed our stomachs with heaping bowls of rich rabbit stew, and shortly after seven, we retraced our steps along the muddy footpath back through San Faustino. Then, we turned east onto another footpath, this one not even wide enough for the two of us to walk side by side. Gigi spoke for the first time. "There is a regular road, Signore, but if we take it, it will add several kilometers to our walk." I tried to imagine what a "regular road" would be in this area.

"Then let's stay on the shorter route," I said.

It was slow and tedious going. There was no moon, and where the path wasn't mired in mud, it was blocked with snow, which we plowed with our "walking sticks"—two thick, gnarled branches trimmed from an olive tree. It was bitterly cold. Even the stalwart Gigi grumbled and cursed as he struggled along. It was close to midnight and I was nearly frozen by the time we reached the farmhouse. Bonucci was right. It was certainly "off the beaten path"! A battered old building, in sad disrepair, it was obviously not the abode of a prosperous family. Margherita's poor flat was a villa by comparison, and Bonuccio's a palace. Like most peasant farmhouses, the ground floor housed the livestock, farm equipment, hay and feed. The family lived on the floor above. I had seen many farmhouses just like this around Gubbio. The one we stood before was just more dilapidated than most. Gigi shouted, but got no response. Now that we were standing still, the cold attacked us with knives. Gigi went from shout to bellow. A shadow appeared in the upstairs front window. Exasperated, Gigi yelled again. "Eh! Ruggero! Si faccia vivo!" (come alive!). The window opened a tiny crack, and a face appeared briefly. "I am here with a good friend of Signor Bonuccio Bonucci, who needs shelter," shouted Gigi. The window slammed shut, and within seconds the door opened. We scrambled up the stairs and into the main room of the house.

"Scusi, Signori," my new host apologized profusely, as he lit a candle in the cold room and prodded the banked fire in the fireplace to life. "Sit! Sit!" he urged us. Despite his prior fear, his sleepiness, and the lateness of the hour, the rites of tradition were scrupulously observed. He went to the far side of the dimly lit room, muttering, and groped among the flasks arrayed on a sagging board that served as a shelf. Returning to the table, he took down three glasses from another shelf and filled them to the brim.

I was nearly frozen, and so tired! I didn't want wine or talk. I just wanted to crawl into the fireplace and go to sleep. For Gigi, it was quite the reverse. A warming glass of wine had been on his mind for the past hour or more. Sleep would not be on his agenda this night, for he had to return to the villa. As soon as the glass was in his hand, he tilted his head back and quaffed it in one gulp. Then, with a roar that resounded throughout the house and out into the hills, he spewed out whatever he hadn't swallowed. Earsplitting curses followed. Our poor host was at first dumbfounded, then his face registered embarrassment. "Oh, scusi, scusi, Signor, what a fool I am! Please forgive me!" Salt, being hard to come by, was hoarded in empty wine bottles, as saltwater. In the semidarkness, Ruggero had poured our glasses from the wrong flask. Still apologizing, he hastened to correct his error. Then he joined us at the huge, rough-hewn wooden table that dominated the room.

While we drank, and warmed ourselves before the feebly flickering fire, Gigi explained our sudden appearance and my presence. He spoke in some sort of local dialect, which I had difficulty following, but which I realized I would have to learn quickly. "Signor Bonucci sends you his regards," Gigi began. The farmer nodded and sipped his wine, waiting. "He has chosen you," said Gigi, with a trace of pompousness, "from among all the others because he knows you can be counted on to handle the very heavy responsibility of being host and protector to his American friend, here." Ruggero raised his eyebrows on hearing that, but said nothing. "He is hiding out from the Fascists and the Germans. No one is to know he is here. He goes by the name of Michele Franciosi—a 'sfollato from Naples, capisce?" The man nodded again. "You and your family are to take care of him, and protect him, for Signor Bonucci, and for the cause of liberation."

Hearing that, our host absolutely beamed. He was immensely flattered to be entrusted with such a big responsibility. In those parts, Signor Bonuccio Bonucci was a man to be respected and accommodated if at all possible. He, Ruggero Bruschi, had been personally selected by Signor Bonucci to shelter this mysterious American, out of the scores of countrymen with whom Signor Bonucci had dealings. What an honor for the Bruschis! As Ruggero poured more wine, I wondered how much of what Gigi said had been directed by Bonuccio and how much Gigi himself had carefully tailored to flatter this backwoods peasant. Finally, Gigi made his farewells to me and took his leave. He would not remain the night, despite Ruggero's urging. Suddenly, I found myself alone with another Italian who was to be my host, in yet another Italian home, which was to be my home.

Ruggero Bruschi was a short, sturdily built man of about thirty-two with dark, straight hair, which he parted on the left and combed neatly back. His round face was ruddy complexioned, and although clean shaven, it bore the shadow of a dark, heavy beard. It was saved from being a formidable face by his natural readiness to smile and laugh. Light, bushy eyebrows shaded clear hazel eyes. His smile revealed only a few remaining, slightly crooked teeth—from a poor peasant's lack of dental care. "Make yourself comfortable, Signore, while I make your sleeping arrangements," he said and disappeared into an adjoining room.

I looked around me. The rectangular wood table at which I sat filled the center of the large room, which was about thirty feet long by twenty feed wide. Ranged around the table were six rush-bottomed, straight-backed chairs. A large open fireplace dominated one end of the room. A heavily encrusted black iron pot, which apparently was used for cooking, was set to one side of the stone hearth. Beside it lay some wrought iron cooking implements reminiscent of paintings of rural colonial America in the 1700s. There was no stove, nor any sink, but it was obvious that the room was kitchen as well as dining and living room for the Bruschi family. A wooden storage counter along one wall, with a few rickety wooden shelves above it, completed the furnishings. The walls were of dull gray stone, as was the floor. A small crucifix hung on the wall above the fireplace. It was the room's only adornment. There were two windows—one at the end of the room opposite the fireplace, and a larger one in the long wall that overlooked the farmyard. Neither had any curtains. I looked around for a place to hang my hat, but there were no pegs in the wall where you could hang anything. The floor sagged rather precipitously toward the middle. It was like a giant saucer. The oaken beams, upon which the heavy squares of stone flooring were laid when the house was built, had bowed over time under the weight of the stone floor, creating the bowl-like curvature. It took me a while to get used to the strange sensation of walking down, then up again, to cross the room.

Before I had had time to adjust to my surroundings, Ruggero reappeared, followed by his entire family. He presented his wife, Adalgisa, who shyly shook my hand. She was a short, plain woman, older than Ruggero, but probably by only a few years, judging from the age of the children. However, she looked at least ten years older. Her wispy, already graying hair was drawn back into a plain bun at the nape of her neck, and her face, neck, and hands were worn and leathery from years of hard work in severe weather. Cosmetics were as unknown to this woman as indoor plumbing. Her slight figure was bent from hard work, but her deep brown eyes were warm and compassionate. Concetta, the daughter, was about fourteen—dark, short, and stocky like Ruggero, and plain like her mother, but not unattractive. The face of the son Giuseppe, called Pepe, a skinny, gangling curly-headed youth of about ten years of age, reflected wide-eyed amazement at this middle-of-the-night apparition. I solemnly shook hands with both youngsters.

I was ceremoniously escorted into the family bedroom—the only other room in the house. It was a large room, too, and in it were two beds—a big, wood-framed bed, with a smaller iron cot aligned right next to it.

The small bed was Concetta's. Ruggero gestured to it. "You will sleep here, please, Signore," he said politely. He waved aside my protests. "My daughter will sleep with us. You do our family honor to be our guest, Signore," he hastened to assure me. "I am sorry our accommodations cannot be better for a friend of Signor Bonucci," he added apologetically. Adalgisa showed me a small screen in one corner of the room. Behind it was the "bathroom"—which consisted of a chipped ceramic chamber pot and a small wooden washstand holding a pitcher of cold water.

I gazed around me, dazed with shock. Never had I imagined anything this poor. I was suddenly struck by what luxury I had enjoyed in my accommodations up to now—even in Gubbio, even at the poor apartment of Margherita Bonucci in Perugia. This was stark, soul-breaking poverty. Yet Ruggero and his family were happy, and proud, at being assigned another mouth to feed, another body to shelter, even a stranger come suddenly into their midst, destroying any shred of privacy left in their huddled family existence. I wondered what Amy and Nancy would think if they could see this. I could imagine Amy's horrified look, and her disdain. I was to learn that the layout of the interior of the Bruschi home, while more modest than most, was not untypical of peasant farmhouses throughout central Italy.

"Now you must get some sleep, Signore," said Adalgisa, quietly. I needed no further urging. After the six-mile, mostly uphill trek I had made, the wine, and the warmth seeping back into me from the fire, I would have been happy to curl up on the cold stone floor to sleep! Shedding only my coat, shoes, and jacket, I fell onto Concetta's narrow bed. It felt surprisingly comfortable. As I hovered at the brink of sleep, I saw the Bruschis all climb into the big bed. Its crossed-rope underframe supported a mattress of coarse linen, stuffed with dried corn husks, which rustled whenever anyone moved. The family settled down, with the two youngsters sandwiched in the middle, heads at the foot of the bed, and the parents on each side of them, heads at the upper end. I was surprised when they all fell asleep almost immediately. Clutching the worn blanket around me, I followed suit.

I woke in the morning to find myself alone. Sitting up, I looked around. In the daylight, it was even drearier than it had seemed the night before. I didn't know how the whole family had managed to get up and slip out without waking me. I shivered, dreading the prospect of having to get up and wash in water I knew would be not just cold, but icy. Ruggero was waiting for me when I stepped into the next room. He had been up for a while, out doing chores. Adalgisa had brewed the bitter, pale liquid that passed for coffee, and she set a cup of it before us, along with a good-sized chunk of coarse homemade bread. As soon as we had finished eating, Ruggero took me outside and showed me several routes leading from the back of the house to a densely wooded spot not far away. "These are your hiding places, Signore," he informed me. "You can remain in one of these for as long as you need to, and you will not be seen." He explained that there would be times I would need to hide out, since the "appuntata," the deputized carabiniere, made the rounds of the farmhouses in the district every other week or so. "It is more of a nuisance than a danger," he hastened to assure me, "we get plenty of advance warning he is coming." He then walked with me to the minuscule spring which gave the farm its name—"Fontanella." Dropping down onto a stump at the bank of the narrow stream, he gestured for me to sit on a flat rock near it. I sensed he wanted to talk, and I was not surprised when he launched into a tale of his recent wartime experiences. When the Armistice was declared, he said, he had been turned loose from his unit, far from home in the north of Italy. Having no sense of geography whatsoever, he had somehow managed to grope his way home, evading German patrols, sleeping under piles of leaves in the bitter cold. I sensed that he was curious about me and was giving me an opening to follow suit and talk about myself, but I chose to pass on that. What Ruggero didn't know wouldn't hurt him, I reasoned. "Your story is very interesting," I told him, "please continue." Expressing himself in his vernacular Italian, Ruggero continued his tale, in great detail. When he had finished, I had a far better understanding of the peasants of Umbria and of how they preserved their indomitable spirit of rugged independence. Ruggero's long, lonely odyssey had taken three full months, and he was relishing the opportunity to tell about his life's greatest adventure to a person of some importance. I praised him for his bravery, which, coming from someone of my stature, friend of Bonuccio Bonucci, was an accolade beyond his dreams.

The next day, I decided to place a ladder near the bedroom window at the back side of the house. The fact that there was only one entrance (and exit) to the living quarters bothered me. It had apparently never occurred to Ruggero that the usually reliable but very informal local system of warning might, on some occasion, fail. He helped me carefully arrange the ladder so it looked like it was just leaning there against the house, near the window, but not close enough to seem placed there for a purpose. Then I turned to my next task. I had some important personal papers with me, that I had kept carefully hidden ever since leaving Nice. Among them were some that were of monetary value—stock and bond certificates—but of no use for the moment, and for them to be found in the Bruschi house would endanger us all. I wrapped them, and my American diplomatic passport, in an old piece of oilcloth, put them into an old tin box, and buried the box under the stairs that led up into the house. As I hacked at the hard, frozen earth with the rusty old shovel, I couldn't help smiling at the thought that the Bruschis had no idea how valuable their farm had just become! I decided to keep my cash—dollars and lire—more readily accessible. I knew that the poor Neapolitan refugee clerk Michele Franciosi would have a hard time explaining how he came by hundreds, fifties, and even a couple of five hundred dollar American bills, not to mention a small fortune in lire, if he were caught and interrogated by the Fascists or Germans, but I decided to risk it, for the time being.

By my third day there, I realized that life at the Bruschis was going to be simple in the extreme. There was no diversion of any kind—no printed matter, no radio, no writing materials, no cards. I longed for a book or an old newspaper to read, to help pass the time. Ruggero would not hear of me doing farm chores. Whether they had worked in the fields that day or not, the family retired immediately after supper, which was served at about six in the evening. Oil for the single lamp was almost impossible to get, and candles were scarce and expensive. By the time Adalgisa finished clearing up the supper dishes, Ruggero had finished smoking his pipe of locally grown tobacco and had had his final glass of wine in front of the fire. He would stand, stretching, and announce, "Well, it's been a busy day, time for some rest." At that, the whole family would immediately retire to the bedroom. It was an unvarying nightly ritual. I wondered how long I could tolerate such stupefying boredom as this. Fortunately, it didn't last long.

That third night, I went to bed just a few minutes after the family. I didn't fall asleep right away—the rustling of the corn husk mattress kept me awake. Drifting in that nether land between sleep and consciousness, at first I thought I was dreaming the loud banging that suddenly shattered the silence. Then, with terrifying awareness, I came awake, heart thumping, realizing the banging was not a dream at all, but at the door! I jumped out of bed, grabbing my clothes, yanked the window open and was scanning the yard, reaching for the ladder, by the time Ruggero got to the door. A touch on my shoulder startled me, but it was Adalgisa, signaling that all was well. I pulled my head back in and slammed the window shut against the cold. The door banger was Gigi, who had returned, bringing Lieutenant Mario Bonfigli with him. I hastily threw my clothes on and joined them, to find that Ruggero had already begun the social amenities. A single candle sputtered on the table, and he was pouring out four glasses of wine. Two chairs, for Lt. Bonfigli and me, had been moved in front of the hearth, where the fire was once again blazing. Ruggero and Gigi withdrew to the table.

Lieutenant Mario Bonfigli was about five feet six inches tall and held his slender but wiry frame in erect, military bearing. He was young, probably in his mid-twenties, every inch the career officer. His merry dark eyes, though, revealed a nature ready to enjoy a good laugh and the fun side of life. After introductions and a few sips of wine, Bonfigli drew a dark, gleaming Beretta revolver from inside his jacket and held it out to me, with a mischievous smile. "Signor Bonucci said that you might like this to cover your nakedness, Signor Console."

"Signor Bonucci was absolutely right!" I exclaimed happily. As I took the pistol from him, I glanced toward Ruggero and Gigi. Ruggero's face reflected his profound awe. Even Gigi's expression showed more respect than usual. By meriting such a rare and valuable weapon, I had climbed several notches in Gigi's esteem, and the mere mention of "Console," in addition to the weapon, had attained me a stature with Ruggero that was beyond imagining. That little Beretta pistol alone represented more wealth than the Bruschi family had ever seen.

We talked for a few moments in low voices. Bonuccio was fine, and he sent me his regards. There had been no response yet from the Allies. But, then, it was too soon to expect one. I knew we needed help, and quickly, to begin operations. As always, I was short on patience. Then, to my surprise, Bonfigli reached into a pocket of his jacket and produced an envelope. I saw Nancy's handwriting on it and eagerly snatched it from his hand. Impatiently, I ripped it open, as Bonfigli, noting my haste, prodded up the fire to give me more light to read by. Tears sprang to my eyes on seeing Nancy's fine script, and I suddenly realized just how much I missed her and all the others.

"Dearest Walter," I read in a blur," Amy and I are well. We and the family miss you. Please be careful. Your friend will be escorting us to the big church. Everything is arranged very nicely. Love, Nancy."

For a moment I was puzzled. Big church? What big church? Then, slapping my forehead, I muttered aloud, "Stùpido! Big church! The Vatican! She means the Vatican! Manfred's going to get them to Rome!" Ruggero and Gigi were staring at me in amazement. They were no doubt thinking that Americans behave in strange ways. I turned to Bonfigli. "Lieutenant," I said urgently, "how soon will you see Signor Bonucci? I need to get a message to Perugia as quickly as possible."

Bonfigli slowly shook his head. "I have several places I must go on to from here, Signore," he said regretfully, then as he saw my face fall, "but Gigi goes back tonight and can take your message to Bonucci."

I turned to Ruggero. "I need some paper and a pen," I said crisply, my tone more commanding than I intended. Ruggero hustled into the bedroom, from whence, after a prolonged conference with Adalgisa, he produced the only paper in the house—a badly wrinkled souvenir postcard. "Don't worry about a pen, Ruggero, I'll get mine," I said, mortified at having made such a thoughtless request in a household that had no ability to use, even if they could have afforded them, such luxuries as pen and paper. To spare Ruggero further embarrassment, I thanked him profusely for the postcard, "This is perfect, just what I need—thank you!" I said. "I must get an important message delivered to Signor Bonucci."

Ruggero drew himself up with pride at having made such a significant contribution to my mission. "I am pleased to be able to assist you, Signore," he said, with grave formality.

Hastily, I penned a note to Manfred in the limited space on the postcard. "Can you advance money for key necessities? Also, kindly present the enclosed paper to your lawyer in Trieste." I couched my words carefully in double-talk, to avoid detection if the message was intercepted. I didn't want the money for myself, but for the partisans—to buy necessary supplies to hold us until we heard from the Allies and got airdrops arranged. I also wanted him to have the bargaining paper I had promised for his friend, since the friend had apparently supplied the necessary fake identification to get Nancy and Amy out safely. I signed the postcard from "Brother Felice at the church in San Faustino" and gave it to Gigi to take to Bonuccio Bonucci. I breathed a silent but fervent prayer that my pipeline would get the message to Manfred quickly, and that he'd come through with the interim funds we so desperately needed.

Then Bonfigli, ever mindful of Bonucci's admonitions that I be protected, said, "We are considering some action in two of the presidios in the near future—in fact, that is what I am going on to discuss tonight. I will talk to them about your wishes. Personally, I see no harm in letting you come along on the mission, as an observer. I'll see what can be arranged and be back in touch with you." Touching his hand to his hat in salute, he took his leave.

We had no sooner closed the door on them when Ruggero turned to me and said, with deep respect, "Buona notte (good night), Signor Console."

"Ruggero! Never say that!" I admonished sharply. "No one must ever know who I am! Don't endanger yourself like that! Michele is the only name you should ever use."

"Sì, Signor Console," he nodded. I sighed, exasperated. I could only hope that his sudden vault to higher status, as my host, would not overwhelm his native caution and secretiveness. But despite the danger Ruggero's new knowledge about me brought, I felt great.

I was sure that Nancy and Amy were already in Rome and safe behind the walls of the Vatican, thanks to Manfred. I was immensely relieved that they were no longer a burden for Margherita to feed, and that the Bonucci family was no longer in danger from sheltering us. I had no way of knowing that the journey had been delayed, and that at that very moment Nancy, Amy, and Manfred were just beginning their dangerous journey. I looked over at Ruggero. "Please Ruggero, go on to bed. I'm just going to finish a glass of wine, then I'll turn in too." He nodded, but didn't leave. Instead, he poured me a glass of wine and one for himself. Then he sat down, across the table from me, watching me quietly. I could only imagine what must be going through his mind. The Italians are very serious about titles. Therefore, because in Italy the title of "Consul," a carryover from Roman times, carries so much more weight than it does in the United States, Ruggero was overawed. He had never before been in the company of anyone so high and mighty as a real Consul, let alone been charged with his care and well-being! He was determined now to be sure that I was accorded the service, and the respect, to which he believed my rank entitled me. He would not go to bed until I did, I knew—just in case there might be something he could do for me. I sighed again. Well, I thought resignedly, Bonuccio has his Gigi, and now I have my Ruggero. I smiled at the sheer ridiculousness of the whole situation. Seeing me smile, Ruggero beamed. Il Console was happy. That was all that mattered. Finishing my wine as quickly as politeness allowed, I got up, and we both turned in.

While it was well past bedtime at Fontanella, it was not so for city dwellers, even with a curfew. Manfred, as I learned much later, was at that moment standing on a corner, in a steady, cold drizzle, about a block from Margherita Bonucci's apartment, fidgeting because the arranged-for vehicle was late. Amy and Nancy were still in the apartment, waiting for the signal to join him outside. To get the vehicle, Paolucci, Manfred's lawyer friend in Trieste, had convinced the police, and their civilian driver, Sergio, that one of the two women to be picked up in Perugia and taken to Rome (Amy) was none other than the mistress of German Field Marshal Kesselring. The other woman (Nancy) was her companion, he said, sort of a guardian of the mistress's safety. Paolucci had further intimated to Sergio that the Field Marshal was intolerant of indiscretion or failure, but knew how to reward those who did him a valuable service. Sweating profusely, Sergio had pledged his wholehearted cooperation with the Field Marshal's wishes in regard to the young women. In fact, he was ready to begin assisting the Field Marshal immediately, he had avowed. And so the rendezvous was arranged.

Manfred was worried. He did not like waiting in the open. He had purposely worn only German clothing, which he had purchased in Berlin. His papers bore a variety of official stamps, most of which related to authorizations for the movement of tank cars. They would pass cursory examination by local municipal guards, but God help him if a carabiniere— or worse, a Gestapo officer—got hold of him. Suddenly, a young German soldier approached. "Haben Sie Feuer, bitte?"(do you have a light?), he asked, politely.

"Surely you're not smoking on duty!" snapped Manfred, with authority. The soldier stepped back a pace, startled. Manfred laughed good-naturedly. "What the hell," he said, drawing out his lighter, "if you have a dry cigarette on a damnably wet night like this, you deserve to smoke it!" He lit the cigarette, declining to have one himself. "Nein, danke," he said politely, "Ich habe genug" (no thanks, I have plenty). The soldier noted the expensive gold German lighter in the flare of light. Thanking Manfred, he went quickly on his way.

The soldier was barely out of sight when Sergio pulled up in the van.

Manfred directed him to a parking place that was in the shadows, then hurried to the house to get the girls. He hustled them into the van, quickly stowing their hand baggage. "Get going," he said tersely to Sergio. "I'm right behind you." He jumped into his green Willys, swung in behind the van, and they were on their way. The bad weather, a stroke of good luck for them, continued all the way to Rome. There were few checkpoints, and, because of the miserable weather, they were subjected to document check only twice. Their hearts pounded each time they were stopped, but after cursory inspection of their papers, the Italian militia guards waved them on. Political prisoners being transported to Rome at the whim of a Field Marshal were of no importance on their watch list.

It was only when the van reached Rome that they ran into trouble. The control point on the Via Nomentana was manned by Germans, not Italians. The van, with the Willys right behind it, pulled to a stop. The senior of the two guards approached, obviously in a foul mood. "You Italians!" he shouted at Sergio. "Will you never learn anything?! It is of no consequence to you if your own city of Rome is burned! Stupido!" The girls, terrified, cowered in silence in the back seat, as a trembling Sergio silently held their sheaf of identity papers toward the irate German guard. "I don't want your damned papers, you idiot!" screamed the guard, pushing them away. "You are the third Italian truck tonight in violation of the regulation about hooding your headlights! Now get the hell out of here and get those headlights hooded! Schnell!"

"Sì, Signore, I'll do that right away." Sergio slammed the van into gear and roared forward.

Manfred, concerned, pulled up to the checkpoint. "Trouble?" he said casually to the guard. "I am Herr Hauptmann." He held out his papers, and an open pack of cigarettes.

"Danke, mein Herr," said the guard, taking a cigarette.

"Take the pack," said Manfred generously. "I have more. Problems with that truck?" He was anxious to know what had transpired.

"Pah! It's these stupid Italians!" snorted the German. "They cannot obey regulations! The headlights were not properly hooded."

"I will certainly speak to the Italian police commandant tomorrow," said Manfred sternly. "Good job that you are so alert. Heil Hitler!" He shoved the Willys into gear.

"Gute Nacht, Herr Hauptmann," said the guard, with respect. Then both guards snapped to attention, each extending his right arm in stiff salute. "Heil Hitler!" they barked, in unison, as Manfred gunned the motor and pulled away.

The van, followed closely by the green Willys with the out-of-date New York plates, proceeded, without further incident, through the outskirts of Rome and right on into Vatican City. There, Manfred delivered Nancy and Amy safely into the hands and protection of Harold Tittman, the ranking Foreign Service Officer in charge of the U.S. delegation to the Vatican at that time.

On February 2nd, Lieutenant Bonfigli showed up at the Bruschis' again. He handed me a packet from Manfred, which had been routed via Vittoria, Valentina, Bonucci, and Gigi. Everyone crowded around me to watch while I opened it, despite Ruggero's gruff admonitions to his family to "stand back and give Signor Michele room." At least he didn't call me "Signor Console," I noted wryly. I was as excited as the family and quickly tore the package open. "Whoopee!" I shouted with joy when I saw what was in it. Italian banknotes! Two fat stacks of them!

I rapidly scanned the note that was with them. "Your fine packages forwarded safely to the main depot," wrote Manfred. "Returning the enclosed for causes you requested. Good luck."

Concetta and her parents stood staring, open-mouthed, at the stacks of bills. It was more money than they had ever seen in their lives. I attained even higher status. Hell, I was now probably equal to a demigod! Handing Concetta one of the packets, I said, "Here Concetta, I need to count this, and I know you are good at numbers—will you help me?" She looked at her parents, who smiled and nodded, bursting with pride that their daughter was smart enough to be able to help Il Console. Swiftly, we counted. Each contained 50,000 lire—over $2,500! Jumping up, I slapped Bonfigli on the back. "Eh, Mario!" I exclaimed jovially, "A hundred thousand lire! Five thousand American dollars! That's more money than either of us has seen in a while, right?"

Bonfigli whistled. "You bet. But I'm glad to see it now," he said.

I turned to Ruggero. Concetta had given them the total, and they were rooted to the floor, eyes wide in astonishment. "Ruggero!" I said sharply.

He snapped to attention. "Sì, Signore?"

"This calls for celebration!" I smiled. "A glass of wine for everyone!" Adalgisa hastened to get the glasses, as Ruggero brought the flask of wine. I turned to Bonfigli. "This will give us operating funds for a while!" Ruggero handed us our glasses of wine, then took his, and I indicated that Adalgisa and Concetta should each have one, too. Pepe, who had never fully awakened, was back in the bedroom, asleep. Hesitantly, they took their glasses. I turned, raising my glass. "To Manfred Metzger!" I said jubilantly. "To Manfred Metzger!" they all echoed, stumbling over the unfamiliar words. "And to the liberation of Italy!" I added. *That* was something they understood, and everyone repeated it eagerly, and drank. I knew the Bruschis had never seen such goings-on under their roof. They would talk about this night for the rest of their lives.

Dropping an arm around Bonfigli's shoulder, I drew him aside. "Can you get this money to Bonuccio Bonucci right away?"

"But of course, Signor Console," he assured me.

I sighed. It was hopeless. None of them would ever see me as Michele, the refugee clerk from Naples.

"The hundred thousand lire could not have come at a better time," he grinned, revealing even, white teeth. "Tomorrow, we'll both go see Bonucci. But tonight, we have other things to do." he said quietly. "Tonight we go out."

"Tonight? Where?" In my excitement, I failed to lower my voice. Bonfigli froze and stared at me as though I had taken leave of my senses. Then I realized my blunder. Fool! I scolded myself. Of course he isn't going to tell me, or anyone else here, what the target is tonight!

He started to say something to me, then changed his mind. "Let's go downstairs," he said quietly. "I have something to tell you in private." At the foot of the stairs, he turned to me, solemn-faced. "Tonight we go to a place in the general direction of west," he said cryptically. "The place we go to must have a name, but even I don't know it. There will be several men in our party. I don't want them endangered. Can you fire a rifle?"

For a moment, I smarted. I knew his confidence in me had been shaken, so I said, emphatically, "Of course I can fire a rifle! Forgive me, Mario, for my question, which I know was imprudent. I've been under arrest, or hiding out, for more than a year. And in the package I received very good news, that two dear friends of mine had made their escape to safety. I wasn't thinking as clearly as I should have been."

His expression changed, and I saw that he accepted my explanation. He smiled. "I am glad to hear about your friends, Signore," he said sincerely. "I know that it makes you happy to know they are safe. But about the rifle." While we were talking, he had walked us to a mound of straw in the livestock area under the living quarters. He reached down into the straw, and, groping around, pulled out an army carbine. "I left this here the other night," he said solemnly, but there was a twinkle in his brown eyes. He handed the gun to me. I took it and checked it out. I had used a rifle plenty of times on my uncle's ranch in Colorado. Seeing me handle and check the weapon over, Bonfigli's confidence was restored. "Tonight, at eight-thirty, leave the house and go to those woods there," he said, pointing to his left. The wooded clump was roughly 200 meters away. He slapped me on the shoulder. "Be on time, my friend." He slipped out the stable door to the back and disappeared into the brush. I was relieved to hear him call me "friend." I really liked Mario. He was intense, but a pleasant and cooperative person to work with.

I examined the rifle minutely, then dry-fired it several times to get the feel of it. In the empty stable, the snap of the bolt was startlingly loud. I carefully placed the carbine under some boards, where I could easily find it again in the dark, and went back upstairs. Adalgisa had done her best to produce a special meal. My chipped earthen bowl was heaped full of pasta and contained more than my fair share of precious sausage. Meat was usually reserved for Sunday only. A glass of wine stood before my bowl, and an extra large chunk of crusty bread was set beside it. A special meal for the warrior, or a good last meal for the condemned I thought, a bit cynically, then brushed the thought aside. This, after all, was what I had been wanting, what I had been waiting to do. I ate heartily, complimenting Adalgisa on the meal. She blushed with pleasure, and Ruggero gave her a rare glance of pride and approval before turning back to his bowl and stolidly consuming his meal. The day had been an especially good one, and I felt sure that the night would be, too.

6

Betrayal and Despair

As soon as dinner was over, Ruggero disappeared, instead of dawdling over his wine, as he usually did. The children were given an errand, which I knew was a pretext, and sent to a neighbor's farm. I went into the bedroom and put on my dark green sweater, the least conspicuous one I had. I pulled a second pair of black pants on over the ones I was wearing, hoping they'd keep me warm. Then I checked the Beretta carefully, loaded it, and slipped in into my waistband. When eight o'clock came, I put on my frayed topcoat, my gloves, and my wool peasant cap. God, I hoped it wouldn't be as cold tonight as it was last night! I knew if it was, my butt would be freezing, no matter what clothes I wore. I could feel a knot of nervous excitement building in my stomach.

When I stepped back into the kitchen, Adalgisa had finished cleaning up after supper. She came over to me and pushed a package containing a chunk of bread and some cheese into my pocket, then looked into my eyes. "Dio sia con te" (God be with you), she said, quietly, making the sign of the cross. She must have known what I was about to do, but she said nothing more. I opened the door and headed down the stairs. Retrieving the rifle from its hiding place, I took a bearing on the trees, the ones Bonfigli had pointed out earlier. As I trotted across the field, I thought of Nancy and Amy. Briefly, while still back in Perugia with Margherita, I had mentioned them to Bonuccio Bonucci, and asked about bringing them into the hills with me. His reply had been an emphatic "No! Absolutely not!" Now, I was glad he had been adamant. They were safe in Vatican City, under U.S. protection again, while here I was stumbling across a frozen field in the Umbrian hills, carrying a carbine.

Suddenly, the brush closed in on me. I tried to find a path through it, to get into the woods. Finding none, I decided to just bull my way through it. I couldn't risk being late for the rendezvous. I had barely gained the trees when I heard a loud stage whisper. "SSST! Sono qui, Signore!" (I am here Sir!). I peered into the darkness but could see nothing. "Eccomi qui" (Here I am), the voice repeated. A shadow moved, and I headed for it. Soon I caught up with it. "We will join the others in a few moments," he informed me, and set off deeper into the woods. I could not see my guide's features, but I followed his shadowy form closely. Soon the muffled voices of several other men came close, joining us. Once through the woods, we headed down the valley, hugging the brush, going about three kilometers. The cold had intensified, but these wiry partisans set a pace that kept me from noticing it, except for my nose, which from time to time I rubbed with my gloved hand to stimulate circulation. Rocks and stubble cut through my thin shoes, and I knew I would have to find boots somehow, before doing this again.

Finally, after cutting across the valley and up into the woods on the far side, we came to a stand of pine, and stopped. Lt. Bonfigli was waiting there. I looked around me, counting up. We were a dozen men, including Bonfigli and myself. We were all armed, though only three of us had army carbines. The others carried hunters' guns—sporting guns of varying caliber and age. Bonfigli spoke. "Now is the time to have your last cigarette." He could have rephrased it, I thought, so it didn't emphasize "last." I had not thought to bring one of my cigars—a mistake I vowed not to make again, as I watched the others enjoy their pipes or cigarettes. Seeing I had none, the youth next to me offered me a cigarette, which I gratefully accepted. Otherwise, no one paid me any particular attention. As we smoked, Bonfigli outlined the evening's plan of action. "When we reach the ambush site," he said, naming a place I didn't recognize, but which brought grunts of recognition from others in the group, "we will divide into two groups of six. One group will take one side of the road, and one the other. Stagger your positions so you are not shooting across at each other. The Germans use this road regularly, and we expect a convoy of at least six to ten vehicles sometime tonight."

I glanced at my watch, and Manfred flashed into my mind. I wished he were here, too—he'd have relished being in the thick of something like this. It was ten o'clock. "Okay. No more smoking," Bonfigli commanded, and everyone immediately extinguished pipes and cigarettes. "Let's go!" He waved us on and we headed out, going at the same brisk pace as before. We walked like that for several hours, across a countryside devoid of anything stirring. We scrambled down steep slopes, over convoluted ridges, and across icy streams. We slogged through mud up to our ankles. I couldn't feel my wet and frozen feet any more. Finally, we halted at the crest of the ridge, and everyone threw themselves down on the ground to rest. "This is the "ritrovo" (reassembly point)," said Bonfigli tersely. "After the 'colpo di mano' (shootout), get back here as fast as you can."

One of the partisans brought out bread, sausage, and cheese. I handed him the ration of bread and cheese Adalgisa had put in my pocket. The food was carefully shared out among us, and then two bottles of wine were uncorked and passed around. Each man took only two swallows, I noted, doing the same. Bonfigli came over and squatted down next to me. "From here on, please stay as close to me as you can. Do not do anything to endanger yourself, Signore." We stood up and moved into place at the road. It was three A.M. Six men took up their positions on the other side. The ambush site was on the crest of a hill, where approaching trucks, in low gear to climb it, would not be moving very fast. Just past us, the road curved away sharply, then dropped at a fairly steep angle, rising again on the far side, to the head of a rocky ridge. Across the road, the brush was fairly thick, and the slope was covered with scrub oak and rocky outcroppings. On our side, an embankment rose straight up for about eight feet. The brush was sparse, but there were a few large rocks that provided good cover.

Bonfigli positioned us so that everyone overlooked the road, but each of us was sheltered behind a rock, or tree, or outcropping. As he positioned each man, he whispered final instructions. He stationed me last—relatively far down the slope. My position was such that most of the action would occur after the vehicles had passed me and were farther up the hill. I knew that Bonfigli was complying with Bonucci's orders—keeping me away from the action and as safe as possible—but I resisted it. I was ready to be in the thick of things along with the others.

I hunkered down behind my rock, trying to concentrate and stay warm. Time crept by like a glacier, so slowly that its passing was almost imperceptible. Once, I caught myself nodding off and countered with a vigorous burst of leg-stretching and face rubbing. To keep myself awake and alert, I mentally ticked off all my resources back home, taking inventory of what Marguerite and Howard would have to live on—in case I didn't make it. Then I imagined us in our favorite restaurant, and I mentally pored over the menu, deciding what I'd order for our reunion dinner. I had settled on shrimp cocktail as a starter and was debating between a thick, juicy prime rib and a porterhouse steak, rare, when the sound of moving vehicles, like a distant rumble of thunder, reached me. "SSST!" The hiss that signaled readiness went from man to man. I held my breath and strained my ears, trying to count how many there were in the convoy as they shifted gears. I counted four—the last two sounded like trucks. Our orders were to stay hidden and not to open fire before Bonfigli did.

The last vehicle had just about cleared my position when the loud, staccato burst of Bonfigli's Mitre, the only submachine gun in our arsenal, rattled everyone into action. His first burst caught the lead vehicle, a weapons carrier with three soldiers in it. It slid sideways, and the man in back dived out and onto the far side of the road. "Sparate! (shoot!), get him!" the partisans yelled. More shots rang out. The second vehicle, a small staff car, tried desperately to steer around the weapons carrier. Rifle fire poured into it from the men on the other side of the road, and the car lurched to a stop, out of gear, its motor racing with a loud, steady whine. Then the first of the trucks, unable to brake in time, rammed into the back of the staff car, completely blocking the road off. "Sparate! Sparate!" (Shoot them!). Shots poured into the rest of the convoy from both sides of the road. "Colpitelo!" (kill him!), shouted someone, as a German soldier jumped down and tried to run toward the woods. A quick shot brought him down.

While waiting, I had wondered if I'd really be able to shoot a man when the time came. Now, as the last truck passed my position, I was up and firing, shouting with the rest in my best barroom Italian. "Darlilo!" (give it to them!). "Non mollate!" (don't let them get away!). I slammed the second clip home and fired. The fuel tank of the second truck ruptured. Whether it was my shot or not, I couldn't tell—there was so much firing going on. With a roar, it exploded, sending flames shooting twenty feet into the air. The driver jumped out, aflame, then fell to the ground. Down the line, barely visible because of the contour of the hill, another truck had been set ablaze, and ammunition inside it began exploding, giving off loud staccato pings like a hailstorm on a tin roof. Further up the line I heard shouts of "Via! Via!" That was the signal to clear out—fast! I turned and ran as hard as I could for the regrouping point.

Later, I didn't remember splashing through the small creek to reach it. As I gained the top of the hill, I turned and looked back down at the blazing trucks and the wreckage of the convoy. I knew that the flames from the ruptured gas tank would be seen for miles. With the noise of the explosion, and the shots, we had probably alerted every military unit in the area. Almost instantly, the others joined me. Bonfigli slapped my back heartily. "Bravo, bene!" (well done!), he commended us. Another man gave the thumbs up, "We stuck it to them!" gesture. There was more backslapping, and the partisan who had earlier produced the bread and sausage now surprised us with another bottle of wine, which we passed among us. It barely went around twice.

Bonfigli turned to me. "Vengo con lei, Signor Console" (I'll go back with you), he said. I was glad to hear that, since I didn't have any idea where I was or how to get back to the Bruschis'. "Give your rifle to Giorgio," he added, "so it won't weigh you down on the return trip. He'll store it with our other arms." A young partisan stepped forward and took the heavy carbine from my numb hands. I was grateful to be relieved of its weight. The lieutenant and I headed northeast along a ridge. He set a fast pace, and this time did not skirt the fields but moved as directly as possible toward the Bruschi farm.

As we strode along, we discussed the ambush in detail, looking for ways we could improve the next one. We had been lucky this time, we agreed, because there had been very little return fire from the Germans. "But after this, Mario," I said, "we had better be prepared. The Germans will undoubtedly provide more protection for their convoys from now on, and it will not be this easy for us." There will also be some reprisals for this one, I thought grimly. The Germans are not likely to take a brazen move like that lying down. But I didn't express that thought aloud. The lieutenant knew the risks—probably better than I.

After about two hours of nonstop walking, Bonfigli halted. I looked around. The first streaks of dawn were beginning to lighten the sky. "Just over that hill," he said, pointing to his left, "you will find a cart track. Follow it to the right. After just a few minutes of walking, you will be home." He stuck out his hand, and I grabbed it and shook it. "Perhaps you should come on down to Signor Bonucci's villa on Sunday," he added. "Sunday is a good time for the officers to gather. The farmers won't be working in the fields, and the women go to church. Everyone is out, so you won't be conspicuous." Then he added, clasping my shoulder, "You did well, tonight, Signore, very well indeed! Go home now, and rest. I will come back again around eight tonight, and together we will go down to Bonucci's and make our report to him." I nodded, thanking him, and we parted.

What Bonfigli had said about it being safe for me to be out in the day-time on Sundays was true, I reflected, as I quickly wended my way in the direction he had indicated I should go. Sunday was a special day every-where in Italy, even in the poorest of countrysides. Whereas minestrone was normally the main weekday fare, homemade pasta with a meat sauce was the favorite Sunday dish, eagerly looked forward to by everyone. Sunday was the day for a stroll along the pathways, after the meal, and a visit and glass of wine with friends and neighbors. It was the day for sitting around the fire smoking one's pipe, and for everyone to do a lot of talking. Since now the city people were often out foraging for food in the countryside, as Margherita Bonucci had done, it was not unusual to see strangers around during the day.

I found the cartpath and turned onto it. I could just make out the farm-house in the distance. Like a horse scenting the barn, and warm hay wait-ing, I picked up my pace and quickly closed the distance to home and bed. It was just after seven when I trudged up the stairs. The family was up, and they all gathered around, happy I was back safely. Seeing my tired face, Adalgisa touched my shoulder in compassion, and made clucking sounds, like a mother hen over a chick. She turned to the others. "Poor man, he is tired, and cold," she said. She began issuing orders. "Concetta, get the Signore coffee! Ruggero, bring wine!" Ruggero moved with alac-rity to bring the flask. I smiled inwardly. Rarely did Adalgisa dare to order him around. But since it was for Il Console . . . Young Pepe was sent to bring more wood for the fire.

They all hoped that, after I'd warmed a bit, I'd give a full accounting of my adventures. I gave only the sketchiest details. "Everyone got back safely," I said, knowing that was their primary concern. "I don't want to tell you much else, except that we were very successful." Ruggero smiled broadly on hearing that. Any success of mine reflected well on him. "For your own safety, I am not telling you more," I added kindly, seeing Adalgisa's face fall in disappointment at the thought that she was not going to hear any good gossip about my night's adventures.

Finishing the last of my boiled barley drink, which everyone still insisted on calling coffee, I got up, stretched wearily, and announced I was going to bed. "I have to go out again tonight," I said quietly to Ruggero. "The lieutenant will be here around eight." He nodded. I went into the bedroom and instantly fell asleep. I had made it through my first firefight without a scratch. Moreover, we had dented a German line of communication without any cost or casualties, except some of our precious ammunition. It was a good feeling, and for me especially it was a big boost in morale. Now I knew that as a partisan guerrilla fighter, I could take the gaffe.

I slept through most of the day and awoke in late afternoon. At first, I thought I was back in Gubbio. I was completely disoriented. Not used to being awake nights and sleeping days, my mind was in a state of total confusion. Pain lanced through my feet and licked at my legs with tongues of flame as I swung out of bed. Bending over, I picked up one of my shoes and looked at it. It was falling apart. I had to get some better shoes, or boots. Dressed, I limped out to the kitchen. After a bowl of hot minestrone, I felt better and went outside to walk around a bit and loosen up. Promptly at eight, Bonfigli showed up, and we headed down the hill along the tortuous route to Bonucci's villa. As we came near, we stopped in a copse of deep brush, carefully surveying the area before approaching the villa. I slipped behind a tree next to the terrace, Beretta in hand, while Bonfigli went to the door and knocked—three soft raps, then two sharp ones. Gigi opened the door and escorted us to the library.

I sensed a coolness in Gigi's greeting and attitude, and that puzzled me. In the library, an unsmiling Bonuccio awaited us. As he poured out three glasses of wine, he addressed Bonfigli in stern tones. "Word is already out about your colpo di mano last night, and I think you should have been more cautious. We don't want to play our trump card on the first trick," he said, with a jerk of his head in my direction.

I interceded. "I was in the safest possible position, Bonuccio," I assured him, "and I wanted to go."

"That may be," he retorted angrily, "but that doesn't make it a smart move by either of you! One slipup could have caused your capture, and that would have cost us dearly." Mario looked at Bonucci sheepishly, accepting the rebuke. Screw that! I wasn't going to sit around and stay hidden away.

"Look," I said hotly, "I damned well didn't come here just to trade one hideout for another!" Glancing my way, Mario gave me a look of gratitude. "Bonfigli was careful for my safety—too careful even—but I have to see some action sometime!"

Realizing my determination, Bonuccio decided to drop the issue. "Well, enough of that," he said calmly. "Now—give me a full report. How did it go? Any problems?"

Relieved that his anger at us had abated, we gladly recounted the details of the previous evening's operation. I expressed concern about our dwindling supply of ammunition. "Hand grenades. We need hand grenades, Bonuccio," I said. "With them, we'd be able to disable the vehicles faster, and limit the amount of rifle fire we'd need." Bonfigli agreed. "Besides," I added, "they're light, and a helluva lot easier to carry and conceal than rifles."

"Very well, Gualtiero," said Bonuccio, "I'll see that some of the lire you gave us goes to procuring grenades."

Mario and I looked at each other, smiling. "Okay!" I said.

"Now you two get out of here," he dismissed us. "You did a good job last night. Come back Sunday, and we'll make more plans. Anything else you need?" he asked me as we walked toward the front door.

"Yes," I replied. "I need sturdy shoes, or boots. I can't go dancing around your rocky hillsides in these ballroom slippers of mine much longer." I lifted a battered shoe for his inspection.

Mario laughed. "You're right, Signore, you're certainly going to need something stronger than those "gentleman's office" shoes! Let's see what we can find for you." He led me down a hallway to a back room, where there were several pairs of sturdy boots and hiking shoes. "See if any of these fit," he said. "There is a good bootmaker in Pietralunga, but boots are expensive, and first we have to find leather." Digging around in what was there, I found a pair of hiking shoes that fit reasonably well and pulled them on. We left quickly and quietly, and we made good time going back up to Ruggero's. For me, the shoes made a big difference. They were already broken in and didn't bother my feet at all. "Thank you, Signore, for coming to my aid with Bonucci," said Mario, as we parted. "I'll see you Sunday, at the villa."

Sunday we woke to a fierce wind moaning at the corners of the house, trying to get in. The sun barely had the strength to pierce the thick cloud cover. Stepping outside, I scented snow in the air. I pulled my collar close, to ward off the wind. Not sure I could find my way back to the villa alone, I asked Ruggero to accompany me. He was delighted. Maintaining a brisk pace to stay warm, we made good time. There were few people about, even though it was Sunday. We saw a few at a distance, half a dozen all told, and passed only one family on the path. Everyone must be staying in by the fire on a day like this. They stared openly at me, which made me decidedly uncomfortable, as they exchanged perfunctory greetings with Ruggero. He did not introduce me.

Shortly past noon, we arrived at Bonucci's villa. "Welcome, Signor Console, destroyer of German convoys," Bonuccio greeted me, smiling mischievously. On hearing that, Ruggero shot me an admiring glance. "The others are not here yet," continued Bonucci," but you, my skinny friend, are in time for dinner." Throwing an arm around my shoulder, he drew me inside. Ruggero stopped in the kitchen to talk to the old cook, seizing the opportunity, no doubt, to embellish my already exaggerated reputation as "destroyer of convoys."

I told Bonuccio I was concerned that Ruggero was overwhelmed by my status and would tend to overplay everything I did. As we warmed ourselves by the fire in the library, sipping wine, he smiled a wicked smile and said, "Already you have gained quite a reputation, Gualtiero. The peasants are saying that the American cowboy Consul blew up and set fire to an entire convoy of German trucks with one well-placed rifle shot!"

My face reddened, and he laughed delightedly. "That's not true, and you know it," I said lamely.

"Of course! But it's good for our sake, and for yours, for them to believe it," he said. "Perhaps we did not play our trump card too early after all." Crossing the room, he picked up a box, and, returning, offered me a cigar. I took one and lit it, drawing on it appreciatively. Before, I had always taken the availability of cigars for granted. Now, such small comforts, rarely available, were a great pleasure. "What else can I do for you, my friend, who has already done so much for us?"

I stared at the glowing tip of my cigar for a moment before answering. "Well," I said seriously, as though about to request a major favor, "the Bruschis are excellent hosts, but as you know, their facilities leave a little to be desired. If you really want to do something for me, what I'd like most of all is a hot bath."

Bonuccio was pleased to comply with my simple request. "That we can provide! But be careful now, you can't go smelling too clean—that would be completely out of character for a partigiano!" We both laughed at that, and he summoned Gigi. "Signor Console needs a hot bath. Please see to it as soon as possible." We finished our wine, smoking in companionable silence, and then I went upstairs. My bath was ready. I luxuriated in the hot water, trying not to think about how long it had been since I had bathed. Months. Not since the Hotel Brufani had I enjoyed the luxury of hot water.

When I rejoined Bonucci, Bonfigli was already there, along with another Italian officer, Lieutenant Biggiotti of Perugia. He brought us up to date on war news. The Allies had opened another front to the south of Rome. That cheered us. Then Bonucci made a dramatic announcement. "With the money from Signor Console, we have procured a stock of new carbines and ammunition."

"Teriffic! Where are they?" Bonfigli and I asked, almost in unison.

"For now they are safe, and no one needs to know where, yet," he replied. "We didn't dare bring them here, so we buried them nearby until we are ready to distribute them."

"You buried them?" I exclaimed, dismayed.

"Don't worry, Signor Console," he said, reassuringly, "we doused them in olive oil first, to protect them, and wrapped them well. They'll be fine. And you'll be pleased to know we got some grenades, too." He smiled at me. "They're Italian made, not as good as the American grenades, but they'll do." I was delighted to hear that, and anxious to get my hands on them.

Soon the rest of the band arrived. Everyone reported on their activities. Bonfigli gave a straightforward, factual report of our raid on the convoy. "There have been no serious reprisals by the Germans, so far," he concluded. "Several farms were searched, and one was burned, but the family had been warned and cleared out before the Germans arrived, so no one was harmed." I was relieved to hear that. Ramsay then suggested we blow up an important railroad bridge located on the outskirts of a small town nearby. A lively discussion ensued, but we decided against that action, because it would endanger too many families. We all agreed that, to the extent possible, we would avoid endangering civilian life and property. We decided our best course of action would be to lie low for another week, to lull the Germans into thinking the ambush was made by a roving band, rather than an organized group in their midst. Passing through the kitchen on my way out, I picked up two links of sausage to take to Adalgisa. After my experience at Margherita's, I was keenly aware of the burden placed upon her by an extra mouth to feed.

On the walk back, Ruggero said little, and my thoughts turned to Nancy and Amy. I wondered what they were doing, and how they were faring. I wondered if they were still at the Vatican. Then I dwelled on Margherita and her family. Bonuccio had assured me they were well, and safe. Did they have enough food? I wondered. Was Lucia's cough any better? Was Valentina risking her safety in helping the partigiani? There were no answers, and not likely to be any for a while, unless I heard from Manfred. I kept my thoughts from veering to my own family back home. That would only lead to self-pity and depression, and I had to keep my wits about me and focused on what I was doing in San Faustino.

The next day was market day in Pietralunga. Adalgisa gathered together a crock of homemade soup, a sack of cabbages, and a bundle of outgrown baby clothes for Ruggero and me to take to market. When we reached the town, Ruggero directed me to the bootmaker Mario had mentioned, and he went on to the marketplace to display his paltry wares. The bootmaker was pleased to welcome someone interested in buying new boots, instead of having old ones patched and mended. I described the kind of boots I wanted. He gave a low whistle, then sighed and shook his head. "Even if you could pay the price for such boots," he said, looking at me doubtfully, "I don't think I could find enough leather for such a job. And the price would be high, very high."

"Well," I said, "I'm a 'sfollato, and my funds are limited, so please get the best price you can, the lowest. But I need boots, so I hope you'll find the leather to make them. I'm sheltering with a family in the countryside near here, and I'll check with you again in a week."

"Si, Signore," he said. "I will do my best to find leather and make you the boots you want." I had told him as little as I could and hoped I could trust him. I needed those boots.

I searched out Ruggero. He had sold the crock of soup for a few coins and had exchanged the cabbages for a rusty crosscut saw. The baby clothes had brought twice what Adalgisa expected. I gave Ruggero some lire and told him to buy Adalgisa and the children a present. He couldn't countenance such extravagance and started to protest. It wasn't Christmas, after all. But I insisted. "Get some wine for us, too," I added. That brought a big smile, and he thanked me warmly and went off to accomplish his mission. I wandered around the market. There was little or nothing to buy, so when Ruggero returned, we headed for Fontanella.

On the walk back, Ruggero assured me I could trust Ugo the boot-maker not to reveal anything about me. "You will have fine boots, Signore," he assured me, "when he finds leather."

During the rest of the week, we tramped around the local area. I wanted the farmers to know my face and become used to seeing me around. A time might come when I'd need one or another of them to shelter me. Wherever we went, we were given a warm welcome and an honored place at the table. Invariably, we were offered the conventional glass of wine, and, after Ruggero had spoken to the host, usually a second glass. Not only that, but I was accorded rapt, deferential attention that was well beyond conventional politeness. I mentioned this to Ruggero as we made our way back to Fontanella. "Ruggero, we're getting a lot of wine, and a lot of attention, from these poor farmers on a weekday. You're not telling them who I am, are you?"

"Oh, no, Signore!" Ruggero protested, self-righteously. "Always I protect your name."

We walked on for a while in silence. I was getting used to the long periods between Ruggero's sorties into speech. I decided to rephrase my question. "Well, everyone has sure been friendly and very respectful. Even the bootmaker. I wonder why they treat me so well after you have talked to them?"

"That is because they have great respect for you, Signor Console," he responded matter-of-factly. "They have never before met an important man who works for Signor Presidente Roosabelta."

I smacked my forehead, peasant style. So that was it! I should have known! My instructions to Ruggero had been to never use my real name, my country, or my title. I had not anticipated, and therefore not thought to prohibit, this kind of circumlocution, whereby he could divulge his new status without breaking any of the rules. Even the folk in this remote area knew who "Presidente Roosabelta" was. I realized I'd have to learn to live with it and to trust Ruggero and his neighboring tenant farmer friends to keep my secret.

Several days later, the Band again attempted a hit on a German convoy, but this time we drew a blank. We waited most of the night, but no vehicles showed up at the ambush point. Disappointed, we trudged wearily home. Sunday came again, and Ruggero and I headed for the meeting at the Bonucci villa. Barely a few hundred meters from San Faustino, a peasant ran out into the road and flagged us down. "No, no, go no farther! Go back!" he called urgently.

"What is it? What's happened?" I asked, skin prickling in alarm.

"Fascisti! A gang of them! They have broken into the villa! You must not go there!"

Damn! Whipping around, we checked the road behind us. There was no one in sight. Scrambling over a low stone wall along the side of the path, we headed for the track back to Fontanella. As soon as we reached the trees, we broke into a run. I was winded by the time I felt we had put enough distance between us and the villa to slow to a walk again. I was terrified for Bonucci, Gigi, and the others. "This is a helluva fix," I gasped to Ruggero. "How do we get word to the others?" His eloquent shrug gave the answer. If I didn't know, how could he possibly know? Well, I decided, I might as well be patient. The "peasant pipeline" will get the news out faster than we could anyway. There was nothing we could do for the time being but return home.

The next two days crawled by. Ruggero and I sat and stared at each other, jumping at every sound. Assunta, the girl who lived at the foot of the hill, was alerted to keep a sharp eye out and to warn us if anyone was approaching. We sent Concetta and Pepe down the road in turns, to keep watch. More than that we could not do. Restlessly, I paced the concave bowl of the room, down, then up, then down, over and over again. What in hell could have happened? Who had betrayed Bonucci? Then, trying to calm myself I thought, maybe it was just a bunch of thugs—vandals. No, the peasant had been clear. Fascisti, he had said. Finally, at dusk on Tuesday, a teenage boy showed up at Fontanella. The news he spilled out numbed me to the bone.

Eight Fascist militiamen had raided the villa early Saturday, thoroughly ransacking it. They were definitely looking for something. I grabbed the dark-haired youth by the shoulder and questioned him closely. "Did they find anything, that you know of, that would incriminate Bonucci, or any of the Band?"

Tears sprang to the boy's eyes. He was clearly frightened. "No, Signore," he replied, "not that day, but there is more."

I sighed. I was afraid of what I was going to hear. "What is your name?" I asked, giving him, and myself, a moment to collect ourselves.

Nervously, he twisted his cap in his thin fingers. "Angelo, Signore."

"All right, Angelo," I said, as quietly as I could, to reassure him. "Tell me everything you know. Did you see this yourself?"

"No Signore, I was not there, but was sent here to bring you the message of what happened." He proceeded with his tale. "The Fascisti, they brought a cart with them on Saturday, and they smashed a lot of furniture there that belonged to our priest!" The youth seemed terribly upset about that. Perhaps he had some family connection with the priest, or the church. "Then they took all the food in the villa, put it in the cart, and took it away." Damn! All the effort and expense in acquiring our stockpile of rations—wheat, flour, sausages, wine, and olive oil—it was all down the drain! But the worst news was yet to come.

"That was all they did that day. But Signor Bonucci heard about it, and the next day he came to the villa, very angry, to inspect the damage. He was only there a few minutes, when four men knocked on the door. They must have been watching for him."

"Militia?" I broke in to ask.

"No, they were dressed in civilian clothes," he replied. "But they were after Signor Bonucci, no one else, because they let two other officers of the Band come to the villa and leave, before Signor Bonucci got there, and they did not come out of hiding or bother them."

"What happened to Bonucci?" I demanded urgently.

The tears spilled over and slid down the youth's cheeks. "They captured him and took him away, Signore!"

I sat back, finally letting my breath out. Christ! This was disaster! Not Bonuccio! "How the hell did that happen?" I demanded. "Why wasn't he warned? Where in the name of God was Gigi? Where were the others?"

"I do not know, Signore," said Angelo miserably, openly sobbing now. "The minute Signor Bonucci opened the door of the villa, the men whipped out submachine guns and hustled him away, without even his coat. By the time the two partigiani officers got the word, it was too late to help him!" I calmed Angelo down, and thanked him for coming to inform us of what happened. Adalgisa served him some hot soup, which he gulped down gratefully, and, having delivered his staggering news, he left.

I sat in my chair by the fire. No one spoke. Bonuccio Bonucci, captured! It didn't seem possible. I tried not to think of the implications for the Band of San Faustino, let alone for myself. I worried hopelessly, and helplessly, about what was happening to my friend. My mind flinched at the prospect of what they'd do to him to get information. I shied from that thought, raging instead at the failure of the warning system. Where the hell were Gigi and the others? Someone had betrayed Bonucci, I was convinced of that. But who? Everyone for miles around loved and respected him. I got up and paced the floor in fury and anguish, smacking my fist into my hand. Ruggero silently poured us each a glass of wine, giving me a sad-eyed look as he handed me mine. Adalgisa and the children had quietly disappeared into the other room. Ruggero touched my shoulder briefly in quiet sympathy, then moved away to sit at the table. He, too, was shocked and lost in thought. If the Fascists managed to torture enough information out of Bonucci, none of us were safe.

Less than an hour later, a second messenger arrived. It was Enrico, a member of the Band, whom I had seen before at the villa. "Bonucci has been imprisoned in Perugia," he informed me tersely, obviously worried. "Colonel Guerrizzi was tipped off in the nick of time, and has disappeared, but his wife and son have been arrested." Hell and damnation! Disaster upon disaster! Enrico left, and I flopped disconsolately into a chair at the table, then stared at the dying embers of the fire. We had lost our two top men, all our provisions, and our military advantage, in one quick move!

I slammed the table with the flat of my hand. Ruggero jumped in surprise. "No, by God!" I said loudly, in English. "We've still got men, and we've still got a cache of weapons somewhere! I'll damn well find out where, and we'll continue. And I'll damn well find out who betrayed Bonucci, and they'll pay for this, if it's the last thing I do!" But I knew there was little or nothing I could do to save my friend Bonucci from his fate at the hands of the Fascists and the Germans. It was already too late for that. God help him. God help all of us.

Walter W. Orebaugh.

Nancy Charrier.

Amy Houlden.

Manfred Metzger.

Manfred Metzger.

Margherita Bonucci and family: Vittoria, Valentina, Lucia, and Franco (Francesco).

Valentina and Franco Bonucci, 1942.

False identity card carried by Orebaugh when traveling in enemy territory.

Exterior and interior of the Shrine of the Forty Martyrs in Gubbio that contains the remains of forty heads of households summarily executed by the Germans in retaliation for a partisan raid.

Countryside of Umbria, near Pietralunga.

San Faustino.

Typical farmer's cart.

The shed at the Rossi farm in Grottazzolina.

Plaque on the wall of Bonuccio Bonucci's villa, San Faustino, Italy: "So that the living will remember those who died under the Nazi-Fascist hell to maintain a free Italy."

U.S. Chargé d'Affaires David McK. Key presents the Medal of Freedom to Walter W. Orebaugh, as Italian Chief of Staff General Raffele Cordona, his mother Imogene I. Orebaugh, his wife Marguerite, and Lt. General C. H. Lee, Commander of U.S. Forces in the Mediterranean Theater, look on. Rome, January 17, 1946.

7

From Diplomat to Guerrilla Leader

The following morning was cold and overcast. The gray of the sky matched my mood. I woke Ruggero and instructed him to go seek out Bonfigli, or any information he could about Bonfigli's whereabouts. I feared that perhaps he and Captain Pierangeli had also been arrested. After Ruggero left, I spent most of the morning watching the approaches to Fontanella through a narrow gap in the shuttered window.

Up to now, even in my bleakest moments in Gubbio and in Margherita's apartment in Perugia, I had believed my diplomatic status might help me some in the event of discovery. Watching for the Fascisti to come after me in this hardscrabble, windswept farm hideout, I suddenly felt terribly alone. A stranger in a strange land. The State Department didn't mean a damn thing here. Neither would my diplomatic passport! I knew that only my own ability and determination could help me now. How the hell will you get out of this one, Walt? I asked myself grimly. I didn't have a good answer. A lot of luck, maybe. And the Fifth and Eighth armies, if they got their butts up here fast enough! It was two in the afternoon before Ruggero returned. Given the situation, the news he brought was good. Bonfigli was safe and knew about Bonucci's arrest. He wanted me to meet with him that night, at the house where he was staying. On the way, Ruggero and I would stop in Pietralunga and listen to the news on the radio at the home of a neighbor of Giovanni Marioli, a good friend of Ruggero's.

Snow flurries began late that afternoon, and I worried that we would leave a trail. But the wind had blown the trail clear by the time we set out for Pietralunga after dark. Determined to exercise greater caution than ever, we made a wide berth around several farmhouses where Fascist sympathizers were reported to be living. Giovanni led us to his friend's house, in the middle of the pitch-dark town. There, after a good deal of fiddling with the dial, we picked up the BBC and got about nine minutes of fairly clear news before the signal became garbled. Sicily, Sardinia, and southern Italy had been returned to the control of the civilian Badoglio government, we learned. The Germans were making a major effort to throw back the Allied forces at Anzio. The Allies had bombed the Abbey of Monte Cassino, which was occupied by the Germans. On hearing that, I looked over at Ruggero and his friend. Neither showed any emotion, but I knew they must have privately grieved at the sad news about the historic old Abbey. Then I realized that, being isolated peasants with little education, they probably knew nothing about the Abbey, so that news would not bring a reaction from them. The broadcaster exhorted listeners to "support the Allies, resist the enemy in every way possible, and, above all, support the Badoglio government."

We slipped out into the wintry darkness again and took off, following the directions Ruggero had gotten from Bonfigli. At one point, taking a wrong turn, we blundered ankle deep into a stinking, half-frozen pigsty. Muttering apologies, Ruggero got us back on track and to the farmhouse where Bonfigli was quartered. An old crone answered my muffled knock. No lamps were lit, but standing in front of the fireplace were Bonfigli and, to my relief, Captain Pierangeli, now our highest ranking officer. We sat before the fire with our glasses of wine.

Bonfigli broke the unhappy silence. "I'm no hero, but I'll be damned if I'm going to turn my back on all we've worked for, and all we've done. I say let's take our lumps, regroup, and carry on. I know that's what Bonucci would have wanted." Tears filled his eyes, and he looked away briefly, clearing this throat, then quickly brought himself back under control.

"You have a point, Mario, and I agree with you," said Pierangeli, "but we must take into account what has happened. We didn't have the proper security, or the proper safeguards, in place. This shouldn't have happened! Bonucci, and we with him, took too much for granted! We can't let that happen again. But I agree—we must carry on with our mission. We'll know now to be more careful about protecting ourselves."

I spoke up for the first time. "We need to get that word out to everyone right away. They need to be reassured. We can't let them think, even for a moment, that the movement, and the Band, is leaderless and in danger of disbanding." Pierangeli and Bonfigli readily agreed. We prepared a message to be delivered to all components of the movement the next day. It would be signed by Captain Pierangeli as commander. I brought up the cache of weapons. We shared every scrap of information we had on it— which was almost nothing. After comparing notes, we agreed that Bonucci had said that he and Colonel Guerrizzi had overseen one person dig the hole, douse the cache with olive oil, then wrap and bury the weapons, and cover the hiding place over to disguise it. We also agreed that we could think of only one person Bonucci would have trusted to do that—Gigi. Since I lived the closest to San Faustino, we decided that I should be the one to question Gigi about the location of the weapons cache.

On the long walk back, I realized that not only did I no longer enjoy diplomatic status, I no longer thought in diplomatic terms. My environment had forced changes in my ethics and my behavior. The guerrilla world I now lived in allowed little room for the practice of "striped pants diplomacy." It was a rough, dog-eat-dog existence, albeit one that was softened by the compassion of the peasants. The next morning, I made an effort to brush my teeth—having failed to practice that civilized nicety for more days than I cared to think about. After forcing down a mug of the ersatz coffee, I told Ruggero to go and get Giuseppe—invoking the authority of the CLN if necessary—and bring him to the Bruschi farmhouse for a meeting with me.

Late in the afternoon of February 17th, Ruggero returned, with a reluctant Gigi in tow. He had not wanted to come, but Ruggero had reminded him that his padrone, Bonucci, would have expected him to cooperate with Il Console in every way possible. As he drank his ritual glass of wine, I watched Gigi carefully, trying to detect any change in his behavior. He acted no differently than he always had.

"These are bad times for all of us," I began. Giuseppe nodded solemnly. "Not just for you," I continued. "Signor Bonucci was doing a great job for us. You know that, don't you?" Another nod of assent. "Now we must close ranks and all work together, Giuseppe." Giuseppe's eyes wavered. I hurriedly added, "I'm not asking you to work for me. You are still Bonucci's man." He nodded again, relieved. "But we need your help," I went on. "Bonucci trusted you with important information. You know things that can help us." Giuseppe looked quizzical at that, but nodded again. I wanted him to say something, anything, but I knew he was a taciturn man by nature, and now would be even more guarded than ever. In a way, I understood how he must be feeling. His beloved Bonucci had been arrested. No one knew his fate. Every one of us was in danger. I took a deep breath and plunged on.

"Giuseppe, before the Fascisti took him away, Signor Bonucci told me and Lt. Bonfigli about a cache of arms he had had buried somewhere. We need those arms now, so we can continue operations. What can you tell me about them?"

Giuseppe turned half away from me. "I can tell you nothing," he stated flatly, without emotion. It appeared to me that by his reaction—the turning away and the terseness of his declaration—he knew something and was hiding it. If Bonucci had told Giuseppe not to say anything to anyone about the weapons, Giuseppe would take that order literally, I knew. He would not tell me, even though I was Il Console.

I adopted a sterner, no nonsense tone. "Giuseppe, you know how important this is! We can't fight the Fascisti and the Germans without those guns! Now please, tell me where the weapons are, Gigi." At my use of the familiar nickname, Giuseppe flashed me a warning look. I repeated the question, addressing him more formally.

"I do not know, Signor Console," he replied gravely. "I cannot help you, because I do not know where the weapons are." Giuseppe was seated at the wooden table. I was standing. I tried reasoning. I tried intimidation, towering over him. He steadfastly maintained he didn't know where the weapons were hidden, and in fact had never seen them.

Exasperated, frustrated, I shouted, "I'll have you court-martialed!"

"But Signore, I am not in the army," he muttered stolidly.

"You are now!" I snapped, infuriated at his failure to disclose the location of our badly needed arms. I whipped out my Beretta and held it to his temple. "Now, damn it, tell me where those arms are, or I'll kill you!" By God, I'd make this man take me seriously! They weren't dealing with any soft city slicker, and they'd find that out quickly! Giuseppe neither moved nor spoke. I stared at him, malevolently. There was fear in his eyes, but no duplicity. He just looked at me, clear-eyed, returning my stare. Suddenly, a wave of self-disgust washed over me. "What am I doing?" I asked myself, half aloud. I couldn't believe I had been ready to pull the trigger and kill Giuseppe! Bonucci's Gigi. I tucked the gun into my waistband. "I believe you, Giuseppe. I'm sorry. Go now."

"Sì, Signor Console." Our eyes met. "If I can find the weapons for you, I will," he said sincerely, and left.

I felt awful. I was still shaking when I went to bed. Would I really have killed that poor, simple man? I knew in my heart that I wouldn't have hesitated to pull the trigger if I had been fully convinced that Gigi was lying, and that in itself scared me. I realized there was a side to my nature that had never been revealed, even to me. I kept to myself on Friday and Saturday, wrestling with my conscience and my sense of duty, sleeping little. Ultimately, I recognized that what was important was that I hadn't pulled the trigger, and that I had sincerely apologized to Gigi for doubting him. I had made the right decision. I slept better Saturday night.

On Sunday, I set out alone for Morena, where our staff meeting would be held. When I got there, most of the other officers were already there. Captain Pierangeli sat at the head of the old dining room table. I looked around. Only Ramsay was there from the contingent of British officers in the area. He told me that the American pilot Joe Withers had left our area to head southward. Pierangeli set a businesslike tone, which instilled confidence in everyone around him. Halfway through the meeting, I gave my report about the arms cache. There was palpable disappointment. However, no one questioned Giuseppe's integrity. Bonfigli said he would conduct an extensive search for the weapons. We agreed we could probably equip fifty or sixty men for combat, with what we still had, but any action we took involving firefights would have to be of short duration, therefore almost a sure thing, until the weapons were found. Not a shot could be fired that was not absolutely necessary. No more recruits would be taken into the movement unless they had a weapon *and* ammunition for it. We moved on to a procedure for requisitioning food to replenish our lost stores. To feed the 120 men we already had was our number one priority. Although the farmers were, for the most part, more than willing to help, many of them were simply not able to. Their own families, and guests, were already overloading their larders. Even in normal times, and these times certainly weren't normal, the average farm household included several generations.

"Any news of Bonucci?" I asked Bonfigli during a brief lull in conversation.

"Only that he has not been publicly executed, and we have heard that he is still alive, but in terrible shape," he said, his eyes reflecting his deep sorrow.

My stomach clenched at hearing that. I knew what it meant. They were brutally torturing Bonucci for information. At the sound of Bonucci's name, a dejected silence had fallen in the room. None of us could bear to think, let alone talk about it. We quickly switched the subject back to arms and ammunition. Lt. Soldatini suggested we attack convoys, and strip them after they were shot up. We disapproved that as too dangerous and requiring too much of our scarce ammunition to accomplish.

Remeccioni spoke up. "There are a barracks and an armory at the garrison at Scheggia, and the force there has been reduced. They must have guns and ammunition."

"I think an immediate raid on Scheggia would be a good idea," said Bonfigli. "Sunday night, because the guards are more lax then." We agreed that more reconnoitering was needed and that, if everything looked good, the operation would go on the following Wednesday night instead.

I left the meeting feeling more optimistic than when I arrived. At least we were doing something! The will to go on was still there. As I walked back to the Bruschi farmhouse, I rubbed my shoulder, which had been paining me lately. I'd have felt a helluva lot better if the details in a message being decoded at that moment in Washington had even been close to the truth: "Orebaugh now with group approximately 1,800 partisans, 80 kilometers from Rome," the cablegram read.

The next morning, when I woke, the family was gone. They were attending the funeral of one of Adalgisa's relatives. Around nine-thirty, I spied a solitary figure coming up the cartpath. Peering out through the ice-glazed window, I couldn't make out who it was, though his step and cadence seemed familiar. I checked the Beretta, then looked once more before deciding to head for the escape ladder at the back bedroom window. Closer now, I recognized the slender, angular form and military bearing of Mario Bonfigli. Strange. It was not usual for him to come around in broad daylight. I went out and hurried down the stairs to greet him.

"Ah, do I have a surprise for you, my friend," he exclaimed, stamping the wet snow from his boots. "Quick, upstairs!" Once inside, I was bursting to hear his news, but he put me off by saying, with a grin, "A good Commandante would offer a poor 'Tenente some real coffee on a cold morning like this."

"Ma che! Real coffee!" I replied. "Who has real coffee around here? You're welcome to this brew if you want some, and it's poor enough, even for imitation!'"

"Ah, but look here!" With a flourish, Bonfigli whipped a foil packet from his jacket pocket, and held it out to me, grinning. "A requisition from a most willing citizen of Umbertide, who happened, by the way, to speak German—once too often." I realized that there must have been a reprisal raid against a German sympathizer.

Just then, the door opened—the family was back. Exclaiming in delight, Adalgisa snatched up the packet of coffee, and immediately began dividing it up, to stretch it out as much as possible. She brewed two cups of undiluted coffee for Bonfigli and me, then carefully wrapped the used grounds to mix with roasted barley grindings later. Favoring us with a rare smile, she brought us brimming cups, then shooed the family out, to do chores in the yard.

When they were gone, Bonfigli drew a larger package from inside his jacket. "And now, for my second surprise." Tearing off the wrapping, he exposed a Mauser machine pistol! I gave a low whistle of appreciation. Bonfigli smiled happily.

Reverently, I lifted it, turning it over and over in my hands. "Wow! Where did you get this beauty?" I asked.

"It's for you, Signor Console," he said. "Should make a hell of a noise." He grabbed the gun out of my hands, and ran around the room, pretending to shoot it, like a kid playing war games. "Rat-a-tat-tat! Rat-a-tat-tat! Got you!" He came back and laid the pistol on the table. "Another present from the man with the coffee," he remarked casually. "Check it over. Tonight you will need it."

Picking it up again I asked, "Who is going?" I didn't need to ask where. It had to be the barracks at Scheggia.

"Well," he said, "there will be you and me. We will be, how you say, 'buddies'."

I was shocked. "That's crazy, Mario!" I protested. "Two of us can't take that on, even with a Mauser!"

He laughed, enjoying himself. "No, no, of course not, my friend. I was only joking. There will be twenty of us. Here, sit down and look." He produced a sketch of the area around the barracks. "We figure there are about fifteen Fascist militia left there. We'll get in early, surprise them, and try to take a vehicle too, if possible, to carry off whatever booty we 'liberate' from them." He chuckled at the prospect. He was certainly in a fine mood this morning! Turning the paper over, he drew a sketch of what he thought the inside of the barracks should look like. Then he gave me directions to a house. "We'll meet there tonight at seven," he said. He also gave me an alternative regroup location, in the event there was any foul-up during the raid. Finishing the last drop of his coffee, he stood up to leave.

I held out my hand. "Good luck, Mario, and thanks! See you tonight."

He brightened visibly at my use of his first name. That was a big deal to him. "So long, buddy," he replied, in English.

I had to smile at that. I walked with him down the stairs, then slipped into the barn area on the ground floor and practiced loading and unloading the Mauser until I could do it with my eyes shut. It would be dark, and I didn't want to foul up. Nineteen other lives might depend on me. Back upstairs, in the bedroom, I checked and rechecked the Beretta, too.

I told Ruggero that I would be gone for a couple of days, and at lunch Adalgisa filled my plate with an extra large serving of pasta. When I was ready to leave, she pressed a package of bread, cheese, and sausage into my hands. As I walked, I noticed that the afternoon's pale sun had warmed the air slightly and yesterday's heavy snow was starting to melt. The icicles, hanging like hundreds of shiny silver ribbons from the bare branches of the trees and bushes, dripped water in a steady rhythm. Damn! A thaw, even a brief one, meant the path would be mud beneath the snow. The temperature was sure to drop again after dark, and the mud would freeze, making the going even rougher. I tried to remember what it was like to drive a car to get where I was going, instead of struggling interminable miles on foot, in the worst weather imaginable, over impossible terrain.

Around sunset, I took out the package and ate some of the meat and cheese. It was seven-fifteen, and I had been walking more than six hours, when I passed the cluster of three houses Bonfigli had described. I made a turn, and there, silhouetted against the horizon in the moonlight, stood the farmhouse where we were to meet. The side path that led up to it was at least 800 yards long, and the last 80 or so yards rose so steeply I had to crawl up it on all fours, struggling for a foothold. Was there no end to this misery? Suddenly, to my right, the ferocious barking of a dog shattered the silence. My hair stood on end.

"This way, Signore," a strange voice whispered, out of the black silence. "Around here."

Groping my way blindly, I followed the sound of the voice. I glimpsed a shadow in movement, but it was too dark to see who it was. We slipped into a low, lean-to type shed. Mario was there, in the pitch blackness, with four other partisans. We exchanged quiet greetings, then left in pairs,

Mario and me last. Cutting across a field behind the ridge, we turned down a lane that paralleled the road into Scheggia. It was only another couple of kilometers, but after slogging through mud all afternoon, it was torture for me. Reaching the town, we backed up against the tightly adjoined buildings and, weapons drawn, ducked swiftly and silently from dark doorway to dark doorway. I prayed that no one had dogs. The moon slept beneath a thick blanket of clouds, and there were no lights anywhere in the town. Even at Scheggia Barracks, the blackout was strictly enforced. We reached the main piazza and dropped quickly into our assigned positions. Bonfigli and I crouched behind the ornate central fountain and waited for Pepe, one of our Band, to begin the action. According to what Mario had told me earlier, one of the militiamen from the barracks had been captured by the Band a few weeks back and relieved of his orders, his tunic, and his weapon. Now Pepe, with a substitute name on the orders, strolled casually across the square to the massive wrought iron gate leading to the military compound, his carbine slung across his shoulder, Fascist style.

Barely daring to breathe, I checked my pistol again, then, as my eyes became more accustomed to the inky blackness, I quickly surveyed the scene around me. The escape route was directly behind me. Mario had positioned me with care. A row of tall trees bordered one side of the piazza. Several of our men were behind them, stationed fifty to sixty yards apart. On the opposite side, roughly seventy-five yards across from the trees, the recessed doorways of dark storefronts provided cover for more partisans. I judged the gate of the compound to be about eighty yards from me. From there, it was only a short distance across a courtyard to the barracks itself. We could see six shuttered windows across the front, on the second floor. The wall and gate hid the first floor from view. I wondered about back entrances. If the Fascists were able to get out the back, then come into the square by way of the side street, we wouldn't get a clear line of fire at them. Suddenly, our position at the fountain, right in the middle of the square, seemed extremely exposed. Fortunately, the fountain itself provided substantial cover. Pepe had reached the gate. Everyone tensed for the rush. He tried the gate, but it was locked, so he reached up and pulled the bell rope. A few seconds later, the shutters on one of the second-floor windows opened, and a soldier peered out. Pepe stepped back enough to be seen. He waved his papers at the man in the window.

"Che volete?" (what do you want?), came the voice from above.

Pepe coolly shouted his false name and a set of numbers from the orders. "Aprite, per favore!" (open up!), he shouted. "I'm assigned here!"

The shutters slammed closed. It's going to work, I thought. We relaxed a bit. Suddenly, we heard muffled shouting, and running, inside the garrison. What the hell? Then—ominous silence. God, what I wouldn't give for a grenade right now, I thought.

I glanced over at Bonfigli, who was watching the building intently. "They know something is up," he muttered. "But they don't know how many of us there are."

"What now?" I whispered.

"Let's shoot them up some—maybe they'll surrender," he replied.

I nodded. Bonfigli was already up on one knee, shouldering his rifle. He aimed at the window where the soldier had appeared, and fired. Instantly, a fusillade of rifle fire poured from both sides of the piazza into the barracks. A woman's scream, from somewhere off to my left, shattered the tranquillity of the town. Then the dogs began. A baby howled. All around us, shutters were being slammed shut. More babies cried, more women started screaming, as we continued to fire into the barracks. It was pandemonium. The militiamen began to fire back at us. They hadn't panicked at all. They watched for the flash from our guns, and, when they had picked a target, they fired.

"Okay! Your turn, buddy!" shouted Bonfigli to me, above the melée. I propped the machine gun on the rim of the fountain and squeezed the trigger. Its loud, staccato bursts startled me, but it had less recoil than I expected. My first burst was aimed low, along the top of the wall. Then I raised up, and to the left, raking a path across the windows on the second floor with my next round. The firing from the barracks all but ceased. "Let's go! Out!" shouted Mario, and he waved toward the church.

As we withdrew toward the church, we covered each other well, with sporadic, but well-placed shots, which discouraged return fire from the windows. Pepe broke from his cover at a full run to join us. Two-thirds of the way across, he lunged forward and fell to the ground, hit. Mario shoved his carbine over to me. "Cover me!" and he was off, running in a crouch toward Pepe.

"The hell with that!" I snarled, dropping the carbine. I rammed the second canister home in the Mauser and covered him with a series of bursts. A new hubbub of screams and shouts erupted all around me. Scheggia must think that the whole war is being fought on its very doorsteps, I thought. Bonfigli had snatched Pepe up and carried him to safety behind the trees. I dropped down behind the cover of the fountain and slid Mario's carbine over to the nearest partisan. "Take this!" I hissed, "and when I start firing, run like hell for the trees!" Both men nodded. Shots began again from the windows of the barracks. The two windows on the left seemed to be firing at the fountain. The others were firing here and there, where they thought other partisans might be. I pulled back little, crouching, and turned to the others. "Ready?"

"Sì!"

"Now!" They bolted to the left, heading for the trees, and I jumped out from behind the fountain to the right. The movement to the left had momentarily distracted the gunners, and, before they could readjust their aim, I fired a burst at the windows from which most of the firing had come. At the end of the burst, I broke for the storefronts to my right. Halfway across the square, I dropped to one knee, swung sideways, and sent off another burst. Then I ran like hell for cover. I saw stone chips flying behind me and thought the Fascists had me targeted, but it was the partisans covering me. I reached an alley behind the church and hustled down it.

"Commandante, is that you?" a voice queried from the shadows.

"Yes!" I replied tersely.

"The 'Tenente is down that way, with Pepe." He pointed with his rifle.

About a hundred meters down the roadway, I found Bonfigli, with two other partisans, tending to Pepe's wound. "How are you doing, Pepe?" I asked, dropping down beside them. I was gasping for breath and dripping with sweat.

"Ah, Signor Commandante, I'm afraid I have disappointed you," whispered Pepe genially. "I was hoping to play my part well enough to go to your Hollywood!"

Bonfigli broke in. "He'll make it all right. But he's going to go around with a big hole in his shoulder for a while."

I reached down and patted Pepe on the forehead. "'You did fine, Pepe, just fine. You had the hardest job of all."

He grinned up at me, teeth flashing white in the darkness. "You didn't do so bad yourself, Signore," he said.

"Nor you, Mario," I said, grasping Bonfigli's shoulder warmly. "That was a brave thing you did. I don't know if I managed to hit anything worthwhile with this thing or not." I held up the Mauser.

"Maybe not," said Bonfigli, "but, like I told you, it makes one helluva racket! I bet there is no one in that barracks with constipation tonight! Or in this town!"

He jumped up, giving the signal to pull out, then turned to me, as I slowly rose to my feet. "Or would you rather stay? We'll rent an apartment in the town," he jibed.

"No, I thought we were hanging around so your lady friend—the one who was doing all the screaming—could catch up to you," I replied with a chuckle, slapping him lightly on the back.

Everything was quiet. The town seemed to be locked up tight. We withdrew in stages, since there didn't seem to be any danger we would be attacked, or followed. "Be careful," Bonfigli warned the men, "and don't get caught with that long thing sticking out of your pants." Despite the pun, his warning was sincere, for come daybreak we were in danger of being seen on the move, toting our rifles and pistols, which would be difficult to conceal. As each one left, they shook my hand. They were still not at ease in my presence, but their "Arrivederci, à presto, Signor Commandante," was a heartfelt one. Each gave a lingering look of respect to the machine pistol in my hand.

Bonfigli and I set off, with two partisans helping Pepe a short distance behind us. Two others remained a half mile behind them, to cover us in case anyone from Scheggia tried to follow us. We stopped frequently to rest because Pepe tired quickly. He had lost a lot of blood. We dug through our pockets and managed to come up with a few bits of meat and bread for him to eat. At about two A.M. we arrived at a fairly sizable farmhouse. Compared to most I had seen, this one looked downright prosperous. "They raise horses, for meat," said Bonfigli. He called out, "Partigiani!" In moments, the door swung open. A very attractive woman, probably in her late thirties, stood there. She was not work-worn, like most peasant women, and she had a slender figure, masses of dark curls, and eyes that glowed like polished coal in the firelight. Silently she led us into a comfortable parlor, then stepped into the next room, leaving us alone for a moment.

I cocked an eyebrow at Mario. "And who is this?" I asked. "She's no contadina, that's for sure!"

"She's a nurse," whispered Bonfigli, "a real one." The other two partisans arrived with a white-faced, bleeding Pepe. The woman brought them in, stirred up the fire, and set water on to boil. Bonfigli poured several glasses of wine. "Now," he said to Pepe, "this is going to hurt worse than your bullet wound."

Pepe stared at him with a puzzled expression. "Why, 'Tenente?"

"Because," laughed Bonfigli, "even though you were the bravest man there tonight, you aren't going to get any wine."

Wine or no wine, Pepe didn't care. That he had our approval was what was important. He couldn't have been a day over seventeen. One day, he would brag about his wound to some beautiful young signorina, and she would tenderly touch the scar.

The nurse shooed all of us, except Pepe, into the kitchen. There, an old woman stood sentinel over the stove, heating a pot of stew. The aroma was so tantalizing that hunger leaped like a flame in our bellies. Silently, she handed another flask of wine to Bonfigli, and he refilled our glasses. I marveled that we could feel so lighthearted! Just coming through with our skins whole seemed reason enough to celebrate. The raid itself had been a complete failure. I wondered if we had enough ammunition to attempt another one. Probably not. One of the other partisans, also named Mario, asked Bonfigli where we were.

"About five miles north of Gubbio," replied Bonfigli.

The young man thought for a moment, then spoke. "Signor 'Tenente, my cousin lives very close to here. He told me about a factory near his farm. Every day, trucks arrive and take away whatever it is that is made there. He said there are no soldiers at the factory, but there are military markings on the trucks."

Bonfigli and I exchanged glances. We were both thinking the same thing. Military trucks meant military goods. We turned to young Mario. "Could you find this place? Or could your cousin take us there?" I asked.

"Certainly, Signore," he said, "it cannot possibly be more than a kilometer from here."

Bonfigli and I withdrew to a corner of the room and went into a huddle. Why not see what we could get at this factory? If we succeeded, we wouldn't have to go back empty-handed. The men could be rounded up quickly—they were sheltered nearby. We decided to go for it, at nightfall, after we'd had time to rest and regroup.

Bonfigli went back to Mario. "What you told us is about to cost you whatever sleep you might have gotten. Do you know your way around here?"

"Sì, Signor 'Tenente," he replied, pleased to be of help.

"Good! Then go and round up our men. Tell them I want them to meet me here, in the stables, tonight."

"Sì, Signor 'Tenente." Bonfigli listed, on a small bit of paper, the locations where the men were quartered. Young Mario took the sheet and was out the door in a flash.

We finished our meal and climbed wearily up the stairs to the bedroom. The nurse was still working on Pepe, but we knew he was in good hands. I did not fall easily into sleep. Bonfigli's snoring reminded me of Amy, and I thought of her, and Nancy, and our life back in the Bonucci apartment. I worried about our supply of ammunition. I wondered, for the thousandth time, where Bonuccio Bonucci might have buried the cache of weapons and grenades. Then I thought about Bonuccio, the man who had come to be my friend. Was he still alive, I wondered? Eventually, I drifted into troubled sleep, to the tune of Mario Bonfigli's deep snoring. It was late afternoon when the old woman came in to wake us. Pepe, his wound cleaned and dressed, had been sent to a safe location. I looked at my watch. It was five o'clock, and I felt a vague uneasiness for having wasted the day. Time to get on with the new plan, and it was a long, tiring walk back to the Bruschi farm.

We were engrossed in planning when the attractive nurse reappeared. "How would you like some real English tea and a cigar?" she asked me, with a smile.

I looked at Mario. "Hey . . . ," I said, "to hell with the war! Let's just stay right here and live like high officials!"

"Ah, yes, wouldn't that be terrific?" replied Bonfigli, "but I don't think you really want to be here when the big shot who owns these cigars comes back." He wiggled his eyebrows, and the nurse laughed softly behind us.

A little later, she served us dinner. Amazing what a difference a bit of influence could make in one's diet! The sausage was meaty and not mostly fat. The pasta was almost as good, and as white, as prewar. Our hostess apologized for the lack of a table covering. I glanced at Mario with raised eyebrows. If she could only see my usual mealtimes—snatched on the run or at the Bruschis' poor table! Table covering indeed! I wondered if perhaps she had bound young Pepe's wounds with whatever tablecloth she owned. I thought of Lucia and the scarf she made me from Margherita's dresser scarf. Amazing, these women. They gave all, uncomplainingly, stinting nothing, to protect their men.

When darkness finally fell, we slipped our packs back on. My shoulder blazed in protest at the burden. The nurse handed each of us a packet of food, and we headed out into the olive grove. "Some woman, Mario," I commented. "Too good for the likes of us!"

"You're right, Signor Console," replied Bonfigli, "but I enjoyed looking, anyway."

The night was starry, and the cold crackled like a crisp wafer on the tongue. It quickly cleared our heads. The men were waiting for us at the stables, and Mario briefed them on the new operation. We sent Antonio ahead as a scout. We were not worried overly much about Germans or Fascists—the Germans were usually in vehicles at night, and the Fascists rarely left the safety of the town or the garrisons after dark. Our only real danger was from other partisan bands who might not recognize us. With no means to communicate with one another, there was no way to know where other groups were at any given moment, or what they were doing. But of one thing we were certain. At night, the Italian countryside belonged to men like us.

The moon had been up for about half an hour when Antonio returned. "The factory is just ahead, 'Tenente," he reported. "Everything is dark. I didn't see any guards, or any vehicles."

"Okay, then let's go," said Bonfigli. "Signor Console, you and I will be point men. The rest of you disperse behind us, about fifty yards off the path on both sides, to cover our backs." We set off at a trot to keep warm and reached the factory in short order.

The building, windowless on the two sides facing us, resembled a huge barn. In front, attached like a lean-to, with a flat, sloping roof, was an office area, and probably also the living quarters of the factory manager and his family. We inched our way silently around the building, keeping to the shadows close to the walls. At the back was a loading door, and in the small area in front of the loading door were empty barrels and crates. A road big enough for trucks came up to, and ran alongside, this side of the building. "We'll have to watch the road," I whispered to Mario. "We don't know when trucks or workers might arrive. Put a man a hundred meters out on each side." He drifted back to the first partisan to pass the order along. As soon as the road was guarded, Bonfigli and I squatted down and devised a plan of attack.

I took four men and we worked our way down, until we were deployed opposite the loading door. As soon as we heard anything from the west end of the building, we would rush the loading door. I prayed all would go as planned. We would be fully exposed once we left cover, and hard-pressed if we had to shoot our way out of this one. Mario took the other four men. Their level of exposure was about equal to ours. He and his men had to cross an open stretch that left them vulnerable to fire from the windows. At his signal, two men scurried across the open space at a low crouch, flattening themselves against the wall next to the smaller of the two main doors.

Bonfigli and the other two then followed, taking up stations next to the larger door. Turning, Bonfigli banged on the door and shouted, "Open up!" Without waiting, he kicked the door in. The wood that was holding the lock splintered. The other two went into action instantly. One smashed the small door in with the butt of his rifle. "Outside! Everyone! Outside, now!" shouted Mario again. At the sound of the lock breaking open, I leaped up, and, waving my men on, bolted across the open space to the loading door. We jammed at it with boots and rifles, but it didn't budge. It was well secured from the inside.

Suddenly, we heard a quavering male voice from Mario's end. "Don't shoot! Don't shoot!" The owner of the voice, a wailing, sleep-befuddled, middle-aged man, appeared. He was quickly joined by a disheveled woman in her nightgown and robe, with a coat hastily thrown over it, and a young boy of about twelve or thirteen. One of Mario's men herded them against the wall. The man beseeched the partisans with protestations of innocence and fervent avowals of his loyalty to the liberation movement. The woman, clutching her coat close, sobbed in fright. The boy, wide-eyed with fear, attempted a facade of bravado, snickering nervously, like a spooked colt. I felt sorry for them.

Mario, meanwhile, had rushed inside and snaked through the building to reach the inside of the loading door. Finding the light switch, he turned it on, calling "Wait! Gualtiero! It's Me, Mario!" to warn us against firing through the door.

As soon as he had the bar lifted, we rushed inside. Stopping for our eyes to adjust to the light, we looked around to see what we had captured. Bins of Khaki-colored material lined one side of the enormous room. Dominating the middle of the room was a piece of machinery that looked like a giant printing press. Along both the far walls were stacks of bundles. Bundle after bundle of . . . blankets! I couldn't believe my eyes. "Oh, great!" I said disgustedly. "Maybe we can beat the enemy by taking their blankets—then they'll freeze to death, and we won't need ammunition to shoot them."

One of the partisans muttered something equivalent to "from your mouth to God's ears, and the sooner the better."

Mario and I conferred. It wasn't ammunition, and it wasn't food. On the other hand, it hadn't cost us the firing of a single shot. For the mens' morale, if nothing else, we needed to bring back something, anything, to show for two nights of walking. Maybe we'd be able to trade the blankets for something of value.

Bonfigli turned to the other Mario. "You know this area. Go and requisition two carts, with drivers. Tell the drivers we can't pay them, but they can have whatever they want from here when we're gone." Young Mario and a companion, probably his cousin, took off at a run.

I took Gastone and went to ransack the kitchen. Might as well see what there was to feed the men before the long trip back. I found two loaves of bread, several links of sausage, and a fairly sizable hunk of hard, dry cheese. Stuffing the provisions into my pockets and inside my coat, I grabbed up two flasks of wine. While the men ate, I posted two additional guards outside. I was getting nervous. Only about an hour of darkness remained.

Shortly before sunrise, Mario and his cousin arrived back with two carts and drivers. We piled them high with blankets. The manager was wringing his hands. "What will I do?" he wailed. "How will I explain? They will kill me! They will murder my family.!"

"Just tell them the people who sent us do not like the quality of your blankets, and we are sending them to Germany where they will be better appreciated," said Bonfigli, as we trundled away with as many blankets as we could safely heap on the carts. We left two partisans to take the manager and his family to an abandoned farmhouse between Morena and Cagli. There, they would be kept incommunicado for twenty-four hours, then released. Bonfigli and I, to avoid risk of being captured together, took separate routes back to Morena.

At mid-morning, I stopped on a hill that overlooked a cluster of ancient stone houses below, the sun glinting off their ocher-color tile roofs. I dropped to the frozen ground for a breather. From the cover of the trees, as I sat munching slowly on my small portion of bread and hard cheese, trying to make it last as long as possible, I could see a group of three women methodically beating wet clothes on the rocks at the side of a small, icy stream. How many years, how many centuries, by how many generations of women, had clothes been washed this way, alongside this very stream, I wondered? A wave of affection for the Bruschis swept over me—especially for Adalgisa, who uncomplainingly bore the extra burden of washing my dirty clothes, along with those of her own family, in this same way. My respect and affection for the peasants of Umbria had grown steadily in the past few months. I had learned to trust them implicitly, and although they were clannish and close-mouthed, and rarely opened up about themselves, they showed me respect and extended to me without question their very special brand of hospitality. The noon bell, tolling from a nearby church, pierced the silence. I thought of the priest who must be pulling the bell rope, and of the profound influence the priests had in the life of the peasants. They were not only the spiritual leader of their flock, but often their real political leader, their psychologist, their doctor, the repository of all the closely guarded secrets of their lives—the parish priest presided over their ills, hopes, fears, and desires, as well as their marriages, births, and deaths.

Don Marino Ceccarelli, "il prete bandito" (the bandit priest) of Morena and the San Faustino parish, was an example of the kind of dedicated cleric who looked after his flock and protected them in every way. Tall, thin, gaunt-faced, in flat black hat and long black cassock, he flew amidst his flock like a spindly blackbird, aiding and abetting the partisans. Time and again he helped us when we were at a loss for somewhere to bivouac. His store of knowledge about where we could safely go, who had what, and which families were sympathizers with the Fascists and Germans, was nothing short of amazing. While he never divulged the identities of the sympathizers, it was not difficult to figure out who they were. Those families whose names he never mentioned were immediately suspect. His help was invaluable. Like many country priests, Don Marino had a good basic knowledge of medicine. There were no doctors in those barren hills. On more than one occasion, we had to turn to him to give first aid to our wounded. Though he was barely into his twenties, his fearlessness, and his love for his people, had already endeared him to the entire region.

With the sound of the bell still reverberating in the clear air, I got up, brushing the crumbs of bread and cheese from my clothes, and continued the long trek back to Fontanella. By five that evening, I had been twenty-four hours without sleep—not a completely unusual occurrence, but there was no sense of overextending myself. I began looking for a friendly farmhouse to stay the night. If it were a matter of choice, I always chose the poorer-looking ones—they were usually safer, and friendlier. As I stealthily detoured around one I had decided not to approach, my presence set the dogs to barking. I had always liked dogs, but now I would have gladly strangled every mongrel in Italy! It seemed that whenever I needed anonymity the most, I offended somebody's damned hound! As I inwardly cursed every dog on earth, the farmer came stomping out of the shed, shouted something to the animal, and it quieted. I consoled myself with the thought that I would probably welcome the dog's barking if I were hiding out at a farm and someone tried to sneak up on me. At dusk, I reached the door of a suitably isolated farmhouse. Sure enough, as I approached, more dogs set up a cacophony of barking. Ignoring them, I strode up the steps and banged on the door. "Partigiano!" I shouted. The second floor door swung open, and I was beckoned inside by a man who could have been Ruggero Bruschi's twin. I stepped into the large, rectangular kitchen/family room. The bustling contadina was already setting an extra place for me at table. I was reminded of Fontanella—this place, too, could have been its twin. It had almost the same long, rectangular wooden table, the same plain, rush-bottomed chairs, several dark pieces of furniture, and, as usual, not a single peg on which to hang hat or coat. Even the floor bowed the same way the Bruschis' did! And here, like almost everywhere, with countless buzzing flies, and countless biting bedbugs, several sons, or daughters, with their respective wives, husbands, and children, lived together under one roof.

With my puritan midwest American background, and my penchant for personal modesty, I never could fathom how anyone managed to conceive a child in these community-living circumstances, where they often slept eight and ten to a bedroom, four or five to a bed. However, it was apparently no problem to them, since there were always children in evidence, or on the way. Talking to the old man during dinner, I gathered I was still about six hours' walk from the presidio at Morena. I asked if I could sleep until midnight, since I didn't want to travel by day. He nodded understandingly and showed me to a bed in the only bedroom. At five minutes to midnight, the old woman woke me, with a shake of my sore shoulder. Pain knifed through me, and I was instantly awake. Damn! I rubbed it, yawning, as I sat there. I didn't know what was wrong with it—must have sprained it somehow. There were no doctors around, so I'd just have to learn to live with it and hope it would go away. I splashed my face with some cold water from the basin, then went into the kitchen. There was a bowl of hot minestrone and a big chunk of bread waiting there for me.

"Mangia! Mangia!" (eat! eat!), commanded the old woman. "It's no good for you to go out in this cold without something to warm your belly." Noting how eagerly I wolfed down the soup, she went to a back room and returned with a generous slab of cheese. "Eat it all. Then I will give you more to take with you. It is not good to travel hungry."

Is there no end to the generosity and kindness of these people? I thought, as I thanked her warmly and took my leave. Five and a half hours later, barely winning the race with dawn, I reached the presidio. As I approached, along the path up the hill, the sentry challenged me. I was pleased that he was vigilant, even at this hour.

Recognizing me, Edoardo the guard jumped at the opportunity to let me know how pleased they all were at the success of our raid. Success? I looked at him blankly. "The blankets, Signore!" said Edoardo enthusiastically. "Che bellezza! We have hundreds of the army's blankets! The people won't go cold this winter! And the garrison at Scheggia—they got a lesson they won't soon forget, eh!" I smiled at his exaggeration, but it made me feel good. The last-minute decision to raid the factory and take the blankets had been a smart one. They were tangible evidence of success of a partisan raid. I staggered to bed, dropping wearily onto a pallet on the floor, with two "liberated" army blankets to cover me and keep me warm.

In our wildest imagination we could never have predicted the hit those blankets would be with the countryside. Why they were so popular remains a mystery to me, but the entire area was seized with "blanket fever" as soon as word got out. The partisans now had something to use as a bargaining tool. Blankets had not been available in the stores for two years, and after the partisans themselves were supplied, families who had been helpful and loyal were given them. They became status symbols. They were traded for food. To own one became a flag of pride to the peasants. A good many blankets were converted into jackets or overcoats, crafted by the talented needles of the local women. Anyone who has spent any length of time there knows what a misnomer "Sunny Italy" is. The weather is brutal at the higher elevations, especially in winter. Coats and jackets, even those made from blankets, were a godsend. Our raid was a rousing civilian success, if not a military one.

Procuring enough food for the twenty-five partisans garrisoned at the presidio at Morena was a constant problem. The men did most of the cooking themselves. As soon as a beef or sheep was procured, it was strung up from the branch of the nearest tree and butchered. The farmer donating it got back the hides and tallow, and the meat was more easily transported back to the presidio in quarters and chunks.

However, none of the men could bake bread the way it was done by the women of Umbria. In truth, doing it never entered their heads. It was a job reserved exclusively to women. The men brought the wood for firing the rounded brick ovens, which were usually situated apart from the house. The baking oven was a structure unto itself, in the back yard of the farm. The men fired the ovens, to get them to the proper heat for baking the bread, but their responsibility ended there. Bread was baked on a certain day, in batches, to last a week at a time. While the oven heated, the women kneaded the dough one last time, and shaped it into oval loaves. When the oven was the right temperature, which the women knew from some mysterious instinct, since there was no thermometer of any kind, they raked the coals out of it, and placed the loaves in the oven in tiers, using a long-handled wooden paddle. Then the door to the oven was sealed shut, usually by slapping wet clay around it as a sealant. Once sealed, the oven was not opened again until the bread was done. How the women knew when that was remained an eternal mystery to me. During all the time I was in the hills, I seldom saw a loaf either underbaked or overbaked. It would have been eaten anyway, I'm sure, since nothing was ever wasted. By the fifth or sixth day, the loaves were pretty hard and crusty, and the chunks had to be soaked in soup or barley coffee to be edible, but they still tasted good to a hungry guerrilla fighter.

With the coveted blankets as bartering devices, less time had to be devoted to food procurement, which left more time for training, gathering intelligence, and planning for the day when the Allied advance into Umbria would call for an all-out effort from the partisans and the peasants. I could see that the partisans were determined to prove to the Allies that they were as courageous and valiant a fighting stock as any country could possibly produce.

Not long after the factory raid, I heard that Leonard Mills, the young student from Perugia, had been detained as a spy. I was astonished. "Come on, now!" I protested. "What gave you the idea that Mills is a spy?"

"We have good reason to believe it," replied one of the officers, stiffly. Several others confirmed that Mills had often been seen prowling stealthily around the countryside. "Also," added the officer, "he's been asking questions about things that are none of his business, and he's been overheard speaking German fluently!" He looked at me triumphantly.

I hadn't given much thought to Mills since January, at the organizational meeting. He was an intellectual, but I knew little about him, except that he was American, doing graduate research at the university in Perugia. His fluency in several languages was one of the reasons he had been accepted into the Band. He had roamed around Perugia, too, asking questions. I felt sure it was only intellectual curiosity on his part, but I could see how it would arouse suspicion. I spoke up. "This is a mistake. Leonard Mills is no more a spy than I am! He is a loyal American citizen." For the first time, my words were having little effect, and I didn't like it. Their minds were made up about his guilt, and I knew that if I didn't do something drastic, and quickly, they might take him out and shoot him. "I must insist, gentlemen, that you take no other action about Mr. Mills until I have conferred with Lt. Bonfigli," I said frostily, in my most formal, patrician tones. I gave them a look that said I expected implicit, unquestioning obedience to my authority. Glancing at one another, they reluctantly acquiesced.

As soon as the meeting ended, I headed out in search of Mario. He was a three-hour walk away. It would take me until five o'clock the following morning to get back. As I trudged along the dark path, I reflected on the irony of my situation. I had never been a night person. I, who had always excused myself early from the endless rounds of diplomatic dinners, receptions, and cocktail parties, was now spending my nights wandering on foot from hill to dale and back again and my days in exhausted sleep in a bug-infested bed in a poor, rundown farmhouse! Sitting with Mario, I explained the Leonard Mills situation as I saw it. The people involved simply did not understand anyone like him. Their backgrounds did not bring them into contact with the types of intellectuals who were always doing research on things around them, to whom everything and anything represented a potential topic to be investigated further, a possible meaning or background to study.

Bonfigli saw my point and agreed to delay any action against Mills, pending contact with the CLN in Perugia for confirmation of what I was saying. By the end of the following week, my observations had been confirmed, and Mills was exonerated and released. Bonfigli and I met with him. He was understandably outraged. He made it obvious to us that he considered his detention an act of lunacy. "Idiots!" he raged. "Those fools would have shot me! THEY should be shot! The world would be better off without them!"

I tried to reason with him. "Look, Mills," I said pointedly, "You'd better just button your lip from here on, and be sensible. In times like these, sometimes individual rights have to take second place to other considerations. I hate to think of what might have happened! Like it or not, you'll have to curb your academic curiosity for the time being and stick to what the Band assigns you to do." Still grumbling, he calmed down somewhat, and I hoped he'd follow my advice and stay out of trouble. I already had more than enough to worry about.

There was another matter bothering me. None of the British officers in the area, with the exception of Ramsay, were supporting our resistance efforts. Ramsay made himself available for staff meetings, gave us advice about explosives and demolition projects, and was generally cooperative and helpful in every way. The others just didn't care what we did. Several times, I stopped by the house where they gathered in the daytime. They seemed to spend more time bickering with each other then doing anything remotely worthwhile. They had a deck of cards and had virtually played the markings off them. They were indolent, bored, and ripe for trouble. Early in March, Bonfigli reported some intriguing, but disquieting news to me. "Eh, buddy," he greeted me one afternoon, with a twinkle in his eye, "your British friends have themselves a 'puttana', and I hear she is quite something! Whoooeeee!" He traced a curvacious female figure in the air with his hands.

"Ma che, puttana! What do you mean?" I asked, surprised. "What are you talking about?"

"Una bella ragazza—a pretty Hungarian woman—has taken refuge with the British officers at Acqua Viva," he replied with a leer, "and they have welcomed her with arms open, if you know what I mean." Bonfigli winked slyly and gave a short, knowing laugh.

A good-looking Hungarian woman, living with the British officers? Playing their whore? "Are you sure, Mario?" I asked. "Or is this a figment of your celibate imagination? Pretty refugee women don't just turn up at remote farmhouses in Italy! No one is that lucky," I added jokingly.

Mario looked offended. "Go see for yourself if you don't believe me," he challenged. "They are very cozy there and, need I add, very 'cocky'! They are enjoying their new lady friend and are not about to question what providence has dropped into their laps, so to speak." Dramatically, he pointed and rolled his eyes heavenward.

"Come on, Mario, you've got to be kidding!" I was still unconvinced.

He turned serious. "No, Signor Console, I'm afraid it is true," he said, looking me full in the eye. "The whole countryside is talking about it."

I decided to drop in on the Brits, unannounced, to check this bit of gossip out for myself. The next day, I set out for Acqua Viva, a farmhouse much like the Bruschis', about an hour's walk southeast of Fontanella. When I arrived, it was about three in the afternoon, and the four officers were, as usual, at one of their interminable games of cards. There was no sign of the woman. I decided to act natural, ask no questions, and see what happened. They chatted idly with me about the state of the Allied advance while they continued their game, but I could tell they were ill at ease. They were well aware that I had little respect for them because of their purposeless existence and their failure to make any attempt to be useful to us or to the war effort. I rarely spent time with them, so naturally they were curious about why I had suddenly dropped by. They were behaving very much like little boys caught with their hands in the cookie jar, hoping I wouldn't find out about their new star boarder.

Enjoying myself, and their discomfiture, I sat back and cooled my heels. I didn't have long to wait. When the Hungarian stepped into the room, I almost gasped aloud. Mario was right—she was a lovely woman! I rose, and introduced myself in Italian. "Good afternoon, Signorina," I said, "I am Michele."

Coolly, she returned my greeting in excellent Italian. "I am Marian," she replied. "I'm very pleased to make your acquaintance, Signore." She graciously extended her hand, keeping it clasped in mine a fraction longer than necessary.

Tall for a woman, she nearly matched my six feet. She flashed me a direct look that was an unmistakable invitation. I felt my throat go dry. We took each other's measure with slow deliberation. Her long blonde hair fell to her shoulders. She wore a dark red sweater that was tight enough to draw attention, but not so tight as to suggest impropriety. Shrugging her shoulders slightly, she brushed past me, and I caught a faint, tantalizing whiff of expensive perfume. She seated herself, in an attitude of languid repose, on the worn divan, patting the empty spot next to her, as she raised a questioning brow to me. I could feel the intensity of the gaze of the four Britishers as they watched this interplay. Their big stake at that moment was definitely not in the game of cards they were playing. She crossed her legs and relaxed against the back of the couch, one arm extended casually along the top of it, thoroughly enjoying her little flirtation. This was no refugee farm wife. This was no frightened damsel, fleeing for her life. She was too well cared for, too sleek and manicured. This Maid Marian of the Umbrian hills was a cultured, worldly woman, accustomed to being pampered and to having her way. Something about her did not mesh. She looked at me archly, in a slightly quizzical way, as if to say "what are we doing here, with all these people?—come, let's get out of here so we can be alone." I returned her gaze with a level stare, trying to give no sign of the effect she was having on me.

Their card game now fully abandoned, the Brits began to mutter and whisper among themselves, their faces growing more tense with each passing moment. I was fascinated by the woman, as one might be by a snake, but I was more than a bit put off by her act—if it was an act. I sensed it was high time I got the hell out of there, before things got out of hand. I had seen for myself that what Bonfigli had told me was true, and now I needed time to recover and sift through what I had just observed. I felt a distinct sense of alarm and foreboding about the situation. As soon as I could, without appearing hasty, I took my leave. "Goodbye, Michele," said Marian softly, lingering over my name, bestowing me with a brilliant smile. Then, with an air of dismissal, she turned from me to the others, addressing them in English, her accent heavily redolent of Eastern Europe. Her Italian was much better than her English. I need to learn more about this woman, I decided, as I stepped out into the frosty evening. The men were more than glad to see me go. No one bothered to show me out.

Taking a deep breath, I began retracing my steps across the drab, gray winter countryside, toward the drab homestead of the Bruschis. After that pulse-quickening blaze of red and gold I had just encountered, my dark, solitary night stretched bleakly before me. I couldn't blame the British officers for being dotty over having her around. Who wouldn't? Still . . . there was something about her that raised my hackles. I decided to be extremely cautious in the future around Marian, the seductive Hungarian. If I ever saw her again. Surprising myself, I realized I hoped I would. Like a Rembrandt, she glowed with life and light, a masterpiece amidst lusterless landscapes and dull still lives. For too many months, I had been restricted to the company of women to whom glamour was as remote as the moon. I wanted to just sit there, staring at Marian for hours on end, enjoying her luminous femininity, inhaling her perfume.

A few days later, I ran into her again. It seemed a stroke of fortune, almost too good to be true. I was delivering one of the purloined army blankets to a family that had been a lot of help to the partisans. Shortly after I arrived there, Marian showed up—ostensibly for a brief visit with the family. I was happy to see her again and especially glad to have a chance to talk to her without the British officers around. Entering the room, she removed her coat and her head scarf, shaking free that incredible sheaf of hair. Apparently surprised to see me there, she greeted me pleasantly, and this time her greeting seemed more sincere, less openly calculating, than the previous time. The flagrant posturing was also absent. "What a nice surprise!" she exclaimed.

"It's nice to see you again too, Signorina," I said with warmth.

She pulled two chairs near the fireplace. "Please sit and visit with me for a while, Signor Orebaugh," she invited softly, indicating the other chair.

I froze, almost visibly, at hearing my last name, a name I hadn't heard spoken aloud in months. My heart began pounding like a trip hammer. How could this refugee Hungarian, lately arrived to the area, possibly known my real last name—let alone pronounce it so perfectly? Fully alert now, on my guard, my mind raced. I was certain I had never revealed my true last name to anyone since leaving Perugia. Bonuccio Bonucci knew my last full name, but he had had difficulty pronouncing it. I doubted that Bonfigli or Pierangeli knew it. Orebaugh was not an easy name, and this woman not only knew it, but had pronounced it perfectly! How, and where, had she gotten it? I didn't think the British officers knew my real name, but that was a remote possibility. Or had she come by it, somehow, in Perugia? Had they tortured it out of Bonucci? Or, worse, had they gotten to Vittoria, or Margherita, or Valentina, God forbid? A thousand horrifying possibilities crowded my mind in those first seconds.

I decided to maintain a facade of social politeness and do some careful detective work. "With pleasure," I said smoothly, pulling my chair close to hers and sitting down. "But you must call me Michele."

She smiled in acknowledgment. Her sheer physical magnetism still overwhelmed me, even though I was now wary of her. With their arduous existence of unrelenting poverty and hard physical work, the contadinas, the country women of Italy, were almost invariably dumpy and unattractive by age thirty, worn out by forty, and old at fifty. Marian Heller, although no great beauty, was a refreshing change. She was not only good to look at, she was charming, educated, polished, and very sophisticated. She was a sparkling, verdant oasis in a vast cultural desert.

Opening her handbag, she pawed around in its contents, finally extracting a small packet of English tea. "Have some tea with me, won't you?" I nodded my assent. The prospect of real tea, along with her company for a while, even though I needed the time to figure out whether or not she was a danger to my safety, was a temptation too powerful to resist. She turned to the contadina, who was, as usual, busying herself in the kitchen. "Boil some water, please," she commanded, imperiously. Ordering others to do her bidding came naturally to her.

Yes, I mused, this woman is accustomed to being waited on. Who is she? Where did she come from? "How did you end up in this part of Italy?" I inquired casually.

"Well, I was living near Naples," she replied. "My husband was in

business there, and when the bombing began, the destruction was so terrible, I was terrified. I decided to come north, to Perugia, where I thought
I would be safer."

Ah, so she had been in Perugia! Alarm bells pinged in my head. "How
long were you in Perugia?" I asked.

"Several months. But then the food situation got so bad in the city! We
couldn't get anything to eat." She pouted prettily, looking at me for sympathy.

"Yes, I've heard there are terrible food shortages everywhere," I acknowledged. She didn't look like she had ever experienced so much as an
hour's hunger. "And what brought you to this remote area?" I probed.

"I heard about Morena from a friend, and I thought I might be safer
and more comfortable here, so I decided to go to the 'macchia,' and here
I am!" she smiled disarmingly. "The British officers were kind enough to
take me in and give me shelter."

Yeah, I bet they were, I thought. "Kind" is hardly the word! The old
peasant woman brought us our tea. We sipped contentedly for a few moments before I spoke up again, with another gentle probe. "Where did
you grow up? In Budapest?"

"No," she replied, "my father was a businessman in the Pest area, but
he died when I was only six years old. My mother was Italian, from near
Milan, and she brought me back to Italy to live after Papa died."

So that's why she spoke Italian so fluently! "I noticed that your Italian
is excellent," I complimented her. "That explains it. You also speak English very well," I went on. "Did you study it in school?"

"Thank you. Not really. I had a Swiss governess who spoke French and
English to me, and my mother had attended school in England and spoke
it well, so she also taught me a lot." She seemed pleased to be telling me
her story, and since she didn't appear to be angling for anything from me,
I relaxed a bit. We sat in companionable silence for a few minutes. Then
she looked questioningly at me. "And you, dear Michele, what about you?
You are certainly not Italian, although you speak it very well. Where do
you come from?" I tensed again, defenses up, though her question was a
perfectly natural follow-on to our conversation.

The psychological need to unburden oneself to a sympathetic listener is
an ever-present danger in the situation of loneliness and deprivation I was
experiencing. I was sorely tempted to just let go and tell her about myself.
I mean, what if she were an innocent refugee, just being polite in asking
about me? But I knew better. God, Orebaugh, you don't trust anything
or anybody anymore! That was true enough. I couldn't trust anyone—and
especially not this woman, at this moment. Her slip with my name was
too much of a coincidence to disregard. "Oh, we'll have plenty of time to
talk about me later on, when we know each other better," I parried casually. "Like you, I'm just one of those poor unfortunates who got caught

in the wrong place at the wrong time." I had purposely peppered my remarks with several words in the dialect of the Trieste area, hoping that would serve to confuse her. "I am a displaced businessman, just trying to survive the war," I added. I tried not to be obviously evasive. Looking at my watch, I got up. "Speaking of business, dear Marian, I could enjoy sitting here over tea with you indefinitely, but unfortunately I have some matters I need to attend to this afternoon, before it gets too late," I said, lifting her hand and kissing it in my most continental manner. "It has been a most pleasant afternoon, Signora," I said, with formal gallantry. Then, with a note of regret, "I look forward to the prospect of enjoying your company again very soon, but now I must be on my way."

Slowly withdrawing her hand from mine, she rose to walk with me to the door. "Please come back, here, again soon, Michele," she said, with slight emphasis on the word "here." "I come here often in the afternoon— at least three times a week. Perhaps we can meet again for tea, and share our stories."

"That would be a pleasure," I said. "Perhaps we will." I held out hope, but made no commitment. Halfway down the stairs, I turned. She stood at the top, framed in the doorway, watching me. "Arrivederci," I called, and waved.

"Arrivederci, Michele," she waved back, smiling, and closed the door.

For the next couple of weeks, I was extremely busy. We carried out several raids—some were successful, some not. There were meetings and organizational problems to solve. I thought a lot about Marian Heller, but I was unable to get back to the farm to meet her again and try to find out more about her. Gossip among the peasants, mostly salacious, kept me apprised of her whereabouts and activities. She remained with the British officers, as their house ornament and recreational diversion. I hadn't spoken about my encounter with her at the neighboring farm, or her mention of my last name, to anyone. I was still turning it over and over in my mind, like a piece to a difficult puzzle.

We began to receive shocking reports, via Captain Pierangeli's partisan network, about the brutal regime now in control in Perugia, which under the "Fascisti Repubblichini" had become worse than could be imagined. The notorious Prefect, Armando Rocchi, and his murderous cohorts, led by Major Carità, had brazenly taken over there and were committing all sorts of atrocities. No one, and nothing, was safe any longer. With these reports, we finally succeeded in getting some scraps of news about Bonuccio Bonucci. He was still clinging to life in one of Rocchi's prisons, but he had been brutally tortured by the Fascists—whipped, beaten, and interrogated almost beyond human endurance, for days on end, during the first weeks after his capture. He had given them nothing, and they finally gave up, but he was reported to be in terrible mental and physical shape. I was very shaken on hearing that, but glad to know that he was alive, even though barely so. I worried constantly about Vittoria, Margherita, and the children. Finally, I asked Pierangeli to try to check up on them for me.

"I will do what I can, Signore," he said, "but we must be very careful—we don't want to arouse suspicion, if it isn't there."

"Absolutely. Do nothing that would bring any adverse attention to them," I said. "I just want to know that they are alive and unharmed."

I thought then about mentioning my concerns about the Hungarian woman to him, but decided to keep my silence for the moment. No point in raising flags until I had something more solid to go on. Something solid wasn't long in coming. Just a few days later, a returning messenger informed us that Margherita and her children were all right, to my great relief. Then he went on to report that Prefect Rocchi, according to rumors circulating in Perugia, was so miffed by the sudden disappearance of his pretty Hungarian mistress, he was no longer restraining his mad-dog minions. He was letting them wreak whatever havoc they wished on the populace.

I was thunderstruck. Could Marian Heller be Rocchi's missing mistress? "Pretty Hungarian mistress," the messenger had said. How many pretty Hungarians could there be, wandering around Umbria, "disappearing?" I went immediately to Captain Pierangeli, and told him about my two encounters with Marian Heller and about her use of my last name. Pierangeli lost no time in dispatching a messenger to Perugia to ferret out more details. Three days later we received information, and descriptions, that convinced us that the hated Prefect's absent Hungarian mistress and Marian Heller, reigning "puttana" of the British officers, were one and the same.

"Signor Console," added Pierangeli gravely, "I have more bad news, I'm afraid. I am fully convinced, from other information the messenger also brought, that Rocchi knows perfectly well where his little chickadee is. In fact, we believe she was sent here specifically to spy on us and to pinpoint your whereabouts for him."

I sat back, trying to digest the implications, if it were true. Her knowledge of my real last name was the key. Either they had tortured it out of Bonucci or the German SS was hot on my tail after our abortive attempt to be flown to Rome following the Armistice. No matter. I was sure now that Armando Rocchi knew who, and where, I was. Pierangeli called an emergency meeting of the officers of the San Faustino Band, to decide what to do about all this. We knew the British officers would kick up one hell of a fuss if we tried to take their plaything away from them.

I was not present at the meeting Pierangeli held, but the heated discussion that took place there prompted him to come to Fontanella the following morning, with two other officers, to fill me in and ask my advice on how best to proceed. We assessed the damage she might have already done to us and agreed that, despite the danger that might have accrued from her being in our midst for so long, she probably hadn't picked up too much intelligence to report back to Rocchi and the Germans. I was not surprised to learn that five of the seven officers present at the meeting had recommended leniency for her. I smiled at that and couldn't resist a barb of my own. "You weren't so charitable when it was Leonard Mills you suspected of spying on us," I pointed out. "You were ready to execute him, without a trial!"

"But this is different!" protested one of the officers vehemently. "This is a woman!"

"So she is," I remarked, "but how would this be handled if you were all still on regular army duty? Shouldn't you follow those rules?"

They stared at me, shocked. "But, but—Signor Console, she is a woman!" they sputtered.

"Damn it, man, I never said she wasn't!" I retorted hotly. "I'm not saying execute her! I'm saying hear the evidence!"

"Of course, Signore," they said stiffly, stung.

"Il Console is right," said Pierangeli decisively. "We will hold a court-martial, tomorrow morning. Go arrest her and bring her to the presidio at Morena," he ordered the two officers. Not daring further protest, they saluted smartly and left immediately for Acqua Viva to take Marian into custody.

The British officers were predictably furious. "You can't do this!" they raged to the two Italians. "Trying her by military court-martial is invalid! She's a civilian! You have no authority to try her! She is innocent of these charges! How could she possibly be a spy—she's just a poor refugee woman!" Nevertheless, the Italians took her into custody, and the next morning a court-martial was convened.

The British officers boycotted it. Pity. They'd have done better to attend. The Hungarian quickly gave the lie to their belief that she was a "poor innocent refugee, incapable of such a deed" as spying. As soon as she was confronted with the charge that she was Rocchi's spy, Marian burst into tears and made a full confession. "Yes, I was Rocchi's mistress," she sobbed. "Yes, he sent me here to spy on you and report back to him! I had no choice! He is an animal," she cried. "What would he have done to me if I had refused? You must understand, and take pity on me! I am only a woman, I had no choice but to do what he said, Signori," she pleaded tearfully.

She was immediately placed under full arrest. The British protested again, but the Italians were adamant. They refused to let her see the British officers. Although I had told the Brits all about Rocchi and the monstrous Carità, and what they were doing to the people of Perugia, I doubt that the British officers ever believed that their Hungarian paramour was a spy, deliberately sent by Rocchi to spy on us, and report back to him on partisan activities. The news of the Hungarian's arrest, trial, and imprison-

ment flew as swiftly as a trained carrier pigeon from farm to farm, valley
to valley. The quip that made the rounds was, "and the Britishers had
their hole shot right out from under them!"

I wondered later why Marian Heller hadn't confessed her spy status to
the British when Pierangeli's men first came to get her. She might have
talked them into detaining her themselves—taking her under Allied custody, which might have worked, and might have saved her life. Who
knows? As it happened, several weeks after her arrest by the partisans, it
was discovered that she had been imprisoned before, once for black-mar-
keteering, and another time as a spy against Italy. Rocchi, impressed by
her good looks and intelligence, had spared her, making her his mistress
instead. Then he had packed her off to spy on us, and pretended she had
disappeared. With this evidence of her former activities, she was tried once
again, this time as a spy and traitor, and was sentenced to death. The
following week, Marian Heller was executed by a firing squad. I felt a
deep sadness when Pierangeli told me that the sentence had been carried
out. I think the thought of her execution was more shocking to me than
the realization that she was a talented and dangerous spy, who would
doubtless have betrayed us all at the first opportunity.

8

"The Man with the Cane"

The only good that came out of the Marian Heller tragedy was the knowledge that Rocchi's sudden need to spy on the partisans, and to find me, was a tribute to our growing strength and disruptiveness. Although Fascist authority still prevailed in the principal urban centers, it had virtually disappeared in the countryside. Outside of Perugia, Gubbio, and the other urban areas, the maintenance of law and order by any arm of organized government had become a farce, if not a total fiction. By force of long habit, lacking any other apparent authority, the tenant farmers began coming to us to pay the age-old tax the government levied on slaughtering a hog. That was another sign of our growing influence. The peasants saw us as the only real government authority in the region.

For centuries, the peasantry of central Italy had suffered under countless ruthless and greedy masters, while wresting their poor living out of an inhospitable, rocky, overtilled terrain. Again and again, they had seen the flower of their young manhood conscripted, to leave the farms and go off to fight and die in conflicts and wars in which they had no real stake, or even any interest. It is not surprising, then, that as a class they held themselves apart from the mainstream of Italian cosmopolitan society and that they harbored a deep-seated distrust of and aversion to government authority. They gathered their few resources about them, and developed a totally family-centered culture, not unlike a return to the safety of the womb, where basic needs like food, shelter, and survival were paramount. Worldly or political matters received scant consideration. The only authority to which the Italian peasant family paid nominal to willing obeisance was the Church. While much has been said and written about the Italians—often in a derogatory sense in regard to their patriotism and martial spirit—what has not been addressed is the warmth and courage shown by the Italian peasants during that period in World War II when the Germans were dug in, the Allies were slow in advancing, and the government of Italy was in disarray.

Dragged into World War II by Mussolini, the peasantry remained stubbornly turned inward, kept themselves closemouthed, and tried to have as little as possible to do with Fascism—a regime they had never understood nor trusted. That is why the solidarity the peasantry manifested in resolutely aiding and sheltering the resistance fighters and the Allied prisoners of war was truly astonishing. Why they risked themselves, and their families, to do it remains a mystery to this day. The fact that their country was occupied by the Germans, and was more or less at war against the Allies, made it an even greater puzzle. History provides us no comparable example of a whole class of society, in any country, acting in this manner. The thousands of Allied prisoners who survived, and were repatriated, did so only because they received help in their hour of need from those peasants. They, like I, can attest to that amazing generosity, selfless warmth, and courage.

True to the highly emotional nature of the Italians, there was, even within the partisan movement, continuous political unrest, and frequent strong, and very vocal, dissension, especially concerning forms of government and the extent of government authority. One afternoon, I engaged in a lively discussion with Ernesto Rossi, the field representative of the Committee for National Liberation (CLN) for the area of Pesaro, who was paying a visit to San Faustino. Rossi was a well-indoctrinated Communist, very capable, and highly educated. I was impressed by him, and that only reinforced my concern that the Communists were making deep inroads in Italy, biding their time, awaiting the outcome of the war. During our discussion, I asked Rossi, "How could the Soviet Union possibly support keeping the Savoy monarchy in power, after King Vittorio Emmanuel showed such wretched leadership during two decades of Fascism?"

His answer made sense to me. "As Communists, we heartily despise the monarchy, and all it stands for. However, for the time being, we see an advantage to be gained by adhering to the symbolic authority the royal family represents and by not further weakening the already fragile structure of the Italian government. That is why the Soviet government has reluctantly decided, at the highest levels, to lend its support to the present ad hoc working relationship between the Allied military authorities and the House of Savoy." Given the widely diverse, and passionate, feelings held throughout Italy, and the difficulty there would be in establishing any kind of working government after the war, I could only agree with that tactical reasoning.

During his visit, Rossi suggested that we establish liaison with the Banda di Cantiano, another partisan group operating in the mountains to the north and east of us. We agreed to that, and two days later, Pierangeli met with Colonel Ernesto Tagliaferro, the career army officer who was commander of the Cantiano Band. They struck up a cordial, cooperative relationship, and we were extremely happy to have established contact with another partisan movement. We decided we'd have liaison meetings every two weeks, to coordinate our efforts. Therefore, I was totally unprepared for what happened a few weeks later.

We had spent a lot of time and effort trying to find the cache of weapons Bonucci had buried, but with no success. What had happened to those weapons was one of the best-kept secrets in Italy. Other attempts to procure weapons and ammunition for our Band had yielded very few. In fact, our activities had almost come to a halt because of the shortage of arms and ammunition. One evening, Bonfigli arrived with welcome news. "I think we might have found some weapons and ammunition, Signore!" he announced excitedly, having barely shed his coat.

I was elated. "How? Where?"

"We had word today, from one of our CLN contacts, that some villagers in the vicinity of Montebello are eager to get rid of a stockpile of weapons and ammunition they are hiding."

"Great Scott, man, this is the answer to our prayers!" I jumped up and banged the table in my excitement. "How do we get them? I'll pay whatever it costs! Where did they get them?"

"Well," he said, "these villagers live down near the Tiber River. When the Armistice was declared, they raided the local garrison, and hid all the arms and ammunition they got from there." Since a partisan movement had not developed in their area, they were concerned that someone might tip off the Germans or the Fascists that they had the arms, which would immediately be confiscated and probably would bring severe retribution down on them. They wanted to get rid of them before that happened.

We immediately dispatched a team of officers to negotiate with the village officials, using food supplies, blankets, and money as payment. After several days of negotiation, a deal was struck. We were jubilant! When Bonfigli came to Fontanella with the good news, I jumped for joy, giving a great war whoop of a cheer. I grabbed a stunned Adalgisa and danced her around the room, much to the amusement of young Pepe and Concetta. Arms, at last! Now we could plan some real raids against the Germans!

"Easy, my friend," laughed Bonfigli, "don't get too carried away! We still haven't figured out how to get them from Montebello to Morena without getting caught."

"Pah!" I said, "That's the easy part! We'll have that solved in no time." However, it wasn't all that simple. The weapons were heavy, and crated, to boot. We couldn't just send fifty men into the town and have each carry out a few weapons. Besides, the villagers and townspeople didn't want the empty crates, with their telltale markings, left there as evidence.

Ultimately, we devised a plan to remove the weapons by donkey cart, two crates at a time, at night. It was a slow and dangerous process. One load came out in caskets, another was concealed under a cartload of manure. One was buried under garbage, and one came out under a pile of rubble from a bombed-out building. Eventually, all the arms arrived safely at the presidio in Morena, and we breathed a collective sigh of relief, then passed around a couple of flasks of wine in celebration. We were in business again—but just barely. We still needed ammunition.

Making my way back to the Bruschis that night, in the dark, I accidentally stepped into a hole in the rutted path, and fell, wrenching my ankle. The next morning, it was badly swollen and black and blue. A couple of nights later, I was still immobilized at the farm, nursing the ankle, when a group of ten partisans from the Cantiano Band pulled a surprise raid on our presidio. Creeping up in the dark, they surrounded the building, and at rifle point, made off with all our newly acquired weapons, the best of the few old ones we had, and just about all of our precious supply of ammunition!

When that news reached me the next day, I was livid. Jumping up, I limped in fury around the room, pounding my fist in impotent rage against tables and walls, hurling every Italian insult and curse I knew at the Cantiano Band. Hell and damnation! Those cowardly bastards would pay for this, by God! What treachery! Ruggero was astonished at my towering rage. Adalgisa was so frightened, she hurried out into the yard with the children. "This," I shouted, "is infamy! The absolute, last goddamned straw! Ruggero! Bring me pen and paper! I'm going to let Tagliaferro know what I think of him and his thieving band!" Ruggero scrambled to obey, producing from only God knows where a musty-smelling, wrinkled half sheet of brown paper. I could barely contain my rage enough to sit and dash off a furious protest to Colonel Tagliaferro. I didn't hesitate for a second over pulling rank, and added some dire threats for good measure. I vowed to Tagliaferro that if he did not rectify the situation immediately, I would personally make it my business to see that the full wrath of the Allies fell upon him and upon every member of the Cantiano Band. With a shaking hand, in a great flourish, I signed "Il Console." Then, somewhat calmer, I asked Ruggero to carry my message immediately to Pierangeli, for transmission to Tagliaferro.

Ruggero was more than happy to go, not only because he deemed it a mission of great status and importance, but also because it would get him out of the range of my temper for the rest of the day. "They will know they are dealing with Il Console," he muttered darkly, as he left.

I didn't have long to wait for a reply. Word came back the very next day that, within minutes of reading my note, Tagliaferro had called the offenders in and given them a fierce tongue-lashing. He had levied heavy punishment duty on them and ordered the other partisans of the Cantiano Band to return the weapons and ammunition to the presidio at Morena

"Immediately!" He sent a note of apology to Captain Pierangeli and me, vowing that he knew nothing of the raid made on the presidio, and certainly did not order or condone it. He assured us that the offenders were being punished. As it turned out, the incident led to the development of a closer, more cooperative relationship between the two groups than might otherwise have been possible.

Shortly after I had come to the Bruschis, one of the neighboring farmers had fashioned a sturdy wooden walking stick for me. I had asked Ruggero to hollow out the lower part of the cane, which he did, working many hours to carve a channel deep into the hard wood of the cane. When it was finished, I tightly rolled the bills and stuffed all my American money into it, concealing the opening with a fitted wooden plug Ruggero made. Thereafter, the cane went everywhere with me, and many of the peasants came to refer to me as "the man with the cane." I was especially glad to have that cane now, as I recovered from the ankle sprain. A raid against the Germans was planned for March 4th, only a few days hence. I desperately wanted to be in on it. As I sat in the Bruschi kitchen, my foot propped up to speed the healing process, I thought about the "Brigata d'Urto di San Faustino" (Shock Brigade of San Faustino)—the official name of our Band, though everyone referred to it simply as "The Band of San Faustino." I wondered why the Germans and the Fascists had made no move yet to challenge our control of the area. It was too good to be true. Rocchi undoubtedly knew our whereabouts. They would move when they were ready, I was sure. In my almost daily inspection visits to the five locations where our men were bivouacked, I stressed the need for constant unrelenting vigilance. I didn't want another incident like the one that had cost us Bonuccio Bonucci and Colonel Guerrizzi.

For their part, the men never failed to ask why we hadn't yet gotten an airdrop of supplies from the Allies. My credibility and power were in question, and I didn't have an answer for them. I knew that the message asking for the drop had been transmitted. I knew the partisans were monitoring the radios, ears ever alert for the code words "abbia fede" and "puoi gioire"—signaling us that the airdrop was on its way to Morena and that we should prepare the bonfires to light the drop zone. But the magic words had not, so far, been heard over the BBC. We had no way of knowing that some months earlier, at a summit meeting, the Allies had decided to route roughly ninety percent of all airdrops to Tito and his partisans in Yugoslavia. My urgent request for the Band of San Faustino had been put on a back burner, for the time being.

March 4th arrived, and my ankle was still not healed enough for me to risk going on the raid. I could only sit at the farm with Ruggero, drink wine, pace, fidget, and wait for news. It was three o'clock the following afternoon before a partisan who answered to the name of Silvio Conti appeared at the door, bringing me a report on the action. Pierangeli and

Bonfigli were both away on CLN business, so none of us had been able to be in on this action. Command had therefore been delegated to Conti, our most senior partisan in terms of both age and experience. I knew him only slightly, but Silvio, whose real name, like those of most of the other members of the Band, will probably never be known, was a veteran's veteran in every sense of the word.

"I took eleven men, Signor Console," he began, "and we arrived at the ambush site, about three kilometers southeast of Città di Castello, just before midnight. We waited about thirty minutes for the convoy to arrive. I waited until the lead vehicle was only about twenty meters from me, then opened fire with the Sten and nailed it."

"Good work, Silvio!" I interjected.

"Grazie, Signore," he acknowledged my compliment with a solemn-faced nod, and continued. "The rest of the convoy piled up behind it, the trucks all hitting one another, and we opened fire and gave it to them good!" His dark eyes snapped, and he drew his short, stocky body up with pride. "We got at least ten vehicles, Signore—trucks, armored personnel carriers, and a command car! Six of them caught fire and burned."

"Any injuries to our men?" I asked.

"No, Signore. One man got a flesh wound from a rock splinter, but it is nothing. We were out of there in five minutes, as ordered, and took very little return fire from the Germans."

"What about retaliations? Have you heard of any?"

"Not yet, Signore, but I am certain there will be some," he responded soberly.

I thanked Silvio for his report. I was pleased that the raid had been a success, but was concerned about what retaliation there would be from the Germans. I told Silvio to tell the men at the presidio to take extra precautions. Less than twenty-four hours later, a platoon of Germans in squad cars randomly selected and torched four farms, appropriating their livestock, and taking two of the farmers away for forced labor service. Although a terrible payment was exacted from innocents by the Germans every time the partisans struck successfully, never once did the peasants complain to us directly or demand that we stop our activities because of their fear of retaliation. To us, it was an inspiring vote of confidence.

Heady with the success of the convoy raids, the Band was ready for bigger and better things. We wanted to make a name for ourselves before the Allies arrived. We wanted them to know the Brigade of San Faustino was there fighting for them. Of the various targets considered, the German arms depot at Gubbio seemed the most attractive. However, to attempt a raid there was extremely dangerous. I urged caution. For a week, we kicked the project around, examining it from every possible angle. Manfred Metzger would probably have jumped at it right away, but I, being more pragmatic by nature, did not like the odds. However, the officers of the Band decided to go ahead with it. They'd make an "assalto lampo"—a lightning strike—at the heavily armed garrison. A squad of twelve was chosen for the raid. They were adamant about not risking me on this one, so I was not among the dozen selected to go, but Bonfigli was, and he brought me a complete report on the raid immediately afterward.

Under cover of darkness, the squad had slipped into the town of Gubbio and made it, undetected, to the massive stone building near the lower town gate that served as the German barracks. The only entry was well guarded by two sentries. To get in, there was no option but to gun them down. Pepe and Vincenzo drew a bead on the two, dropping them with single, almost simultaneous shots, and the others rushed quickly to drag the bodies aside. The ten men then entered the compound, leaving Pepe and Vincenzo in place of the two German sentries. So far, so good. Then their luck went sour. They heard the sound of running feet coming from every direction. The Germans outside the wall began shooting, and Pepe and Vincenzo fired back. The partisans inside the wall heard Pepe and Vincenzo returning the Germans' fire. They knew it was time to abort the raid and get out of Gubbio—fast! Covering the stairway with several machine gun bursts, they raced for the opening in the wall, where Pepe already had the gate open for them. Gaining the street, they broke for the escape route, zigzagging along the side wall and then dashing into a narrow alley. As they ran along the dark street, seven German soldiers came pounding toward them, firing. The squad split up, ducking into doorways for cover, then one by one they dashed out, shooting, and scampered to the next cover. In the melee, Vincenzo and Luigi were hit. The others grabbed them, and dragged them along as they continued their daring escape.

"Everyone made it back safely, and the two wounded men have been treated and are mending without serious complications," finished Bonfigli.

"Well, we got off lucky that time Mario," I said, "but was it worth it?"

He thought a moment before answering me. "I think so, Signore," he said. "Although we didn't pull off the colpo as planned, Pepe and Vincenzo got two automatic rifles from the dead German sentries, so we have two valuable weapons to show for our effort. And, we did polish off two Germans and showed them they are not safe any more, not even in their own back yard!"

I wasn't fully convinced it had been worth the cost, but grudgingly allowed that something was better than nothing. At least we hadn't suffered any major casualties. And, the men were proud of themselves and their bold attack—and that was important to maintaining morale.

The raid on Gubbio made it imperative that we exercise greater control over our use of ammunition. "Well, we'll just have to do things that won't take ammunition, but will keep us nipping at their heels," remarked Bonfigli a couple of days later, as we surveyed our nearly depleted supply.

"Like what?" I said caustically, thoroughly discouraged about the ammunition situation, with no sign of an airdrop coming.

"Well, let's see. For one thing, we can do some of the things we did before—change some of the road signs around, and remove others. Everyone who lives around here knows the roads anyway—the Germans are the ones who will get lost." He laughed mischievously at the thought.

"You know, Mario, that's not such a bad idea. We should always take actions that we can accomplish, with very little effort and almost no risk, that will confuse or delay the enemy. Let's try to accomplish several missions like that every week."

Mario, pleased that I approved of his idea, went off to confer with the men and assign tasks. For most of March, we engaged in almost daily activities, from the mundane to the significant. The weather was milder, and we sent two or three of our squads out on the prowl every night. We avoided depleting our remaining small supply of ammunition, and we prayed daily for the code words on which our future existence hung. We desperately needed supplies, but now, more than anything else, we had to have ammunition, and soon, or we would become helpless quarry for the Germans and Fascists to hunt down at their leisure. It was at about that same time that I heard I was being actively sought by the Fascists and Germans. They had learned from Captain Bice Pucci, who had been at San Faustino in January, and who had turned informer, that I was the driving force behind the San Faustino partisans, and that I had been successful in coming up with money to finance our activities. That information, in the hands of the enemy, was enough to put a death sentence on my head—and indeed on all of our heads. We entertained no illusions about that.

The night of March 22nd, I was sleeping, with one ear cocked as usual for any unfamiliar sound. A loud pounding on the door brought me fully alert, before it roused anyone else in the family. Ruggero woke too, and hustled to answer the door as I hovered at the back window, ready to bolt down the escape ladder. Adalgisa was already at her station in the doorway, where she could see the front door and signal me to go, if necessary. The children had not stirred. Adalgisa gave the "it's okay" sign, and Ruggero appeared in the bedroom with two roughly dressed partigiani. They were in a state of high excitement. "Signore!" they said, "we have news, big news!"

"Sit," I whispered, indicating my cot. "What is it?"

Ruggero and Adalgisa handed around glasses of wine. The two men drank theirs in grateful gulps, then one said, "A huge force of tedeschi (Germans) in busloads, maybe as many as fifteen buses, Signore, have come from the direction of Cagli and are heading toward Pianello. They are different from the Germans in Perugia and Gubbio. They are wearing black uniforms, with skull and crossbones insignia. We thought you should know right away."

I sat back, stunned. SS troops! The elite of the German army had been sent to get us! My heart began pounding. Fifteen busloads—five or six hundred of them! They were being brought in for some kind of sweep of the area, for sure. The Germans were finally going to make their move. "Are you sure of this? That there are that many?"

"Si, Signore," Antonio, the senior of the two affirmed. "We saw them ourselves—there were more than ten buses full, we know. The Cantiano Band has already engaged them near Pianello. They will need help. We hurried to give you this news."

"Of course. Thank you. You did well, very well, and I'm glad you came quickly." I grabbed some clothes and threw them on. We went into the next room. I sat at the table, with my wine, and tried to think calmly. Ruggero and the two partisans took up stations at the foot of the table, and sat silently watching me, awaiting my orders. If the incursion proceeded on as it had started, the SS would enter our zone of operations from the east. They were now well within the Cantiano Band's territory, where a partisan line of defense had been drawn earlier, and that line would at least slow the German advance, and buy time for reinforcements to get there. "Ruggero," I said, "take Tullio and go alert all our combat squads. Tell them what is happening. Tell them to get to Pianello, and we'll reconnoiter there."

Ruggero nodded, gulped down a cup of hot coffee, took some bread and cheese from Adalgisa, and left with Tullio.

I turned to Antonio. "Can you show me the way to Pianello?" I asked.

"Of course, Signore," he replied. "I will be honored to take you there."

I looked at my watch. It was five A.M. We wolfed down some food. Then Adalgisa tucked the usual packet of extra rations into my pocket and, at the door, murmured the ritual "go with God." This time, though, her eyes showed fear. I knew just how she felt. Impulsively, I leaned down and hugged her close. Poor soul, and poor souls like her, I thought, always having to stand by, to wait and wonder what their fate would be—a fate determined not by themselves, but by the men they bore, and nurtured, and married. I stepped quickly into the predawn cold. At the foot of the stairs, I groped my way into the dark stall and retrieved my carbine from its hiding place. I would have preferred the Mauser, but there was less than a clip of ammunition left for it. As we set out on the long walk to Pianello, which lay about twelve or thirteen kilometers to the northeast, the trees, silhoutted against the pale morning sky, stood at attention like a forbidding line of storm troopers. I knew we'd really be put to the test this time, and I hoped we'd all be equal to the challenge.

As we proceeded along, Antonio filled me in on the terrain around Pianello, where we'd probably make our stand against the SS troops. "We will move past Pianello, in all likelihood, Signore, and up the valley, which is set like a tilted bowl against the mountain. Its upper rim is bordered by a line of steep, sharp ridges."

"Do you think we can defend from it?" I asked.

"Probably better from there than anywhere else," said Antonio. He spoke little, but was definite when he did. "From the valley, we can yield ground bit by bit, if we have to, as we work our way up to the ridge. Just on the other side of the upper rim is an old farm track that runs along the perimeter of the ridge. It has been worn into a rut, about four or five feet deep, under the rim. It will provide us excellent coverage from anyone attacking from below. That is where we'll make our final stand, if need be. It is a good place," he concluded; "May the Blessed Virgin grant us the strength to defeat the tedeschi maiali!"

We had been walking for just over two hours, keeping close to wooded areas, when the first sounds of distant shooting reached our ears. I stepped from the cover of the trees, shielding my eyes from the sun, which glowed like a burnished copper disk through a curtain of smoky haze. I could barely make out the rim of the valley, which was laid out exactly as Antonio had described it. Quickening our pace, we saw that the battle was already joined. As we neared an outcropping of rock, two partisans jumped from behind it, and with a quick arm wave, motioned to us. Ducking around the edge, we found eight of our men, and to my relief, Bonfigli was one of them. He looked up and smiled. "Well, good day, Signor Console," he greeted me. "Now, finally, you will see some real action, eh?! Probably more than any of us bargained for, but that's war, no? Let me know if you want to check out early, eh?"

He knew that would get to me. "Hell, ME check out?" I said. "Hah! You, with your skinny legs, could make a run for it now and get away, but I'm too old for running away! So just tell me where you want me, and give me my orders. I'm ready for action, and you're wasting my valuable time," I grinned.

Turning serious, Mario pointed upward to a spot about halfway along the rutted road on the right side of the ridge. "That's where I want you. Choose good cover, and tell your men to make every shot count. If we're not careful, we'll run out of ammunition before noon."

I took eight men and, keeping low, we made our way to the old farm road and followed it along under the cover of the rim to the spot Mario had indicated. Finally, sheltered behind a large rock, I had my first chance to unsling the carbine, which had been weighing me down ever since we left the Bruschis. I looked at the battle unfolding below me. Once again, I noted, Bonfigli had positioned me as far out of harm's way as possible.

Down the valley, to my left, I could see the points from which the Germans were firing. There were small mounds of dirt and rock where they had dug in, after their first, almost suicidal charge up the steep slope.

Dead bodies of SS troopers littered the slope, mute evidence of the devastating hail of fire that had poured down on them from the two heavy, water-cooled machine guns the partisans had positioned above. From time to time, a German would leap from cover and heave a grenade, but invariably the grenades fell short of the mark. They were also firing mortars, but the trajectory was difficult, and very few landed near the rim where the partisans were holed up. I could see now what Antonio meant— this was the perfect place to make our stand against the Germans.

It was ten-thirty, and I had just taken out Adalgisa's food packet to assuage my hunger pangs, when a runner came out of the woods to my right. "Signor Commandante! Commandante Tagliaferro wants you and your men to go occupy those positions." He pointed to the left side of the valley, which was sparsely defended by a few of the San Faustino Band.

"Okay!" I said, grabbing up my carbine, all thoughts of food gone. "How do we get over there?"

The runner grabbed my arm and led us back up and over the crest of the ridge. We followed him along, and he showed us another point where the track curved over the western edge, from where we could make our way down. As we crouched in our new position, still on the periphery of the battle, Bonfigli arrived. He had twenty or so men with him. "Good work, Signor Console," he said, in greeting. I breathed a sigh of relief. I was afraid he might be angry that I had changed positions without first consulting him. Bonfigli took charge immediately. This was his kind of fight. He directed our men to positions on the western third of the line, which permitted the Cantiano Band to reinforce gaps in the middle and at the eastern end of the line. "You, Signore, over there," Bonfigli directed me. He placed me to the far left, right below the notch that was our withdrawal path. I dashed to my position and flattened myself down onto the ground, swinging my carbine into position. Looking around, I was pleased to see that my rocky nook formed a natural gun port. To fire on me, the Germans would have to draw a bead through a narrow gap between two rocks, whereas I could direct my fire to a wide area that extended from the center of the valley to the extreme left. Our orders were to carefully pick our shots, to conserve ammunition.

By one o'clock, the Germans had advanced enough to make a rush on the road to the far right, where the Cantiano Band was defending. Tagliaferro had realized the possibility and had ordered all remaining grenades shifted to that sector. When the rush came, grenades rained onto the SS troops, driving them back with heavy losses. From then on, aside from another minor, unsuccessful rush by them, the situation remained at a standoff. By three-thirty in the afternoon, although we really hadn't been severely pressed, we had expended a lot of ammunition just containing the sporadic rushes by the SS troopers, and we were running dangerously low. Our San Faustino force, though not as heavily engaged as our Cantiano comrades, was down to its last cartridges. Bonfigli summoned me to a joint meeting of officers to decide our next move. I could sense the officers felt that to withdraw now, besides being dangerous for the Bands, might give the populace the impression that the Italians had "turned tail and left." Too often they had been ridiculed. Though forced by the numerical superiority of the SS troops into a defensive stand, the officers didn't want us to be the first to disengage.

"Well, we don't want to get into a siege situation, either," I pointed out. "We'd better take stock." We were vastly out-armed and outnumbered, but even so, we had managed to inflict heavy losses on the enemy. "How many German dead are there? Do we know?" I asked.

One of the Cantiano officers spoke up. "My men counted over one hundred dead. There are at least forty wounded."

"What about the partisans?" I asked.

"We have had only minor losses so far, Signore," said Bonfigli. "Two or three of the Cantiano Band have been killed, and there are about twenty-five wounded from both bands."

"Ammunition?" I asked.

"We have almost none," said Bonfigli, dejectedly.

"We're almost out, too," said Tagliaferro, "and we don't have any more food for the men, either."

"Well then, I think we should devise a plan of withdrawal," I said, practically. "The Germans are at a definite advantage now, which will only improve with time, and there's no sense in our taking unnecessary losses. Let's get as many of the men as we can out safely, and then lay low for a while. There will be hell to pay for this, but it has been a big victory for the partigiani. You have taken on the most elite force of the German military, and inflicted heavy losses on them, with very few men and almost no arms. The Allies will surely commend you for this effort."

On hearing that, the officers looked at one another proudly. "Grazie, Signor Console," said Tagliaferro. "We hope so."

"I assure you," I said, "history will reflect the bravery manifested here today by you and your men. But now, we should try to live to tell the story."

We decided on a plan of withdrawal that would have the area cleared of partisans by four-thirty. First to go would be those who were completely out of ammunition. There was no need for them to remain. They would be followed by those who were billeted the farthest away. Last to depart would be the two machine guns and their crews. Enough ammunition would be saved to cover their retreat.

I returned and gave instructions to my men. Three of us shared our remaining chunks of bread and a couple of swallows from my water bottle. I noticed that fire from the Germans was diminishing along with ours. Even so, they were firing ten rounds to our one. Shortly after four, I motioned to three of the men to leave. Then it was my turn. I slid my three remaining cartridges over to the man on my left and began slithering backward up toward the lip of the hill. Making our way toward the woods, we stayed close together, in box formation, but once we reached the safety of the woods, we split up. Each man was on his own. The Germans, too, must have seen enough action for one day. There was no further sign of them. The slight warmth that the sun had provided was absent in the dank, cold muskiness of the pine woods. I was exhausted. Gritting my teeth, I plodded along, knowing full well I had ten to twelve kilometers of rough hills to cover before I would reach shelter. I decided to head for the presidio, which was closer than Fontanella. That way, if the Germans followed us, they would be met by armed partisans, instead of an un-armed family. At the edge of the woods, before heading out into the open fields, I dropped down on a rock and drew the stub of one vile, home-made Italian cheroot from my shirt pocket, and, lighting it, I sat quietly smoking for a few minutes. Some reward, I thought cynically, staring at its glowing tip, as the acrid smoke curled into my nostrils. When darkness fell, the ground froze, and the muddy route turned into rough and uneven ridges, which bruised my feet through my boots, and tripped me again and again. By the time I reached the presidio, my feet were a swollen, bruised mass. I could give no more than a tired, perfunctory nod to the sentry, as I passed him. I had no sooner stepped inside than I was sur-rounded by my comrades, all of whom were congratulating me and clap-ping me soundly on the shoulder, making me wince with pain. I was as glad to see them as they were to see me. The men who remained behind had not been idle. Scouring the countryside, they had foraged flour, meat, and a pile of firewood. They had even procured three demijohns of red wine! The beef stew warmed our stomachs, the roaring fire warmed our frozen bodies, the wine relaxed us, and, disregarding my exhaustion and my throbbing feet, I joined in the retelling of how our own San Faustini, together with the Cantiani, had fought the elite German Waffen SS troops to a standstill. Everyone was duly impressed.

The next day, I had to pry my pain-wracked body from the pallet. I was sipping coffee in the mess area when Bonfigli appeared, looking as worn as I felt. "Well, Mario, that was certainly something yesterday!" I greeted him. "We can all be proud of ourselves for what we accom-plished."

"Yes, Signore, and I'm pleased to tell you that none of our men were seriously wounded. Two got flesh wounds, and have been treated by Don Marino."

We were on our second cup of coffee when a messenger from the Can-tiano Band arrived. "Did the machine gun crews get out safely?" we asked anxiously.

"Sì, Signori," he replied, "the disengagement went exactly according to plan. The Germans pulled out about fifteen minutes after we did. We tried to go back later that night to retrieve any German weapons we could and to make an accurate count of the casualties, but the Germans had taken their dead away. The peasants of Pianello report that many fewer men got back on the buses than had gotten off." We knew that we had killed at least 100 SS troopers. The official report from the Germans, much later, showed that German losses were 170 killed, 63 wounded. Our own losses were a mere 3 fatalities, 10 wounded.

We had barely digested the Cantiano report when a second messenger arrived, from Captain Pierangeli. "He wishes to see you, Signore, and Lieutenant Bonfigli, and the other officers, immediately," said the runner. "He said that it is a matter of great urgency." I groaned aloud. It would take two hours of walking to get to the meeting site! Seeing the look of anguish on my face, the messenger added, "The captain sends his apologies. He knows you must be tired."

An hour later, I set out. It was on that walk that I vowed to myself that if ever I got out of this mess alive I would never again take an extra step, or go any distance on foot. Little did I know what lay ahead. When I arrived at the rendezvous, all key officers were present, including two representatives from the Cantiano Band. Pierangeli congratulated us on the previous day's success, then queried each officer about ammunition. The responses made him shake his head sadly. "My fellow officers," he said gravely, "we couldn't possibly be in a worse situation than we are now. Just when we are in a position to make a real contribution to the war effort, and just when we might desperately need to defend ourselves against the Germans, we cannot put together the ammunition for even one small raid. I'm afraid we'll have to disband." At a loss for further words, he sat down, almost tearfully. There was silence for a few minutes.

Then Bonfigli spoke. "Yesterday, our concerns were for the immediate battle, and the ammunition we needed to sustain it and get out of it alive. Now, we must face the future. If we cannot continue, we lose the confidence and support of the countryside. They have learned to count on us when they need us, and we on them. If we don't continue, this whole zone will fall back under the control of the Germans and Fascists within a matter of days. We must figure out a way to carry on!"

Everyone nodded assent, but after a half hour of discussion, no one had come up with a feasible plan. What the Germans had not been able to accomplish by direct confrontation would now be theirs by default. The partigiani of Umbria had run out of the supplies necessary to continue the resistance movement. The meeting continued throughout the day. Finally, in the late afternoon, one of the officers said, "We need to send someone through the German lines to the Allies, to appeal to them directly for help, for an airdrop."

Everyone turned to stare at me. Who else but me? I was an American. I was an American diplomat. I had a passport that would immediately establish my identity to the Allies, as well as an Italian identity card to use between here and there. Without arms, I was unsafe now in Pietralunga, since the Fascists and the Germans knew my whereabouts. There was bound to be retaliation for what we'd just done. And lastly, and most importantly, I had credibility—I was someone the Allies would believe. I shifted uncomfortably in my seat, thinking, as they all continued to stare at me. I certainly didn't relish the thought of wandering across hundreds of miles of Italy, hoping to make it to friendly lines. But I also realized I was the best and most logical choice, and that this was the partisans' only hope for continuing.

Finally, I cleared my throat. "You're right. Reaching the Allies is our only chance. I'll go," I said quietly. If a bolt of lightning had struck in our midst, it couldn't have had a more galvanizing effect. What had seemed a hopeless cause suddenly took on new life. Everyone crowded around to shake my hand and pound me on the shoulder—the sore one, of course. The air of excitement was electric.

Pierangeli took control of the meeting again. "All right, now. It is decided. Il Console will try to get through to the Allies and get us an airdrop of ammunition and supplies. He cannot go alone. We must send someone with him who knows the countryside, who can protect him, and help him get there alive." He looked around at the circle of faces, then turned to me. "Il Console, you are free to choose any member of the Band you wish, to go with you." The others nodded their agreement.

I thought for a minute, but my mind was in a whirl. Names and faces flashed before me. "I'd like a day to think it over, while I make my preparations to leave," I said.

"Of course," said Pierangeli. "How about if we meet here again day after tomorrow? At noon?" I agreed that would be a better time.

Leaving the meeting, I suddenly felt light-headed, as though I had drunk too much wine. The prospect of leaving the Band and having to cross enemy lines was a powerful intoxicant to a mind and body already strained to the limits of physical endurance. I decided to go back to the Bruschis— it was closer than the presidio—and besides, I wanted to ask Ruggero's help in choosing my traveling companion. I started to fantasize about life back home, if I got through to the Allied lines. I would be with Marguerite again. Would little Howard even remember me? Would Marguerite recognize me? For eighteen months now, I had been running from either the Italians or the Germans. I hadn't had a hot bath in over two months. I stroked my long, scraggly beard and tried to imagine a barbershop shave, with hot towels, and after-shave lotion. Holding a woman again, and making love to her. Lying in bed on a Sunday morning and talking to my wife—in English. For the first time in months, loneliness, and a wave of homesickness, washed over me. Chiding myself, I blinked back tears and strode resolutely up the path to Fontanella.

The whole Bruschi family welcomed me back enthusiastically, and I realized just how much of a family they had become to me. I cared deeply about each and every one of them. I didn't know how to tell them I'd be leaving them, for good, and very soon. As Ruggero poured me a welcoming glass of wine, I made no effort to hide my excitement. I told them all about my experiences of the past two days, including what had transpired at the officer's meeting I had just attended. Everyone suddenly stopped whatever they were doing and turned to look at me, wide-eyed. "When will you leave, Signore?" asked Ruggero respectfully.

"In two or three days, at the latest," I replied frankly. On hearing that, to my dismay, Pepe burst into tears, and ran from the room. Then Adalgisa started to sniffle. "I will need someone to go with me, Ruggero, and I'd like your help in deciding who it would be best to take."

"I will go with you, Signore," said Ruggero, without a second's hesitation.

"Yes, Signore," said Adalgisa, surprising me, "Ruggero should go, to see that you get there safely. We will be all right here until he returns."

I was deeply touched by their generosity and willingness to sacrifice for me, but I couldn't risk Ruggero, and the family. And while I had no doubt that Ruggero was dependable and solid, or that he would lay down his life for me, he wasn't the right man for this venture. I needed someone with a sense of the cloak-and-dagger nature of this mission. Someone strong, yes, but also someone who had a more outgoing personality and plenty of imagination, cunning, and daring. But who? Gently, I refused Ruggero's offer to go with me. He accepted my decision without question. That evening, Adalgisa, Ruggero and I sat at the table and reviewed the names of possible candidates. We found some reason to reject each one. Suddenly Ruggero's eyes brighted. "Giovanni . . ." he began, "Marioli!" I finished, slapping my hand on the table with a big smile. Ruggero beamed. We knew we had the man for the job! Even Adalgisa was smiling and nodding her head in agreement, although I'd have never believed we'd find anyone that she'd agree was acceptable.

Giovanni Marioli, about my own age, was a member of the Band and had been a friend of Ruggero's since childhood. He was a lot like Manfred Metzger, but with darker coloring and a slender, more athletic build. There was always a merry twinkle in Giovanni's steel-gray eyes, and, like Manfred, he got a big kick out of pulling off a practical joke. In my dealings with him in the past, he had impressed me as nimble-minded, but able to make calm judgments; daring without being reckless; gregarious, and completely unpretentious. He was just the person I needed! My main concern was that he was married and had two young children. I asked Ruggero to go to Pietralunga, where Giovanni lived, and tell his friend only that I wanted to talk to him about an "avventura rischiosa," (dangerous mission) and if he was interested, he should return to Fontanella with Ruggero in the morning to see me. I also asked Ruggero to inquire in Pietralunga about my boots. Somehow, Ugo the bootmaker had finally found the leather, and was making them for me. While Ruggero was gone, I began preparations for the journey. It would mean hundreds of miles walking through dangerous country and high, mountainous terrain, so we'd have to travel light. I pushed all my remaining American bills into the hollow in the cane, dug up the box beneath the stairs and took my U.S. passport out, then reburied the rest of my papers.

Just before lunch the next day, Ruggero returned with Giovanni. Before we sat down, Giovanni, acting like a magician, reached slyly inside his jacket and, with a grin and a dramatic gesture, whipped out my new boots! I grabbed them from him, exclaiming in delight, and immediately tried them on. Medium-high and beautifully crafted, they gave me a thrill of pride and possession—a real feeling of elation. They fit my feet perfectly! Now, at last, I would command "rispetto"—respect. I had noted, on entering a farmhouse for the first time, that glances were instantly directed toward one's feet, not the face. That was not surprising. In the rocky countryside of Umbria, with no vehicular transportation, how one was shod was more indicative of status than anything else. We finally had enough of admiring my boots and turned to our lunch.

As we ate, I outlined the problem and the plan. Giovanni listened intently, saying nothing. Ruggero looked alternately at me, then at Giovanni, head swiveling as if watching a tennis match. I could tell he was dying to see what his friend's final reaction to my proposal would be.

When I finished, Giovanni sat, turning it all over in his mind for a few moments. Finally, he spoke. "I am honored you have chosen me for this mission, Signore," he said, without undue emotion, "and I am ready to go with you, whenever you say. I ask only that you write a statement for my wife and children, in case I don't get back, so that when the Allies come, my family will be taken care of."

That response assured me that we had chosen the right man for the job. "Of course," I replied. I composed a brief document, stating the nature of Giovanni's mission in accompanying me and that I considered this a formal assumption of financial responsibility for him and his family by the United States. I further stated that I expected the United States to indemnify the Marioli family in the event that Giovanni did not return to them, safe and unharmed, from this dangerous mission on behalf of the Allies.

After some further discussion, Giovanni carefully folded his document, placing it in the jacket pocket, and left. "I will return in two days, Signore, with a detailed plan for the first leg of our journey."

I shook his hand, looking him full in the eyes. "Grazie, Giovanni," I said, with deep sincerity. "The Band, and I, will be forever indebted to you and the Marioli family."

The next day's meeting was a long one. The officers heartily approved my choice of Giovanni Marioli, and we immediately turned to other matters. The first task was to list priority items for the airdrop. Then, a description of drop zones, codes, and signals. Naturally, ammunition, grenades, explosives, and automatic weapons headed the priority list. Pierangeli, after some deep thought, said, "I think we need to ask for a radio-transmitter, and if at all possible, a man to operate it." We agreed that should be next on the list. Then came a fairly long list of medical supplies. I smiled at the fourth request. Not wishing to appear demanding, they asked for leather, rather than boots. Item by item, the list was pored over, reviewed, and revised. Finally, I was given the approved list.

Then Bonfigli stood up. "Well, buddy, it is not all take and no give, as you say," he said in English, smiling, and, reaching into his pocket, he pulled out a silk aviator's map of Italy. Spreading it out on the table, they conferred for a few minutes among themselves—not without some heated and emotional disagreement—and finally traced on it the route they felt would be the best, and safest, for me to follow. I looked, and my heart fell. I could see it meant slogging southward through the steep, tortuous terrain of central Italy, over high mountain passes, straight down through the Apennines, to somewhere south of a line drawn from Anzio to Ortona. It would be a nightmare journey.

Pierangeli then produced a rare and valuable bottle of brandy, a gesture that touched me very deeply. He poured each of us some, and we all raised our glasses in a toast. "To the safe return of our leader, Bonuccio Bonucci!" he said, and we all echoed "Sì! To Bonuccio!" and drank a sip. We had had no further news of Bonucci, and could only pray he was still alive. Bonfigli raised his glass. "To the safe journey of our friend, Il Console!" "Sì! To Il Console!" came the echo, and I felt my eyes misting over as we drank again.

I raised my glass. "To my dear friends of Umbria, and to the liberation of Italy," I said, my voice breaking slightly.

"To Umbria, and to Italy!" they shouted, and Pierangeli added, "And to the Allied victory!" as we drained our glasses. Then each man came to me in turn, to solemnly shake my hand, and give me an "abbraccio" (embrace).

Finally, as spokesman for all, Pierangeli said, "Good luck, Signor Console. We have been fortunate, and honored, to know you and to have you with us. You have been a good leader, a good soldier, and a good friend."

Mario Bonfigli walked with me out the door, his arm across my shoulder—or rather across my back, since he was a good four inches shorter than I. As I turned to leave, he grabbed my hand and shook it repeatedly. "So long, buddy," he said, in English. I could see tears standing in his eyes. It struck me that it was unlikely that I would ever see him, or any of them, again. I turned away and headed blindly down the path. For the next two days, I spent my time meeting with Giovanni and making preparations for the journey. I wanted to get to know him very well. My life might depend on this man's ability to cope with any crisis that arose along the way.

In going carefully through my things, deciding what to take and what to leave behind, I came upon a letter I had never opened. I realized with a start that it had been hand-delivered to me over a week ago, by a CLN agent, and I had tossed it into my bag without opening it, intending to get to it later. Then, with so much happening, I had completely forgotten about it! Hastily, I tore the envelope open. The letter was ten pages long, handwritten, in a cramped, European-style longhand that I didn't recognize. I ruffled through to the end to see the signature. The writer was a Mr. Foster, a name that rang not the slightest gong of memory with me. I began reading.

Foster claimed he had met me once in Trieste, where I had been of service to him in some diplomatic capacity. He rambled on and on with details of his problems, both personal and financial. Impatiently, I plowed on through it. He claimed he was being held under house arrest near Ancona on the Adriatic Coast, was in danger of a nervous breakdown from the stress piled on him, and wanted me to contact the Swiss Legation on his behalf. I laughed, shaking my head in wonder as I read. I was about to toss the letter aside, as nothing more than the frustrated ravings of a lunatic, when the footnote—a page-long "P.S." in the same handwriting—caught my attention. In it Foster wrote:

You might want to try contacting an agent known as "Quinto," the British A Force agent for the Le Marche region. Quinto has direct contact with the Cingoli Band, the major partisan movement in the area. He can be contacted through a peasant family named Rossi, whose farm sits at the base of the hill, about 600 meters west of the road, on the outskirts of Grottazzolina. The Rossis can put you in touch with Germano, who knows how to contact Quinto. Quinto arranges for resistance supplies to be delivered behind the German lines by Mas boat, and sets up the transport of military escapees to the Allied lines on the return trip. If you could arrange for Quinto to get me out, I'd be most grateful.

I sat, thunderstruck, after reading that. If even remotely true, it was very valuable and highly sensitive intelligence, and Foster, whoever he was, was foolhardy for putting it on paper. Or else someone was desperately trying to get critical information to me. My heart lurched. Could it be Manfred? Was Foster's use of Trieste, when Manfred and I had met, a clue? I knew from my initial meetings with Bonuccio Bonucci that A Force existed. I pulled out my map and searched for Grottazzolina, a town I had never heard of before. There it was, in the Le Marche region, just as the postscript had said! I studied the map carefully. To reach the Allied lines from Pietralunga, it was a much shorter trip to go across to the Adriatic coast, where we might get a boat, than to head south along the mountain chain, on foot, over the route Pierangeli and his men had indicated. The information in the letter, if true, could shorten our journey by weeks! Time gained was precious. My heart pounded with excitement. If the letter WAS from Manfred, as I suspected, I had to trust it, and use the information in it. I prayed it wouldn't turn out to be some kind of trap, or crazy wild-goose chase. Nevertheless, I knew I had to give it a shot. It was far better odds than traipsing over endless mountains in winter with little or nothing to go on, hoping to get to the Allied lines safely. Not that getting to the Adriatic would be easy—I'd have to cross the mountains on foot to get there, too. But fewer mountains, fewer miles, and fewer days.

Just then, Giovanni arrived. I carefully reread the footnote. "Foster," whoever he was, could not possibly be making all this up, I concluded, after the second reading. It was worth checking out. If this Quinto person existed, he was the answer to our prayers. I hoped that the crazy sounding "Mr. Foster" was really Manfred. I looked up at Giovanni. "My friend," I said, smiling, "it looks as if there's been a big change in plans!"

We set out on the Monday evening following Easter Sunday, in the gathering dusk. Under my coat, I wore my good luck charm—Margherita Bonucci's white dresser scarf, the one little Lucia had embroidered with the American Eagle, the one that had been my signal to Bonuccio Bonucci. In my knapsack were provisions for the next day's meals, prepared by Adalgisa and Concetta. Pepe had scrubbed and polished my cane, and at the last minute, had shyly offered me his wool cap, which, although much too small for me, was now clapped jauntily atop my head. I had left Adalgisa some money, which she protested taking, but I insisted, and had given each of the children a small souvenir to remember me by. Ruggero was at my side, carrying the knapsack I had put together for the journey. He had insisted on accompanying me as far as Pietralunga, where I would pick up Giovanni. As we left Fontanella, after a tearful goodbye to Adalgisa and the children, I handed him my Beretta and indicated he was to lead the way. He stepped out in front, the Beretta in hand. As we started down the worn and rutted path, I stopped for a moment to turn and look back at the place that had been my home these past three months. Framed by the dilapidated old farmhouse, the baking oven in the yard, and the trees beside the little stream, stood a tearful Adalgisa, hair blowing in the wind. Concetta, like a young colt, was at her side, hugging a sobbing Pepe. When I turned, they all gave sad little waves. "Buona fortuna, Signore, vada con Dio!" (Good luck Sir, God be with you!) called Adalgisa. Like the moment when Lucia Bonucci reached up and put the scarf around my neck and hugged me, and that first taste of the Christmas goose at Margherita's, with everyone gathered around the table, I knew I would carry the image I was seeing, a treasured photograph in my mind's eye, for the rest of my days. I waved back, then reluctantly turned, and left Fontanella.

What would it be like for these people, I wondered, when the devastating turbulence of the front of the war swept through here like a howling, raging tornado? Here, everything seemed peaceful and timeless. And here, as elsewhere, everything was relative.

It was well after dark when we reached Giovanni's house. He swung the door open on the first knock. After the obligatory glass of wine all around, Ruggero stuck out his hand, ready to leave, and I shook it. Then we embraced warmly. I couldn't allow him to leave with such a sad face. "Ah, Ruggero," I teased him, "you came with me only so you could sample the wine of the Casa Marioli!"

His round face creased into a warm smile, though tears glistened in his eyes. "No, no, Signor Console—I had to come along, so I could taste the wine first, to see if it was good enough for the likes of you!"

And so, laughing, we parted ways for good—he, to return to life at Fontanella, and I to go on, with Giovanni, to whatever unknown adventures lay before us.

9

The Long Trek to Grottazzolina

Giovanni's wife, Zelinda, set out huge bowls of minestrone. "A journey should never begin on an empty stomach," she declared. I showed Giovanni how to use the Beretta, which Ruggero had reluctantly relinquished to him, and checked over my own recently acquired Colt automatic. I asked Giovanni if he knew how to use Italian grenades, six of which I had managed to cajole out of Bonfigli. He said yes, he had used them before. We concealed the grenades on him, since I wasn't sure I would be as good with them as he would. "If challenged, we'll use grenades for a group, pistols if there are only one or two of them, okay?"

"Okay." Giovanni grinned with pleasure, like a small boy, as he repeated his first word of English.

Neither of us mentioned the obvious—that it would be certain death, for him at least, if anyone caught us out, armed, after curfew. My diplomatic passport might, just might, save me from a firing squad—but only to be subjected to God knows what else.

"I have a nice surprise for you, Signore," said Giovanni, with a smile, as we got ready to leave Tuesday evening. "We'll be going by bicycle for the first leg of the journey. A trusted friend of mine will be here with them shortly."

"Hey, that's great!" I said. "How did you manage that?" I was pleased. Given what lay before us, any relief from walking was welcome. Promptly at nine, Giovanni's friend Oreste arrived, with two extra bicycles. I insisted on paying him for the use of them. In turn, Oreste insisted he would accompany us as far as Branca, a town about forty kilometers away. Initially, I was against it. It would be hard enough for two to be inconspicuous, let alone three. And on bicycles, at that.

"But Signore, I think it might be a good idea," said Giovanni. "Oreste knows the back routes to Branca, and the terrain, like the back of his hand. He can get us there safely, by skirting Gubbio and taking back roads. He also has a cousin in Branca, who will give us lodging the first day. Then Oreste can bring the extra bicycles back here, one at a time."

Hearing that, I readily agreed to have him go with us as far as Branca. After quietly handing some lire to Zelinda, I suggested we get on our way. Oreste and I waited outside while Giovanni said his farewells to his family.

The moon, which by then had risen high, shed a pale silvery light on the hills as we pedaled toward Gubbio. At first, I had difficulty balancing myself and all my gear. I finally managed to fasten the cane across the handlebars, where it wouldn't get in my way, and that helped some. On the steeper hills, I barely had the strength to keep up with Oreste and Giovanni, who were obviously more used to this kind of exertion than I. After what seemed like an eternity, with my calves and thighs on fire from the strain, we crested the last hill and began the long, easy coast down to the plain of Gubbio. After a short stretch, Oreste slowed, signaling us to stop. I was grateful for the chance to catch my breath, as we listened to his instructions. "About 200 meters ahead, at the road to Umbertide, bear left and ride hard. Stay close together. After about 800 meters on the highway we'll cut right onto a smaller road. We don't want to stay on the highway any longer than we absolutely have to."

I certainly agreed with that. We hit the highway pedaling like mad. Despite the coldness of the night, I was sweating. The two shadows I was following suddenly darted right. I followed suit, and before I knew what was happening, I was sliding on gravel and hurtling head first over the handlebars, landing in the grassy ditch next to the road. Unaccustomed to European handbrakes, I had grasped the handlebars too firmly, as I made the turn, locking the brakes. My two companions, hearing the commotion behind them, stopped. As I remounted, embarrassed but fortunately unhurt, I heard Oreste laugh softly and mutter to Giovanni, "Behold! The next Campione d'Italia (biking champion of Italy) has been found!" I laughed too.

"Let's put you in the middle," said Giovanni, "so we don't lose you along the way." With me between them, we set off again, and about an hour before daybreak, we arrived at the outskirts of Branca. Oreste's relatives, the Panfiglios, welcomed us with open arms. Out came bread, and the inevitable wine, while a pot of ersatz coffee was prepared.

Oreste, as he left to return to Pietralunga, said "Take good care of my important friends, here, eh?" He needn't have worried.

Over the coffee, which Signora Panfiglio improved by sweetening it with some of her precious store of honey, we talked. I explained the general direction and purpose of our journey, without giving them too many details. "I will help," said Signor Panfiglio. I wondered what he meant, and thought for a minute he might be offering to accompany us. As soon as breakfast was finished, Panfiglio left for work. His wife shooed the children out of the house and showed Giovanni and me to the bedroom. Within minutes, we were sound asleep. When we awoke that evening, in time for dinner, we found all the Panfiglios gathered at the table, dressed in their Sunday best. The excitement of important guests was not an everyday occurrence, and, heeding Oreste's admonition, they were determined to put their very best forward for us.

We did Signora Panfiglio's delicious meal justice, but I winced at the thought of the dent she must have put in her larder, and her finances, to lay such a magnificent table for us. First, there was a rich minestrone, with meat in it—probably chicken. Then a decent egg pasta, dressed with a sauce that actually had pieces of meat in it. I savored each mouthful before swallowing it. The bread was crusty and not too coarse. For dessert, the lady of the house produced "cenci," a sort of cruller made of dough, rolled, twisted, fried lightly in oil, and sprinkled with honey. With it, Signor Panfiglio served us glasses of sweet dessert wine. The meal was holiday fare—a very special treat. Giovanni said he thought it was probably the best meal the family had had in years. I could almost say the same. I rose to express our thanks, telling them I had never been shown a higher or more generous order of hospitality than I had received from them that night. They beamed. Then Signor Panfiglio said, "I have been successful in satisfying your request."

"What request?" I asked, puzzled.

"I have arranged for a horse, a cart, and a driver to take you on the next leg of your journey," he said, as though it was the most ordinary thing in the world. "He will be here before daybreak in the morning."

Openmouthed, I stared at him. Then it struck me. In our conversation that morning, I had remarked to Giovanni that I wished we could ride a cloud over the mountains instead of walking over them! Signor Panfiglio had undertaken to find us a cloud to ride—over the first mountain peak, anyway. I was astonished. "Grazie, grazie, Signor Panfiglio," I said, fervently. "You have no idea what a great help this is to us."

"It is nothing. Do not think of it," he replied politely. When bedtime came that night, they insisted that Giovanni and I take the one bedroom. Where they, and their six children, slept that night I have no idea.

Shortly before dawn, we piled into an old straw-filled wooden cart. The tired horse matched the cart in age, as did the cantankerous owner of the whole decrepit outfit. Giovanni and I covered ourselves with some loose straw and a smelly old blanket, and enjoyed the novelty of being transported, jouncing about, over the rough road across the Marchigiano spur of the Apennines, which divides Umbria from the Le Marche region. As we bumped along, we chuckled more than once at the running stream of colorful and imaginative curses the driver rained down upon his poor old horse. After five hours of mostly uphill travel, he drew up and dismounted. "This is it," he grumbled. "I go no farther. Get out, and be on your way."

We got down, stretched, and looked around us. We were at a crossroads, somewhere in the general direction of Macerata, probably near the little town of Cancelli, I figured, consulting the map. We had no idea which way to go. The driver was no help. Anxious to be gone, he turned the cart around and bid us goodbye in the same surly tone he had used to curse the horse. Then, just as he reached the first curve, he turned around in his seat and shouted, "Buona fortuna!"

Giovanni and I looked at each other and broke out laughing. "See, I told you he was a softie," Giovanni remarked dryly. Our journey had so far been easy. We had not had to walk, and not a single vehicle or human being had passed us on the road.

We sat in the shade of a tree, behind some bushes, and ate our lunch. Then we tucked our remaining bread and cheese into my knapsack and filled our empty wine bottle with water from a nearby stream. Refreshed, we set off again at a brisk, but comfortable pace. The warm sun felt good on my aching shoulder. It was a pain that didn't go away. Since I hadn't injured it in any way that I could think of, I finally decided it must be some sort of bursitis or tendinitis. Shortly after two, we saw a group of men filing down the mountain to our left. They seemed to be spelling each other, carrying something heavy and awkward. As we neared the base of the mountain, we encountered one of them. He looked tired and disheveled. At Giovanni's questioning, we learned that he, and others of the local partisan band, had engaged the Germans the day before, and had suffered a number of casualties, including several killed. The men we had seen coming down the mountain were carrying their wounded. Once at the foot of the mountain they had quickly dispersed, not wanting to risk further retaliatory action by the Germans. Now on the alert, we bid the partisan farewell and good luck and then continued on our way. As the evening advanced, we began looking for a likely farmhouse in which to shelter for the night. It was dusk, and we were still searching, when suddenly, from behind us, came a soft, but insistent "ALT!" We halted. "Now, very slowly and carefully, put your hands on your head." These words were spoken in a dialect that I barely understood. My first thought was that it was all over for us, we had fallen into the hands of a local Fascist patrol. Then, as I turned my head slightly to glance back, I saw that these men were not wearing militia uniforms. They came up to us and patted us down, relieving us of our weapons, and Giovanni's precious grenades. "All right, now, lower your arms, and turn around." "Don't try anything," another warned, unnecessarily. I knew that these men had to be partisans.

Greatly relieved, I thought back to a few hours earlier, when Giovanni had commented that the trip so far had been uneventful, almost dull. I

wondered what he was thinking now? I ventured a question to our captors. "Who are you? What are you up to?"

"More to the point, who are YOU?" snapped the older of the two.
"And what we are up to is placing you under arrest."

"Why would you do that to two fellow partigiani?" I asked. They looked
startled. "I am an American diplomat, recently a member of the Banda di
San Fa . . ."

A hand went up, cutting me off. "SILENZIO!" (be quiet!). Then, more
calmly, "have you any identification to prove it?" I produced my passport
and my forged identity card. Giovanni produced his identity card. The
partisans examined our documents at length. "The beard is not much of
an improvement," the younger one commented, looking from my passport photo to my face. I didn't dare laugh. "Come," he ordered, and with
one leading the way, and the other covering us from behind, we left the
road and set off down a narrow path.

"Where are you taking us?" I asked. No answer.

After about twenty minutes, we reached a cluster of farm buildings.
There were a good many young partisans around, all equipped with Sten
guns. This was no insignificant, poorly armed partisan force, I realized.
We were led into the house, where we were able to quickly establish the
truth of our identities to the officers billeted there. We were questioned
about what we had seen on our trip and what was happening in the San
Faustino area. I filled them in as frankly and fully as I could. Then I followed up with some questions of my own. "I envy you your equipment.
How did you manage to get so many Sten guns? We had almost no arms
to work with."

"This is the headquarters of the Garibaldi Division of the Cingoli Band.
We are one of the largest partisan movements in central Italy, so we have
gotten Mas torpedo boat shipments of supplies and arms from the Allies."

My heart lifted on hearing the words. They were the Band Foster had
named in his letter! And the boats he had mentioned also existed! I was
tempted to reveal the contents of Foster's letter to them, but no one had
mentioned A Force, so I decided to keep silent. The Cingoli Band was a
formidable and well-organized resistance unit. The San Faustini were definitely country cousins by comparison! We were comfortably housed and
fed that night in the old farmhouse that served as their local headquarters.
Giovanni enjoyed a new gastronomic experience—his first taste of American "Spam." To eat meat from a can was a novelty to him, and for days
afterward, he extolled the virtues of Spam to anyone who would listen.

The next day, our weapons and grenades were returned to us, and we
were escorted back down to the valley road leading to Camerino. "Give
Camerino a wide berth, Signori," advised Vincenzo, our escort. "There is
a large garrison of Germans there. Also, the town is on a major highway,
and German convoys are constantly passing through. It is wise to avoid

the area if you can." He turned, saluted us, and took off. Grateful for that information, we immediately changed our original plan, and instead chose a route that would avoid any of the main roads leading to Camerino. We walked all day, following the twisting path of the Patenza river, down the valley in the direction of Camerino.

Giovanni was a good-natured companion, and once more I was glad that I had chosen him to accompany me. At lunchtime, giving me a wink and a sly grin, he whipped a can of Spam out of his shirt. He was as intrigued as a child with the metal key that peeled the can open. Though it never had been a favorite of mine, I must admit the Spam certainly hit the spot with me for lunch that day. Any meat besides dry sausage was a rare treat. By nightfall, having taken various side routes to avoid the main highway to Camerino, we realized we were hopelessly lost. We came to a crossroads, and a short distance from it we saw a farmhouse. It was much too close to the intersection to serve as a refuge for the night, but we thought we could at least get some directions from the people there, before continuing on. Giovanni went to the house to make inquiries, while I stood back in the shadows, out of sight. As he raised his hand to knock, the door swung open. Giovanni froze for a moment, then, muttering "scusi," he turned and broke into a dead run. Seeing that, I also took off. Running with a knapsack flapping and slapping at your back is no way to run for your life, but my feet were pounding the road as fast as I could move them up and down. Giovanni quickly caught up and passed me.

"What the hell is going on?" I shouted as he whizzed by. I could hear yelling from the house and risked a quick look back. Four armed men had emerged.

"Militia!" panted Giovanni. That terrifying pronouncement had the needed effect. I found strength I didn't know I possessed and ran faster than ever. After a few minutes, I knew I wouldn't be able to keep up the pace.

"Run!" I called to Giovanni. "Don't wait for me! Just keep running!"

"What the hell does it look like I'm doing?" Giovanni shouted back. "I'm running!"

Just then, shots rang out. Three of them. What a hellish time to be wearing a light tan raincoat, I thought. A bullet zinged by my left ear, so close the concussion was like a sharp blow. The firing continued as we dashed around a curve. I didn't dare turn to see if we were being pursued, but the crack of rifle fire seemed to be receding. Then I saw Giovanni dive off the road, into some bushes. I followed, and together we slithered and wriggled away from the road for about 100 meters. The firing ceased.

We lay there panting, trying to catch our breath, listening for any sounds of pursuit. After a few minutes, hearing nothing more, I got up. Motioning for Giovanni to follow me, I slunk along behind a row of trees, following a shallow ditch, until we were far enough away from the road to feel relatively safe. Stripping off my knapsack and throwing it down, I

announced loudly, "Now, I need to take a leak!" Givoanni doubled over
in laughter as I calmly relieved myself against a tree.

"Run!" he mimicked my shout to him as we were running from the
Fascists. Seeing my startled expression, he laughed even harder, tears
streaming down his face. "What did you think, I would take an afternoon
stroll down the road, while those Fascist bastards were shooting at my
ass?" Catching his mood, I started laughing too. Soon we were both
howling. "Hah!" he pointed at me. "You with that pack flapping and
your long legs churning—you run like a camel up to its knees in sand!"

"Well, you should have seen your face when they came to the door!
'Scusi' " I mimicked derisively, in a high falsetto, and that set us off again.
It was a long-overdue nervous reaction, and a hell of a lot better than not
being there to laugh at all.

To be on the safe side, we waited a full hour, resting, before going on.
The sky was beginning to lighten when, through the swirling dawn mists,
we saw, perched atop a nearby hill, the chocolate-frosted wedding cake
tiers of the town of Camerino. From the direction of the streaks preceding
the sun's imminent arrival, we were happy to see that we were coming
out of the hills well to the northeast of it. Giovanni suddenly stopped and
pointed over to his right. A lone farmhouse stood about 200 meters away.
He raised a questioning brow to me. I hesitated a moment. Did we dare
chance it? We had been on the road since six the previous morning, and
we were both ready to drop in our tracks. I nodded yes, too tired to even
speak. "Back in a minute," he said, "but if I turn and run, you head for
that stand of trees over there." He indicated a small, dense thicket about
100 yards to my left.

"Okay. Be careful. If it looks good, just signal for me to come on in,"
I said, dropping down into a shallow ditch by the side of the road, from
which I could cover Giovanni and watch the door to the house. He saun-
tered up to the building and, after cautiously climbing the stairs to the
second-floor living quarters, rapped on the weathered wooden door. Thank
God no dogs started yapping! I could see him talking earnestly with the
person who came to the door, then he pointed in my direction, and I
tensed. He said something more, then turned and with a short, piercing
whistle waved me in. I breathed in relief. It was safe. I loped across the
field and met him at the top of the stairs. We had to brush past several
people to squeeze into the crowded kitchen. I looked around in amazement. There were at least two complete families gathered there, including
grandmothers, aunts, babies, and children of all ages. There were also
seven or eight assorted " 'sfollati," besides us. It was a mob scene. Clouds
of flies were buzzing around. Everyone was talking at once, and no one
seemed to be listening to anything that was being said by anyone else.
They were like a barnyard full of chickens, all cackling, darting here and
there, pecking and scratching.

The welcome warmth of the fire thawed our weary bones. "Are you hungry?" asked one of the old ladies.

"Sì, Signora," replied Giovanni. "We have not eaten, except for a chunk of bread, since yesterday."

The old woman looked horrified. "Ma, poveracci! Che disgrazia!" (you poor things! how terrible!), she said, turning immediately and yelling, to the room in general, "Eh! some food for these poor men. They haven't eaten since yesterday! Angelina! Qualcosa à mangiare, per favore!" (something to eat, please!). This had the effect of doubling the decibel level in the room, if that was possible, as everyone commented, again to no one in particular, on the fact that we hadn't eaten since yesterday. It also sparked frenzied activity from two of the women—one of whom, presumably, was Angelina.

"Here, Signore," said the other one, solicitously, getting up from the table and indicating her empty chair, "Sit, sit—rest yourself. You must be tired near to death." That was closer to the truth than she could have imagined! I dropped gratefully into the seat. One of the men jumped up, indicating that Giovanni should take his place at the table. Cups of hot barley coffee were quickly brought and put in front of us, and we sipped, dunking chunks of bread in the hot liquid, and wolfing them down.

The old woman watched us, hawklike, nodding approvingly as we ate and drank, punctuating our every swallow with a cooing murmur of satisfaction, like a nurse with two very sick patients to be coddled. Then Angelina set a "frittata," the Italian version of an omelet, before us. Saliva rushed into my mouth at the sight and smell of it. Besides never wanting to walk an extra step, I hoped that once I got out of this, I would never in my life be this hungry again, either! We tried, unsuccessfully, not to bolt the omelet down in huge bites, like starving animals. It was the most delicious thing imaginable. "Grazie, Signora," I said to Angelina, laying my fork down after consuming every last morsel on my plate, "you have made life worth living again, with that delicious frittata."

"Think nothing of it, Signore," she replied modestly, beaming with pleasure.

I glanced around the room. How in hell she fed this mob, I couldn't imagine, let alone any strangers who wandered hungry to her door!

An older man, who seemed to be the master of the house, approached us. "Signori," he said apologetically, "I am sorry there is no space here for you to sleep. But you are welcome to sleep in the barn." He meant the adjoining structure that housed the oxen and cows. At that point, I didn't care where I lay down. We were safe, warm, our hunger was assuaged, and more than anything else now, we just wanted to drop down somewhere, anywhere, and sleep. We thanked everyone and went out to the cowstall.

Inured to dirt and farm smells though we were, the stench that assaulted our noses when we opened the stable door was overwhelming. I looked at Giovanni with a pained expression. He returned the look, then shrugged, and, holding our breath, we entered the fetid place. The stalls must not have been cleaned for a week or more. Scrabbling around, we searched out some fresh straw, and, strewing it around, we each prepared to bed down next to a cow. Pointing to the largest of the three animals, who had turned their heads to stare with mild disinterest at us, I said to Giovanni, grinning, "You take that one, Giovanni, I can see she has eyes for you."

Patting the cow on the head, he rejoined, chuckling, "Yes? Well, she'd better let me sleep and not expect any action from me tonight!" He settled in beside her.

Snuggling deep into the straw next to my own cow, I was soon warm, if not exactly cozy. The bitterly cold wind whistled around the corners of our haven, and although I didn't want to think about what we'd smell like later, I was glad to be in here with our warm, bovine companions, and not outside somewhere, where the temperature was several degrees below freezing. Although I was vaguely aware of my "bedmate" stirring from time to time as she was watered or fed, I never really woke, and we slept most of the day that way.

Late in the afternoon, one of the youngsters came sidling into the barn to wake us. Staring at me with great, round dark eyes, he said, "Mamma says you should come up now—there is dinner ready for you."

We washed ourselves, as best we could, in the icy water of the stock trough. Giovanni entertained the children by juggling the grenades for them, something he enjoyed practicing, wherever we happened to be holed up. He certainly succeeded in catching everyone's attention with his little trick. They were usually more than impressed—it scared them out of their wits. Giovanni loved it, and so did the children. "All right, Giovanni, put your toys away and let's go eat!" I said, and we trudged upstairs—he still juggling grenades, a gaggle of awestruck children following him. As we stepped inside, I noticed several people wrinkling their noses in distaste at the odor emanating from us, but there was nothing we could do about it. Politely, they said nothing.

Angelina urged us to "Mangia! Mangia!" as she dipped into the giant pottery bowl in the center of the table and spooned out huge helpings of the piping hot spaghetti, cheese, and tomato dish. Once more, the old woman hovered nearby and watched us, clucking and nodding in approval as we ate. We needed no urging! Not knowing when, or if, we'd see another hot meal, we obligingly stuffed ourselves. Then, sated, we toasted the assembled group with our remaining few sips of wine. They all smiled genially and joined us in the toasts.

Our hosts, and many of the others, gathered around us as we got ready to go. At the door, Angelina handed me a wrapped package, which I knew contained bread and cheese, and her husband gave Giovanni a flask of wine. The old woman then made the sign of the cross over us, saying "Vada con Dio" (go with God), and I felt a wave of nostalgia for Fontanella and the Bruschis.

Thanking them for their hospitality, Giovanni added, with a merry twinkle, "My girlfriend for the night, your cow, was very simpàtica, dear friends." Everyone laughed uproariously at that, and we made our way out into the night, their laughter echoing down the stairs behind us.

About two inches of iced-over snow crunched softly beneath our feet as we walked across the field, and I knew there would be more snow as we moved higher up. Even worse, the drizzle that had fallen during the day had turned the trail into a muddy mess, which meant that all the back roads and trails would be impossible to negotiate—especially in the dark, as the temperature dropped and they froze. Giovanni stopped and stared at the steep and slippery quagmire of a trail that stretched before us. Then he shook his head and sighed, turning to me. "We cannot do this, Signore! No way! Even in summer it would be difficult, but now—I'm afraid we'll just have to risk staying on the paved highway."

I nodded. "Yes, it looks that way, doesn't it—but I hate the idea. It's a main highway from Rome to the Adriatic." On the map, we could see that the highway ran from Rome to the Adriatic coast at Loreto, where it connected to the coastal highway leading to the port city of Ancona. The portion of paved highway that would take us through the mountain pass, where we could branch off onto a less traveled secondary road, was at least eight or nine kilometers long. From the map, the town of Calderola lay just west of our route, a bit off to the side of the secondary road.

"We'll have to move as quickly as we can," said Giovanni. "Do you think we can jog most of the way to the pass?"

"I'm sure going to give it a try," I said determinedly, setting off at a brisk trot. I didn't want to be on that damned highway one minute longer than we absolutely had to!

As stretches of the road steepened, we were forced to slow our gait somewhat, though fear urged us on. The snow was crusted with a thin, brittle layer of ice as we neared the summit, and I prayed the road would not ice over completely until we were through the pass and down the other side. To my right, out of the corner of my eye, illuminated by the moonlight reflecting off the snow, I could see the unprotected sheer drop down to the river far below us. One slip or misstep and we'd be over the edge, plunging hundreds of feet into the river's icy waters. We were close to the summit when we stopped for our first break. We leaned against a spindly tree, panting. The ground was wet, and too cold to sit down on. We were just stepping back onto the road again when we heard the unmistakable drone of motors below us. Trucks were laboring up the pass, in low gear. We scrambled off the road, and took cover in some bushes growing on the slope, under an outcropping of rock where the roadbed had been cut through the sheer face of the mountain. Dropping down, we pressed ourselves flat on the cold, snow-covered ground, clinging desperately to the thickest branches of the brush to keep from sliding down the slope. Barely daring to breathe, we clung there and waited for the trucks to pass. I prayed our handhold would not give way under our weight, and willed myself not to look down.

Giovanni turned his head toward me and whispered, "Don't worry, Signore, the Germans won't need to see us, they'll smell us long before they get here!" He chuckled softly. I grunted, too cold and frightened to respond. Gingerly releasing one hand, I tapped a finger to my temple, then to him, to indicate he was nuts. Hell, at least he could laugh at a time like this! "But it is no big problem," he concluded irrepressibly, "one whiff and they'll pass us right up—figuring anything that smells so bad has to have been dead for at least a week!" He laughed aloud at that, and I winced. I was sure whoever was coming would hear his laugh echoing across the roadway.

We stayed well out of sight until about five minutes after the vehicles had passed, then laboriously we pulled ourselves up to the top of the slope and scrambled back onto the highway again. Soaked from the wet snow and our own sweat, and with the biting cold wind that tore through the pass, we were soon in a near-frozen state. Shivering, we decided to run as fast as we possibly could, not only to keep from getting frostbite, but to get us through the pass and off the highway in a hurry. By the time we were over the pass and had turned onto the secondary road, I was lathered in sweat, and my lungs hurt so badly I was sure I had pneumonia.

"Giovanni!" I gasped out. "Look for shelter—I have to rest—can't go on!"

"Haystacks over there!" he panted, pointing to a field just ahead and to the right.

We veered off the road and jumped into the nearest haystack, burrowing deep. We thought the hay would shield us from the icy wind, and keep us warm enough to cool down gradually. We learned a quick and miserable lesson to the contrary. The hay not only gave us no insulation from the cold, it was damp from the rain that had fallen earlier in the day. We'd have been warmer in a snowbank. The temperature was somewhere in the twenties, I figured. We stuck it out another fifteen minutes, but could take no more. We emerged from our freezing burrow, brushed ourselves off as best we could, swinging our arms and stamping our legs vigorously to restore circulation, and set off again at a run. After dog-trotting for half an hour, the last thing on earth we expected was to round a turn, and run smack into the center of the town of Calderola! From the map, I had expected it to be off to the side, at a distance, not seated comfortably astride the road we were on.

Skidding to a halt, we scampered over to the right and hunkered behind a cypress tree, from where we peered down through the center of town. There was no sign of life, so we decided to chance going through. We were too damned cold to stop and make any alternate plans. Sticking to whatever shadows we could find, we began slowly working our way through the town. The moon, like a lighted globe above us, hung full and round and bright. I was convinced I could have read a newspaper by its stark, cold light. Suddenly, we were facing a tiny piazza. Two rows of small young trees ran along one side of it, and from the looks of them, they would afford us very little cover. Cautiously, we sidled along, staying between the rows of trees. A movement to my right caught my attention. I glanced over—and froze in my tracks, stopping so suddenly Giovanni bumped into me from behind. "What is . . ." the sentence died on his lips. At the end of the line of trees and slightly to the right, five uniformed men hove into view.

They caught sight of us at about the same time we saw them. Moonlight gleamed on white Sam Browne belts that marked two of them as carabinieri. The other three wore the garb of the Fascist militia. All were armed. Fear, like thousand-legged spiders suddenly dumped from a jar, prickled along my arms and ran up my neck. "Get a grenade out—quick!" I hissed.

"Done!" Giovanni whispered back.

Slowly, carefully, I drew the Colt, and held it ready, but with the muzzle pointed down. Giovanni shifted his pack slightly and moved his right hand, with the grenade, close to his mouth, where he could quickly pull the pin with his teeth and heave it into their midst. Watching them intently, we continued quietly along the length of the piazza. For their part, they stood like a group of statues, staring at us, as though seeing ghosts, or an apparition. We passed not fifteen feet away from them—two ragged, unkempt strangers who had materialized out of nowhere—and they never challenged us, or so much as moved a muscle. Gaining the opposite end of the piazza, we quickly slipped behind a large building, and I let my breath out in a "whoosh!" Without a word, we broke into a run and didn't pause until we were a good half mile out of town. We came upon a small mountain stream, in a deep cut below the road. Clambering down its steep bank, we hid in the bushes beside it, weapons at the ready. We waited about five minutes, but nothing happened. There was no alarm, no pursuit. Why had they, with the odds in their favor, not reacted? Were they moving ahead of us to set up a roadblock? It was long past curfew, so we had no right to be out, let alone armed, strolling casually through their town.

"Let's leave the road and head for the fields," I whispered. "It will be safer." Giovanni nodded agreement, and we took off across a field and up and over the top of a small hill. The bright moon led us like a guide, lighting our way, so that by the time dawn peeked over the hills a few hours later, we had put several kilometers and several steep ridges between ourselves and Calderola.

"Time to find some breakfast and a bed, Signore," said Giovanni, glancing at the sky. Our friendly moon had scampered for cover, and daylight, our biggest enemy, was arriving in a great burst of orange fire.

"Look for a farm—a poor one," I said.

"That should be easy enough," said Giovanni dryly. "I haven't seen many rich farms, or palazzos, here in the middle of nowhere!"

After about fifteen minutes more of walking, we found the kind of poor, isolated farm we were looking for. Giovanni went to check, then came back to report to me. "I listened with all my ears, Signore," he said, shaking his head in frustration, "and I could hardly understand them, but it seems to be safe there, and at least I know we are welcome."

Wearily, we made our way to the house. Once again, the greeting we received was warm and sincere. After bowls of hot minestrone, we were shown to the family bed to sleep. In the evening, I watched the woman prepare the family meal and again was struck with amazement at the generosity of these folk of the Italian countryside. While she and her husband sat down at one end of the table to a simple supper of minestrone and a piece of bread, Giovanni and I, at the other end of the big wooden table, were given heaping bowls of pasta, some cheese, and a link of sausage cooked with onions. When we asked directions, spreading our map out on the table, the woman exclaimed in delight over the silk, touching it with gentle fingers, as her husband's stubby, work-worn finger traced out the route we should take. "What a rich country America must be," she commented softly, fingering a corner of the map. "Even your maps are made of silk! Imagine!" After supper, she wrapped a small package of food for us. "Stay out of trouble, and make your mothers proud," she admonished us, like we were small boys.

Near midnight, we paused to rest a bit near a small stream. Giovanni, always hungry, suggested we eat, so we took out the bread and sausage the woman had given us and ate it as we sat on a large flat rock in the cold night air. "I wish we had some wine to wash this down,"said Giovanni, plaintively, but no genie appeared before us to grant his wish.

"Well, you'll have to be satisfied with water from the stream here," I said. "A quick drink and we'll be on our way. I want to make San Ginesio before dawn."

"Well, I just hope that San Ginesio doesn't send out a welcoming party like the one we saw in Calderola! My heart can't take that twice in a row," said Giovanni, and putting his hand over his heart in a dramatic gesture, he dropped to the ground next to the little stream. In the bright moonlight, the outline of his face was mirrored in the shimmering water. Standing behind him, I smiled down at the image, and was startled to see my own unkempt, virtually unrecognizable face reflected next to his. We were certainly a frightening-looking pair.

"Look at us, Giovanni!" I joked. "Would this sight make our mothers proud?"

"My mother would scream and faint at the smell, before she even saw me," replied Giovanni, his even white teeth flashing as he laughed.

I'm so glad I have him along, I thought, as I stared at the outline of our two faces, mine fully bearded, his with several days' growth of whiskers, wavering there in the water. I shuddered to think of what this trip would have been like alone. Giovanni abruptly plunged his fist into the water, shattering the reflection and sending it undulating away, in wider and wider circles, until it disappeared completely. Scooping up a handful of the icy water, he gulped it down. Dropping down beside him, I did the same.

I glanced up at the sky. Fast-moving clouds were scudding in waves across it, the dark, foamy edge of one already lapping at the moon, blackly obscuring a quarter of its shining face. "We'd better get moving, Giovanni—it looks like we're in for a weather change." A few hours later, wet and miserable from a steady, cold drizzle, we stood facing San Ginesio. The road ran right through town, as it had in Calderola. We edged our way in, then cautiously slithered down the narrow, cobbled streets, groping our way in the darkness. The sound of rushing water, from a fast-flowing river nearby, pervaded the town, and not another noise was heard over it. Suddenly, above me, a gust of wind caught a shutter and banged it against a wall, sending me jumping in fright, my hand automatically clasping the butt of the Colt. Not even a dog barked. We were about ten minutes past the town, when Giovanni finally spoke. "Whew!" he said, "that town gave me the creeps! I think everyone must have been dead there."

"Well," I said, "lucky for us that they were—or heavy sleepers. But, never mind them, we're still very much alive, wet, and hungry, and we'd better start looking for our place to sleep the day away!" I shivered miserably, cold rain dripping from my cap onto the back of my neck. Would I ever enjoy a normal life again? I wondered. One where the nights would be for sleeping, and I could be awake and among people during the daylight hours? I, who used to be a happy daytime creature, now moved about stealthily, and only in the dark of night.

Our next lodging was at the small, modest cottage of a widow, not far from town. It wasn't the type of isolated farmhouse that we usually chose, and it was near enough to town to make me apprehensive about it, but we were soaked to the skin and left with no other choice. Assunta Lombardo was tiny and cheerful, around fifty, I judged. "Phew!" she said frankly, as we stepped through the door, wrinkling her nose at the smell. If she was frightened by the appearance of these two rough-looking strangers, she didn't show it. "You certainly need some dry clothes, and a bath." She bustled to the fireplace and filled the cauldron there with water from a large pitcher, swinging it over the fire to heat. When it was warm enough, she left the room, and we took turns sponge bathing from the hot water, and changed into our second set of clothes, which had stayed pretty dry in our knapsacks. "I'll wash these while you sleep," she said briskly, returning with some food. Scooping up our filthy, wet clothes, she dumped them into the hot water we had used for bathing. "I think the sun will come out soon, and I can dry them in a sheltered place in the back yard, where they won't be seen by anyone."

"Grazie, Signora," I said gratefully. "Clean clothes are a big luxury for us poor 'sfollati."

Sipping the hot coffee she served us, I looked around the room. It was a well-furnished little place—several cuts above the average poor farmhouse. The few pieces of massive, dark furniture gleamed from polishing, the windows were dressed in lacy curtains, framed by dark side drapes, and a worn maroon, oriental-patterned rug covered most of the rough marble floor. There were even a couple of oil paintings on the walls, in addition to the usual framed religious and family pictures. Massaging my bruised and aching feet before pulling my boots back on, I decided to chance a question. "Signora Lombardo, is it possible, do you think, for us to hire a horse-drawn vehicle, a cart of some sort, to take us for the next portion of our journey?"

She thought a minute. "Hmm! I don't know, Signore. Let me think about where you might get a horse and cart. That is not an easy request." She went over to the fireplace and began vigorously scrubbing our clothes, twisting and wringing each piece. There was no soap, of course, but a good dunking in hot water would help rid them of the worst of the dirt and smell we had accumulated. Suddenly, she straightened up, murmuring, "Forse, il dottore!" (perhaps the doctor). She turned to me. "Perhaps il dottore can help you about your transportation," she said, drying her hands on her apron as she came across the room. "He is not a medical dottore," she explained, as though it mattered, "but a person of learning. I think he favors the Allies, and he might help you find a horse and cart for hire, to help you get to where you are going."

I brightened at that news, all thoughts of sleep gone. "Give us directions to his house, Signora, and we will go right now and ask him," I said.

As we left, I told her to expect us back in an hour or so. At the doctor's house, after several prolonged rounds of knocking, we finally roused an old woman, who reluctantly let us in. Fortunately, I didn't tell her who we were, or who had sent us. "I'd like to talk to il dottore, Signora," I said politely. "We have heard he might be able to help us hire a horse and cart for our journey. I am an American officer, and we are trying to reach the Adriatic coast."

Motioning Giovanni to stay and guard the front door, I followed her into a large, well-furnished parlor. Clutching her hands together nervously, she said, "Scusi, Signore, but my husband has been very sick. It will be a few minutes until he comes down to see you." With that, she left the room and didn't return. Strange. I sat alone, fidgeting uncomfortably. Minutes dragged by, and there was no sound in the house except the ticking of a clock on the mantel above the fireplace. Alarm bells began to chime in my head. Our reception by the lady of the house had not been very cordial. All my instincts had always warned me against asking favors of anyone in the upper classes. They simply didn't have the same generous attitude toward strangers in need as the poorer country folk did. Just as I had decided to forget the whole thing and bolt out the front door, I heard a slow tread on the stairs that led to the second story. A few seconds later, il dottore, a bent, balding wraith, entered the room, leaning heavily on a cane. He shuffled with agonizing slowness across the room and seated himself in a straight chair opposite me. He didn't offer me so much as a greeting or a handshake. After giving me a careful once-over, in complete silence, he looked me balefully in the eye, and I knew that something unpleasant was about to happen.

Without preamble, he sat forward, hands folded over the top of his cane, and attacked. "Assassini!" (assassins!), he snarled, hoarsely, his voice barely above a whisper. "You have abandoned all semblance of civilized behavior, you English!" He lifted the cane a fraction of an inch to point it toward me, a look of loathing on his face. "You bomb populated areas, even peaceful Macerata—an offense that even the Russians, those barbarians, are not capable of! We know what you are doing—you are determined to destroy, to obliterate, the great heritage and culture of Italy!" His eyes grew wild and his voice rose an octave. "You cannot stand it that it is OUR art, OUR music, that the whole world celebrates! Yes, great art and music are Italian, not English!" As he ranted on, his face flushed a mottled red and his eyes, wide and furious, bulged from his head. I was sure the man would have a stroke right there. My own temper rose at his diatribe. I jumped up to leave. I gained the door, and was reaching for the handle, when "Wait!' he thundered, no longer the weak, frail invalid of a few minutes ago. "I am not finished with you, Inglese!"

"Well, I'm damned well finished with YOU," I retorted and whipped out my Colt, pointing it at his head. He froze, turning several shades paler. "Now, go over there and sit down!" I ordered. He quickly obeyed, his tremors becoming quite pronounced. "Look at the clock," I said. His eyes swiveled from the gun to the clock on the mantel, which read ten-fifteen. "If you so much as move a muscle for fifteen minutes after I'm out that door, I will come back here and blow your head off! Depend on it!" I barked. "And not a word to anyone about our little visit, understand?" Terrified, gasping for breath, he nodded mutely. Then I caught sight of the telephone, an antiquated wooden affair, attached to the wall. Damned if he'll call the carabinieri down on us with that! I ripped it out of the wall and flung it across the room. It landed near the old man's feet, and he jumped in fright.

"Signore," he said, pleadingly, "my horse is lame, and could not possibly pull a cart."

"What do I care about your damned horse?" I retorted. "I don't want anything from you! And another thing, I'm American! And you'd be damned lucky to have the Americans liberate you, you. . ." I sputtered, searching for the words in Italian ". . . horse's ass!"

Giovanni jumped in alarm on seeing me. "Signore! What is it? Put the gun away! What the hell happened?"

I strode down the little path between the gardens, fuming. "Just walk calmly, Giovanni, and smile. We're two guys on our way to visit our sick aunt."

When we were out of sight of the doctor's house, we broke into a run, not stopping until we were at the foot of the lane that led back to the widow Lombardo's house. Then we slowed and nonchalantly strolled up the path to her door. I quickly filled Giovanni in on what had happened. "Accidenti!" he said malevolently.

Signora Lombardo had been watching for us, and she admitted us immediately, wringing her hands, obviously distressed. "Oh, oh, Signori, I'm so glad you are back safely! I made a terrible mistake! The recent bombing at Macerata destroyed il dottore's big house there! Now he hates the Allies!" So that was it.

"It's all right," I soothed her. "It wasn't a good experience, but I don't think the dottore will do anything to bother us." With that, we fell into bed and slept most of the day. Since it was Sunday, and we wouldn't arouse suspicion by being out, I decided to use the afternoon daylight hours to cover most of the remaining distance to Grottazolina, which looked to be about a six-hour walk from Assunta Lombardo's cottage. As promised, our freshly laundered clothes were dry, and after a hot meal and our farewells, we headed down the road.

It felt good to be out in the pale afternoon sun, with full bellies, dressed in clean clothes. I had even trimmed my beard a bit, so I didn't look so bedraggled. "Eh, Signore, we sure smell good, now, no?" smiled Giovanni, pleased that our barnyard smell was gone. "The Signorine will all be happy to see us coming, two such handsome Signori as we are. They won't turn their noses up, and make faces any more!" He laughed, and began whistling a sprightly tune as we walked along. That it was Sunday served us well for this leg of the trip, because there were not likely to be any German or Fascist patrols or convoys on the roads. We made good time, without incident, and it was just before midnight on April 10th when we reached the area we sought. Following the instructions and directions given in the mysterious Mr. Foster's letter, we had no difficulty locating the farm of Francesco Rossi. It stood isolated, a prosperous looking stone edifice, in good repair, at the foot of the steep hill whose crowning glory was the ancient, crumbling town of Grottazzolina.

Seeing the farm, excitement surged through me. All the information in Foster's letter so far had proven exact. It meant that the contact named Quinto probably existed, too. "This is it, Giovanni!" I exulted. "This is our link to the Allies! We made it! The worst is over!" Clapping him jubilantly on the shoulder, I strode ahead of him up the path, climbed the stairs, and banged confidently on the farmhouse door.

10

Airdrop at Morena

No one answered. I banged again. I could hear sounds from within, but the door didn't open. Finally, from behind it, came a muffled voice. "Who is it? What do you want?"

"I am here to see Francesco Rossi. We need shelter." I waited. Nothing happened. "I am an American officer," I added, "and I have an Italian companion with me." Someone else must have joined the person on the other side of the door, because I could hear two voices, raised in discussion. Exasperated, I called, "I have come to meet with Quinto!" More voices from within, but the door remained shut.

An old man's voice quavered, "Go away! We will not open the door! Go elsewhere for shelter!"

I was not prepared for that. To be summarily dismissed at the end of a long and frightening journey was more than I could take. "Signori!" I shouted. "You MUST open the door! I am an American officer, with an Italian partigiano friend, and we were sent here to contact Quinto! I have a passport and we have papers to confirm our identities, if you will only look at them. Please let us in!" Inside, there was more conferring. Another voice, which sounded like a younger man, came through the door. "We will not open the door tonight, but if you come back in the daylight, we will speak to you. Go away now."

Exhausted, cold, and discouraged, with no idea where we could go to find shelter, my endurance snapped. "If you don't open this door," I threatened, "I'll throw a grenade through your window!" Giovanni gasped, and looked at me in horror. I instantly regretted the threat—not because I wouldn't have done it—but because I knew it would be a stupid move. A grenade would only bring all the police and militia in the area swarming.

A strong male voice responded sharply, "I wouldn't do that if I were you, Signore! If you are who you claim to be, you will be welcomed at daybreak. If you need shelter for the night, go to the shed in the back and sleep there."

I knew we had no choice but to accept their terms. Furious, I turned and Giovanni followed. At the back of the yard we found a small wooden shed. Double doors creaked on rusty hinges as I lifted the wooden door latch. We stepped inside, pulling the ill-fitting doors closed behind us, and peered around, looking for some straw to bed down on. There was none. The bitter wind that whistled in around the door and through the chinks in the wood made it impossible to lie down on the frozen earthen floor. Crouching in the farthest corner, we huddled together. It was like being in a large, empty refrigerator, with a fan blowing on us. For the next five hours, we were two of the most wretchedly miserable human beings on earth. We shook and shivered uncontrollably, teeth chattering, as the minutes and hours to daybreak slowly ticked by. They're going to hear from me in the morning about THIS welcome, I vowed grimly. I'll have a few things to say to them! From time to time, when the cold became unbearable, and we were in danger of falling asleep and freezing to death, we'd jump up and stamp around the shed, blowing on our hands, trying to keep circulation going.

As the night wore on, I turned the events at the door over and over in my mind. I realized that I couldn't blame the Rossis for not opening the door, or letting us in. I had been foolish to mention that I was an American officer and that I wanted Quinto. To have opened the door after that would have been tacit admission of association. What if it had been a trick, and I were Fascist militia? Their fate would have been sealed. They were pretty sharp all right! At no time had anyone on the other side of that door admitted anything—not even that it was the Rossi farm!

Miserable though we were, Giovanni couldn't resist giving me a couple of verbal jabs—" 'This is it? The worst is over?' Hah! If the 'worst' is over—I don't want to see what the best is!"

I couldn't feel my hands and feet anymore. Our bellies growled with hunger. We weren't sure we'd get a welcome, or a meal, in the morning. We weren't even sure we'd live until morning! I knew how Giovanni felt. "This is pure hell, my friend, I know, but we can't give up," I said, encouragingly. "It will be better in the morning. Please, God, just get us through the next few hours!" I prayed.

When the first pale ray of light filtered through the cracks, I was up and shaking Giovanni, who had dozed off. "Up! Let's go!" I urged. "That sonovabitch said daybreak, and it's daybreak, and I'm not waiting another second!" I fumbled with numb fingers for my passport, while Giovanni, yawning, stamping like a horse, dug in his pockets for his identity card. Still stamping, trying to get feeling to return to his feet, he limped to the doors and opened them. Swirling mists of cold, gray dawn swept in. We stood in the doorway and stared up at the farmhouse door. There was no sign of life.

As I started across the yard, the door opened, and a sturdy old man wearing brown pants and sweater, and a wool farmer's cap, stepped out and beckoned to us. "Ah, Signori, scusi, scusi," he called in the quavering voice I recognized from the night before. "My apology! It is so dangerous now! We must be afraid of people who come in the night. Scusi, per favore!" he apologized profusely. As I approached, I held out my passport and began again to explain who we were. "No! No," cried the old man, interrupting, "much too cold our here! Venga! Come inside." He waved aside our documents. "Inside! Not so cold."

There was a roaring fire in the fireplace, and we made a beeline for it, holding our hands out to warm them. It was a large kitchen, even for such a prosperous-looking farmhouse as this. We turned our backs to the fire, to warm our backsides a bit, and the old man began introductions, starting with himself.

"I am Francesco Rossi," he said, with dignity. My heart skipped a beat. So it WAS the Rossi farm! "And this is my wife, Giulia." He then presented his two sons, Gino and Carlo, and their families, and Graziella and Mariana, his two "zitonelle"—his unmarried daughters, and more than a half dozen grandchildren. I understood why the kitchen was so big. There were at least fifteen people, or more, in the Rossi household.

Signora Rossi motioned for us to sit down. "Poveracci! You must be starved!" The kitchen was obviously her domain, and she ruled it smoothly and easily, in a very kindly way, as she directed members of the household to their assigned tasks. "Mariana, per favore, some hot coffee and bread for our guests." Immediately, we were served.

Francesco Rossi, still apologizing for not admitting us during the night, joined us at the table. "I am sorry to have had to put you through such a terrible night, but you must understand—if it was the Fascisti, or the Germans . . . we knew they would not stay the night in the shed!" That was true enough. No human that didn't have to would have opted for that torment! "Now, please tell me what you need me to do to help you, Signori," he said kindly.

I explained who I was and what my mission was. "I need to get in touch with Quinto, either directly, or through Germano, as quickly as possible." When I mentioned the two names, Francesco nodded. "Can that be done?" I asked anxiously.

"Yes, it can be arranged, Signore. I don't know how quickly, but we will try."

I was elated to hear that, but pressed him anyway. "It is very important that it be done soon."

"Yes, Signore, I know. But now you must rest. You are exhausted."

Calling one of his daughters over, he said, "Show our honored guests to a clean bed, so they can sleep."

"Sì, Papa," she replied and bustled off to prepare our sleeping arrangements.

Then he turned to the younger children. "We have important guests who need rest—you will be quiet while they sleep."

"Sì, nonno," they answered respectfully and fell silent.

The two sons, and most of the others, had already eaten and gone. I looked around the cheerful kitchen. Francesco Rossi was not wealthy, but he had managed his resources well and was more comfortable than most farmers. The house was large, and its furnishings were a cut above the norm. The floors were tiled with colorful ceramic tile. The place was very clean, and no flies were in evidence. It was obviously a well-run household.

"Before you go to sleep, Signori," said Francesco, rising, "I will show you our hiding place. The Fascisti sometimes send patrols out for food, and sometimes they come here." He led us into one of the bedrooms, which I assumed was the one we would be using. There was a massive four-poster bed in it. He indicated we were to move the four-poster to one side. The three of us accomplished that, and, slipping one gnarled finger around a bolt-head embedded in the floor, Rossi swung open an ingeniously designed trapdoor. Taking a kerosene lamp from the sideboard, he lit our way down into a large underground hideaway. The area was spotlessly clean, with whitewashed stone walls and a hard-packed dirt floor. It had two simple but comfortable cots against one wall. The other three walls were lined with shelves and storage bins. I looked around me in wonder. There was flour and olive oil. There were large raffia-sheathed flasks of wine. Hanging from the rafters were dried sausages, salamis, and hams. From other rafters hung clusters of dried grapes. Francesco Rossi and his wife were prudent, thrifty farmers. They were also crafty and imaginative.

Back up in the bedroom again, with the trapdoor carefully closed, I eyed the area critically, but its outlines were virtually invisible. "You are clever and resourceful, Signor Rossi. You should be proud of what you have accomplished."

"Grazie, Signore, but this I do not only for me and my family, I do it for the Church. We must always remember to repay God for His goodness to us." I soon discovered that the Rossis were the most Catholic, and the most devoutly religious family I'd ever met, or ever would meet.

Giovanni and I had to share the big bed, but we had something I had almost forgotten existed—privacy. In less time than it takes to say it, we were snuggled under the warm blankets on the bed and sound asleep. I was roused by a soft knocking on the door. Giovanni, deep in slumber, hadn't stirred. I went quickly to the door and opened it a tiny crack. "Yes?" I whispered.

"A man is here to see you, Signore," said Simonetta softly.

I looked at my watch. We had already slept the day away—it was five o'clock in the evening! I quickly tiptoed over to the basin, splashed cold water on my face, rubbed the sleep from my eyes, and raked my fingers through my hair. I noticed that the pain in my shoulder had lessened considerably. A decent sleep in a good bed is probably all I needed, I thought, as I hurried along to the kitchen. A stocky, dark-haired peasant, dressed in rough blue trousers and a coarse-knit maroon sweater, awaited me there.

"Buona sera, Signore," he said, with deep respect, cap in his hands, "Mi chiamo Germano." (my name is Germano). A quiet man, who looked to be in his mid-forties, Germano didn't look much like a resistance fighter, I thought. But then, neither did I.

"I'm very pleased to have found you, Germano," I smiled in greeting, extending my hand for a handshake. I beckoned him into the next room, where there were no eyes or ears around but ours, and said, "Io voglio Quinto" (I want Quinto). I repeated it, for Germano understood only the local dialect. It was the phrase that was supposed to unlock access to Quinto.

"Not possible." Germano stated flatly. My heart sank. "Quinto is not here." All sorts of dire possibilities flashed through my mind. Maybe he's been captured, or killed. Maybe the whole exfiltration program has been stopped. Then Germano spoke again. "Two days maybe, he should be back."

I let out a sigh of relief. "Germano, it is very, very important that I see Quinto as soon as he gets back. It is important to Italy and important to the Allies," I said. Then, for emphasis, "Tell him the American Consul wants to see him." When he heard the words "Il Console," Germano's eyes widened. "Do not worry, I will personally get your message to him, Signor Console," he said, deferentially; "I will say it is most urgent."

"Thank you, Germano," I replied gravely, looking directly at him. "You are doing me a great service."

"Grazie, Signore, but it is nothing," he said. With that, we returned to the kitchen, and he took his leave.

Supper was served promptly at six. The men were seated and served first. That was the custom in many Italian households, especially where several generations were housed under one roof. After a long, sincere grace was said, we were served heaping bowls of hot pasta with garlic and cheese, followed by a delicious rabbit stew, with plenty of bread for sopping up the gravy. Signora Rossi, with her daughters and daughters-in-law, waited on us. After the meal, we retired to another room, to smoke and talk about the war, while the women and children ate their dinner and cleaned up the kitchen. The household operated in perfect harmony, with Signor and Signora Rossi as benevolent rulers of their respective domains—farm and household. No one, from the eldest son to the smallest grandchild, would have dreamed of questioning their wishes or challenging their authority.

I enjoyed my few evening conversations with Francesco Rossi. Although nearing eighty, he had a keen intelligence and wanted to know what I thought Italy's role in the world might be, after the war. He had had little exposure to the outside world, but was current on the news and very interested in America and "Roosabelta." I was deeply impressed with the man's sincerity, with his profound faith, and with the solid values he taught his family. As I fell back into the warm bed that night, I thought deeply about the truly good men in the world. In my experience, men like Francesco Rossi were few and far between. Sadly, they rarely held, or controlled, the levers of power in the world.

The next day, Germano returned. Beckoning me into the next room, he nodded toward his companion. "Ecco Quinto. (this is Quinto)."

Quinto was a dark, solid-looking fellow, about five feet ten inches tall. He was about my age, with nothing special about him in looks or bearing that would command a second glance. It took a bit for me to accept that this was the redoubtable Quinto. Later, I learned to appreciate that part of Quinto's success was that he did not appear different, or special, but there was no question of his toughness and fearlessness as a partisan fighter.

"Could I see your identification papers, please?" he asked me politely.

"Of course." I went to the bedroom to get them. "Quinto's here," I muttered to Giovanni, at his questioning look. He quirked a brow, and gave me a quick, thumbs-up gesture. Quinto examined my passport, and Foster's letter, minutely. I stated and restated my case to him, as emphatically as I could. "Many lives, and many partisans, depend on me getting out of here and back to the Allies quickly—by the first available boat," I finished.

"I understand perfectly, Signore," said Quinto with respect, but noncommittally. "I don't decide who goes out first, but I will do my best to get you there and ask that you get out as quickly as possible. More than that I cannot promise." He gave me a direct look as he spoke.

"I know that, Quinto," I said, "and I'm grateful for any help you can give me. Any help," I emphasized.

"You should know," he said, "that during the dark moon period coming up, the Mas boats will be making more contacts, so your chances of getting out quickly should be pretty good now." At my hopeful look, he continued, "I say this because, one, you have relatively high rank, and, two, you have very good reasons for needing to reach the Allied lines more quickly than the others."

On hearing that, I felt reassured, and I grabbed his hand and shook it warmly. "Thank you Quinto. I'll need all the help I can get. Tell me about this Mas boat evacuation program." He proceeded to fill me in, confirming that it had had its ups and downs during the seven months since the Armistice.

Throughout the fall of 1943, Mas boats, as the Italian motor-torpedo boats were called, were used effectively by the Italians to evacuate a number of Allied personnel from points along the Adriatic coast. However, as winter set in, with its bad weather, some of the boats had been diverted to other military uses. The Mas boat evacuation program had been virtually at a halt since mid-December. "Now, with the coming of spring, more boats are available again, so your chances of getting out are much better than they would have been a month ago," he concluded.

Germano, who had not spoken a word since introducing Quinto, but had paid rapt attention to everything that was said, then jerked his head toward the door.

Quinto immediately turned to me. "Now, I must be going," he said, "but I will be back in a couple of days. Be ready to leave on very short notice."

"Don't worry about that," I assured him, "I have lived that way for over a year now."

"Good," he said, "then you understand how it is. Do you have any more questions, before I go?"

"No," I said.

"Quinto Silenzi, at your service," he said, reaching out to shake my hand. "I'll be back for you very soon. Be ready."

"Grazie, Germano, for bringing him so quickly," I said, shaking Germano's hand sincerely. Then they were gone, Germano leading the way.

At last I had some time to spend with Giovanni. During the week that we had trekked across the mountains together, there had been little opportunity for conversation. We had been too harried, and too exhausted, to give attention to anything besides staying alive and finding food and shelter. At the Rossi's, while I waited for Quinto to come back for me, Giovanni and I had our first chance to talk in a leisurely way, about things beyond our immediate needs. The range of his mind surprised me. For one whose formal education was limited to one or two years of rudimentary schooling, he had managed to acquire, through observation and astute questioning, a sound understanding of dealing in a complex environment and had mastered the art of getting along with people.

Giovanni questioned me about America, a subject that had apparently occupied his thoughts a good deal. "Where is America, exactly?" he asked.

"Pretty much due west of here, Giovanni, about 6,000 kilometers," I replied. "If you left where we are, and headed due west, you'd probably hit New York City."

"Six thousand kilometers! Eh! That's a long way!" He thought for a moment, then asked, "What is there beyond New York?"

I tried to think of a simple way to answer such a broad question. "Well, America is a big land mass, Giovanni, big! From east coast, say New York, to west coast, say San Francisco, about five thousand kilometers of land. Then is another big ocean, the Pacific, even wider than the one between here and New York."

He thought about that. "But then, what is beyond that?" he persisted, childlike.

It dawned on me that here, in the year 1944, four and a half centuries after the days of Magellan and Christopher Columbus, this man was still grappling with the concept of the world as a vast, flat expanse, with an end—a dropping off point—somewhere, rather than as a sphere! Giovanni couldn't read, had probably never seen a globe or a map of the world, and no one had ever talked to him about such esoteric things, so his understanding of the world's physical shape was no different from that of his ancestors, several centuries back! I was astounded. I explained the world, and the universe to him, in very simplistic terms. He quickly grasped it. He listened, mesmerized, drinking it in, soaking up knowledge like a sponge. Educated or not, Giovanni was quite a man. Courageous and loyal to a fault, he was capable of being devious with strangers, but not so with friends.

He had gotten me safely through, and now that I had established contact with Quinto and A Force, his mission was finished, and it was time for him to return to his family. On April 14th, 1944, we said goodbye. Solemnly, he handed me back the Beretta. Alone and unarmed, he could travel easily and without suspicion, a simple countryman caught far from home and family, due to circumstances of war. A weapon on his person would be a death warrant. I offered him some money, but he refused. He was a very proud man and had been my partner on this trip. He was friend, and partner, to Il Console. As he walked from the Rossi farmyard. I vowed that some day, somehow, I would find a way to repay this man the debt I owed him, in a more meaningful way. The next day, a messenger—another peasant farmer—came to tell me I should be ready to move that night.

The close-knit Rossi family had achieved a level of peace and well-being, even in the midst of war, that I deeply envied. I had never, in all my experience, seen anything like it. Nothing in these chaotic times, or in this broken land, I reflected, could vitiate this family's faith, its love and respect for the land, and its ability to live in harmony and hang together. Francesco and Giulia had achieved a higher order of life than most mortals can ever aspire to. I prayed fervently with them on that last afternoon, not only for myself, but for all of Italy and for the Italians. No one, I reflected, and nothing, should have the right to interfere with fundamental goodness like that of the Rossi family. In my room, I carefully packed my knapsack and thought about my own family. I vowed that some of the things I had just seen and learned at the Rossi's would be values I'd instill in my own household, if God allowed me to return safely. I thought warmly of Marguerite and Howard, and of our parents. I was so deep in my thoughts, the soft knock on the door startled me. Isa, the little eight-year-old granddaughter, had come to escort me to dinner.

"Look, look!" she cried, clapping her hands delightedly, laughing up at me. "It's a party!" And what a party it was! The table groaned under its load of meats, pasta dishes, all kinds of vegetables, and, of course, desserts. We stood in the kitchen, heads bowed, as Francesco quoted scripture and asked a blessing on me and everyone there. Then we all sat down, men and women and children together. We were at the table, eating, for more than two solid hours. Each adult proposed a toast to me and to my success. When it was all over, I felt I needed and wanted to succeed in my mission as much for the Rossi family, and their faith in me, as for my comrades of the San Faustini. Shortly after eight that evening, Germano and another partisan arrived, and I took my reluctant leave of the Rossi family. Tears flowed on all sides as we said goodbye. I realized that in that very short time, I had come to care deeply for them.

Germano was armed to the teeth, with a Sten gun in hand, and a bandoleer and several grenades slung around his neck. He led the way, and his buddy, also armed with a Sten gun, guarded my back. Within a couple of hours we had reached a location from which, Germano said, we could get to the Adriatic fairly quickly—within no more than an hour. The hills bordering the Tenna River valley area, like those in most of central Italy, are like a tangled nest of serpents, slithering down to drink from the Adriatic Sea. Their descent is so steep, they bite deeply into the soft sand of the beach, to keep from falling headlong into the surf. The coastal highway and coastal railroad line have been hacked out of those stone jaws clamped down on the very shoreline. Here and there, a few hardy rivers manage to bend and turn and wiggle their way through the maze. Dotting their banks are tiny towns and fishing villages, clinging to the rocks like lichen. It is where the Tenna River meets the Adriatic that I would be making my attempt to escape by Mas torpedo boat, explained Germano, as we struggled along.

Suddenly, he stopped and pointed to a dilapidated farmhouse. 'That is where you will stay tonight. There are other Allied military there, also waiting to be evacuated." From the outside, it was no different from any of the hundreds of farmhouses I had frequented since joining the partisans, possibly a little more rundown than most, and certainly several cuts below the Rossi farm. Although the interior was as drab and colorless as I expected it to be, what was waiting there was not. The atmosphere was decidedly different—startlingly so, for one who had lived almost exclusively in the company of Italians for so many months. Crammed into the main room of the farmhouse were half a dozen or more British officers, some of them very high ranking, and one American flyer. As I greeted each one, the others looked me over, frankly staring, and whispered comments to one another. The first to greet me was Brigadier E. W. D. Vaughn, the nominal leader of this coterie. He was a big, imposing figure, who radiated confidence and command. His was the epitome of the build, bearing, and look that most men only dream of achieving. His clear hazel eyes swept over me, his well-trimmed mustache twitching slightly at the sight of my scraggly, unkempt beard, and the smell that no amount of washing in cold water could eliminate.

I shook his hand. "Good to see you," I said, politely.

"Same here, I'm sure," he responded, in clipped tones. "You'll want to meet Brigadiers Combe and Todhunter here," he said, maintaining the strict order of rank and precedence as he handed me off to Generals J.F.B. Combe, D.S.O., and E. J. Todhunter. Both were of average height and build. Combe was a carrot top, his pale, guileless face liberally sprinkled with freckles, while Todhunter was darker, with gray eyes, and a narrow, sharp-featured countenance. They greeted me, and in their turn presented Captains J. G. Kerine and G. E. Ruggles-Brise. Kerine's hair was almost a golden wheat color, and he had the patrician look that comes from a background of nannies and governesses, private schools, and the right clubs. Tall and lean, he at first seemed quiet—almost shy—but as I got to know him better, I found that when he did speak, it was with an air of assurance that inspired confidence.

Ruggles-Brise was about thirty years old, the shortest in stature of the bunch, but the most cheerful and outspoken. He had the kind of squat, heavy-set body that runs to softness and paunch in the middle years, and his ruddy, clean-shaven face was capped with a thatch of thick, straight brown hair. "How d'ye do?" he said, with a grin, his pale blue eyes gleaming with mischief. He held out a square, stubby-fingered hand. "Welcome to the boys' club! Bloody boring lot, we are, but we'll have to do."

They were all so in character, I felt like I had walked into the middle of an English movie. Ruggles-Brise, in his turn, presented a young lieutenant who out-titled them all—Lieutenant the Earl of Ranfurly. A wiry, sandy-haired man of about my own age and height, his Lordship greeted me with a quick smile and a firm handshake. "Hullo, Orebaugh," he said, "Glad to have you join us." He had a pleasing voice, and his accent was more cultured than most I had heard. My beard and unkempt appearance did not seem to bother him, though he was meticulously clean-shaven himself, and his clothes were barely rumpled.

All of them were in mufti, sporting an assortment of garb—probably whatever they had been able to scavenge since being turned loose to wander on their own. However, with the possible exception of Ruggles-Brise, they all managed to look as though they were still in full military uniform. "Where were you captured?" Ranfurly asked me.

"Monte Carlo, in late 1942," I replied.

His eyebrows rose. "Monte Carlo! You mean . . . ? You can't be serious," he said, as I nodded yes, "I should like to hear THAT story!"

"I'm sure you'll get plenty of opportunity to hear it," I laughed. "It's quite a story. Where were YOU picked up? Shot down?"

"No," he said, "they got most of us in the North African Campaign. Brought us back here, and then when the Armistice was signed, they just turned us loose. Same with you?"

"Not quite," I answered. "But that's another story. I've been fighting with the partisans in Umbria." Up went the eyebrows again, and he looked intrigued.

At that point, the young American interrupted. "Hey Ranfurly, enough bull! I can't wait any longer to talk to another Yankee!" he exclaimed, clapping me on the back.

"Same here!" I said happily, shaking his hand. "Walter Orebaugh, Wichita, Kansas—State Department."

"Jack Rieter, Chicago, Army Air Corps, Lieutenant," he said crisply, mimicking my shorthand method of introduction. "Good to see you, Walt! It'll be great having another American around to defend the boorish ways of the colonists! These English blokes are still convinced we Yanks are untutored savages." We all laughed.

Excusing myself to the Earl of Ranfurly, I drew Rieter aside for some private conversation. "Tell me," I began, "how long have you been waiting here?" Before he could reply, two Italians in khaki uniforms arrived and announced we'd be moving out immediately. My hopes rose. All conversation ceased, as we scrambled for our gear and headed for the door. "Who are they?" I managed to ask Rieter, amid the hubbub.

"A Force, Bari Command," he replied, as we shouldered our packs and followed them out. "They're in charge of the exfiltration operations in this area. They're very sharp, and VERY well-trained, from what I've seen."

With the Italians leading the way, we worked our way down toward the Adriatic. It was shortly after three A.M. when they stopped at a remote farmhouse. "You'll stay here for now," said the senior of the two Italians, in fairly good English. "Figure a way to sleep. There are many of you, little room." An understatement. The family was already asleep in the one bedroom, so we tried to find places to bed down on the floor of the kitchen. The fire had been banked to embers. We pushed the table against one wall, and Ranfurly and Rieter promptly set up under it. Being the newest arrival, with the others already paired off by rank, I ended up close to the hearth, sharing a pallet with Brigadier Vaughn. It was warmer there, but if I slept at all, it was no thanks to the Brigadier, whose stentorian snoring outshone even Amy's.

The next evening I was in a foul mood, and not happy to find we had to move again. This time, we went back up the river a short distance. Our destination was a charming, whitewashed, well-to-do country villa, whose bougainvillea-draped marble terraces were shaded by a wide terra cotta tile roof. Two more officers had joined us, bringing our number to ten—a sizable number of "house guests," even for such a large villa.

At the soft call of our guide, the front door was thrown open, and we were greeted, in English, by a tall, very striking woman, who looked to be in her early sixties. "I am Helen Salvadori," she said, giving me a brilliant smile. "Welcome to our home." Her graying blonde hair was swept up and pinned to the top of her head. She was an imposing figure, in a modish lavender wool dress, accented with a single strand of pearls. A large sapphire, its color the clear deep blue of the ocean, with a wave of sparkling white diamonds cresting over it, adorned the carefully manicured hand she held out. Two other women, younger but as stylishly dressed and coiffed as our hostess, directed us to a cheerful, sunny dining room. We seated ourselves at the long table, whose dark wood gleamed with the patina of years of polishing. It was centered with a silver urn filled with fresh flowers. "First, some warm breakfast, then off to bed with the lot of you," ordered Signora Salvadori, coming into the room.

Breakfast was a marvel in itself. Copious amounts of food were presented in charming, well-appointed surroundings, and the conversation at table was conducted entirely in English! Professor Salvadori, the elderly "padrone" of the villa, was a highly regarded writer and teacher, well-known in intellectual and academic circles in Italy. I had heard of him while stationed in Trieste. He had earned quite an international reputation for his acerbic criticisms of Fascism. The Salvadoris, we learned, were virtually marooned in their villa because of restrictions placed on them by the Fascist government. It was dangerous for them to help us. Nevertheless, they were determined to help the Allied cause in every way possible. They had given the Cingoli Band free access to their villa. Situated on a hill overlooking the river, with clear views to all roads and paths around, it was particularly well-suited for use as a way station.

After breakfast, the daughter, Amelia Salvadori, showed us to our bedrooms. I was billeted with Ranfurly, and when we got to our room, we found to our amazement that not only did we each have our own bed, but they were made up with fresh linens! We didn't spend any time in small talk, but fell into the beds and were almost instantly asleep. That evening, after a solid sleep and a most welcome hot bath, we gathered in the parlor for a glass of sherry before dinner. I sat on the couch and chatted with Helen Salvadori. "I am pleased to be here, Signora," I said, "but concerned about you taking this chance, and endangering yourselves to harbor fugitives like us. Aren't you afraid of what will happen to you if you're caught?"

"Oh, piffle!" she replied. "The local Facists are afraid of my husband. They don't want to enhance his reputation for verbally hitting the mark on them, so they leave us pretty much alone and don't pay attention to what we do."

Just at that moment, our attention was distracted by the man in question. Someone must have made a comment that set Signor Salvadori off, because he was venting his spleen against the Facists, the Germans, and the Allies alike. Although in his late seventies, the professor had not lost his talent for the well-placed barb, and the British were now his hapless target. "Tell me, is there something in British genes that adversely affects the eyesight?" he inquired archly, surveying the circle of British officers. He fixed his piercing brown eyes on Brigadier Todhunter. "Well?" he challenged.

"Not that I know of," replied Todhunter warily, his curiosity piqued, "why?"

The professor had his opening. "Why? Hah! Your futile attempts at knocking out the few paltry bridges, and the coastal road, all completely unsuccessful, have become monotonous! What a bore! Even with the whole area lit up like daylight with those infernal Bengal flares of yours, you've not been able to score a single hit! You must all be half blind! You British couldn't find a volcano if it erupted up your noses!" The professor cackled, enjoying his barb.

The Britishers had gone red in the face. "Now see here . . ." sputtered Brigadier Vaughn angrily, leaning forward in his chair.

"That's what I'm saying," interjected the old man. "Your English pilots CAN'T 'see here!' That's the whole problem!" Everyone roared with laughter at that, and Vaughn subsided good-naturedly. However, later that night I wasn't so sure the professor's taunts hadn't somehow reached the ears of the Royal Air Force. I was thrown from my bed when an errant bomb from a British bomber, undoubtedly intended for the Tenna River railroad bridge, landed almost on top of the villa.

The next morning, I finally met the A Force agent in charge of evacuation arrangements, Lieutenant Cagnazzi. A South African of part-Sicilian parentage, "Cag," as everyone called him, was a lean, dark-haired, wiry bundle of energy and a crack intelligence agent. His specialty was behind-the-enemy-lines activity. He was a man of action, a doer, and would not let go of anything until he got results. I took an immediate liking to him, as did almost everyone who met him. He had been dropped off, along with another agent, near the port of San Giorgio a few weeks earlier, and had promptly established an incredible communications network, with the help of the partisan bands. "My main mission," he said, "is getting the top brass among the Allied evaders, like you, out of here—quickly and safely."

"I'm glad to know that, Cag." Briefly, I outlined my situation, and my mission, to him.

"I'll do my best for you, Signor Console," he said. Cag was responsible for much more than just getting us out. He was also involved in getting weapons and supplies to the resistance movements operating in the area. "I knew you were on your way," he said, grinning, his even white teeth flashing in his swarthy face, "before you even met Germano." At my surprised look he added, "I have a pretty good communications network set up with the partisans."

"So that's why Quinto showed up so quickly after I contacted Germano!" I said.

"Yes. Germano didn't know that we were waiting for you to make contact. I had heard about you from the Cingoli partisans who detained you overnight. Had they gotten word to me before you left them, I'd have made contact with you there."

"Then you also know that a lot of lives depend on me getting through to the Allies as quickly as possible," I said.

"Yes, sir. And I want to tell you that I am honored to meet you, and appreciate all you have done for the partigiani and to help the Allied cause. But tell me—I'm curious about how you found out about Quinto, up there in the middle of nowhere in Umbria. Has our communications network extended that far?"

I wasn't sure how much to tell Cag, because above all, I didn't want Manfred's name mentioned. I thought for a moment, then said, "Well, it was very strange. Someone sent me a letter that told me how to contact Quinto."

"A letter?" He was instantly alert. "Who sent you a letter?"

"It was signed by a Mr. Foster," I said; "I don't remember ever meeting him, but he claimed in the letter that he had met me several years ago, in Trieste, when I was with the U.S. Consulate there."

"Oh. Yes, I know Foster," Cag nodded, visibly relieved. Now it was my turn to be surprised! "I saw him just a couple of weeks ago, in Cagli."

"You did!" My heart began a trip-hammer rhythm. I tried to stay calm. "How old is Foster?" I asked. "What does he look like? What does he do? I have absolutely no recollection of the man." I wanted to see if the description Cag gave me fit Manfred, or anyone I knew.

"He's an older man, balding, kind of strange. Tall, very skinny. Always complaining." Cag grimaced, his dislike of the man obvious. The person he had just described was definitely not Manfred Metzger. I felt a twinge of disappointment. Nor did Foster sound like anyone either Manfred or I might have known. Manfred had absolutely no patience with complainers. My curiosity was really piqued.

"What's this Foster person, whoever he is, doing in Cagli? His letter sounded like he's a borderline nut case."

"He was a manager for Shell Oil. Got detained when the war broke out and has had all kinds of problems since. He's a big whiner, and he wants us to get him out," said Cag, "but there are others who are higher on our priority list than Foster—like you and the Brigadiers. Foster's not in any real danger so far, and we'll get to him before long."

I expressed my concern about the contact information written in the letter and about Foster being a potentially dangerous security leak. "Somebody better muzzle him before he blows your cover, and gets Quinto and Germano killed," I warned.

"Don't worry, Signore, we'll take care of that little matter immediately. Foster won't write any more letters, I assure you. None that we don't see, anyway," Cag replied grimly. Before I could respond to that, he was up and striding away. So the mystery of Foster's identity was finally solved! I think I was disappointed to find that he wasn't my friend Manfred in disguise. In any case, I was grateful to Foster for putting me on to this connection, even though his intention in doing so was directed toward his own interests, not mine. At the same time, I was angry that he had so thoughtlessly risked the security of several A Force agents and a lot of high-ranking Allied officers.

I was champing at the bit to get on with my mission, and therefore I was not an easy person to be around. I had ceased being a reserved, polite diplomat many months ago. I was not an "officer and a gentleman." I was a partisan—a guerrilla fighter, not accustomed to lolling around at a villa, doing nothing, exchanging polite chit-chat. The British officers, especially the Brigadier, chided me for my impatience. For my part, I couldn't understand their complacent acceptance of delays and "red tape." I was not just waiting around to be repatriated, I had a job to do, a mission in which time was extremely critical. With every day's delay, the Band of San Faustino was more exposed, its activities further curtailed. I wanted to assure their safety and well-being and the Band's continued operation. Of course I was impatient!

The afternoon of April 18th, Cag called us together. "We are coming into a 'no moon' phase on the calendar," he said. "This is the safest time to try to get you out. Three consecutive nights have been set up by A Force headquarters, and the first try will be tonight." A murmur of surprise and excitement flew around the room. All discussion stopped when Cag started speaking again. You could have heard a pin drop. "Be ready to leave as soon as darkness falls. By then, we'll have gotten intelligence reports on German and Fascist patrols and convoys in the area, and we can proceed by routes where we'll have less risk of unwanted encounters." He briefed us on alternate routes, rendezvous points, hideouts, and signals. Every man was to memorize the recognition signals—a pattern of flashing lights—in case called upon to be a signaler. "I'm sure you all understand that during the hours you are out tonight, you will be at considerable risk. Stay close together, and follow your escort's instructions to the letter."

I immediately went to my room and started putting my gear in order for departure. By nine that evening, I was more than ready. Quinto was our point man, and I was glad to see him again and to have him in charge. We moved out in the darkness, following the course of the Tenna River, heading for the coastal highway. In single file, we made our way laboriously across country, walking up and down and around the twisting hills, dropping to the ground instantly at a hand signal or a whispered command. It was slow, tedious going, and it took more than an hour to cover two or three kilometers. Several of us had our own weapons, and Quinto and the other partisan with us were armed with Sten guns, but given the large number of enemy troops in the area, it was little protection. Finally, we reached the steep embankment just above the highway and the railroad line that ran along beside the beach. Carefully, we slithered down, and then, like a herd of clumsy deer, we bounded across the highway and the tracks, leaping into the protection of the deep brush a few feet below the railroad bed—in a narrow strip between the rail line and the beach. At that point, only a couple of hundred yards separated the railroad from the beach.

Crouching low in the tangled scrub, we worked our way toward the water. When I reached the edge of the brush, I was taken aback. I had not expected the beach to be so wide! Getting across it without being seen would be difficult enough. Boarding a boat undetected, fully exposed like that, even more so. I checked my watch—it was close to midnight. A cutting, icy wind was blowing in off the water, and we hunkered down as best as we could to ward it off. Peering into the gloom for signs of a boat, our ears strained to pick up any stray sound. Quinto and his fellow partisan guarded us to the north and south, and two of our men, armed, were stationed as rear lookouts, watching for any activity from the direction of the tracks and highway. After what seemed an eternity, we heard a low, throbbing rumble from out at sea. No one dared speak, or even breathe.

Quinto advanced stealthily toward the water and began flashing the signal toward the sound. Eyes aching with the effort not to blink, for fear we'd miss something, we watched for a return signal from the Mas boat. Seconds ticked by. No lights or recognition signals came from the sea, though the engine noise increased, indicating the boat was coming in closer to shore. We waited, hopes high. Then, incredibly, the sound of the engines began moving away, and slowly faded in the distance. There was no sound except that of the waves—the steady, rhythmic swoosh and slap of their unending assault on the shore.

We were stunned. For some unknown reason, the Mas boat had decided not to come in for the pickup. Quinto gave us the signal to pull out, and slowly we worked our way back up to the railway line, clambered and struggled back up the steep embankment above the tracks and highway, and retraced our tortuous route in the dark, stopping only when we reached the prearranged rendezvous point. "You can smoke now, if you like," whispered Quinto, in an attempt to boost our morale. Dejectedly, shielding the light of the flame with cupped hands, we lit up, and sat silently smoking.

A voice, barely above a whisper, suddenly broke the deep silence. It sounded like Ruggles-Brise. "Well, dammit all to hell!" he swore. "Just plain dammit!"

Another voice rssponded with a terse, clipped "Right-O!" That about summed it up. The disappointment in the air was almost palpable.

We arrived back at the villa just before first light. Within minutes, Helen Salvadori was up and in the kitchen, brewing pots of tea, and making toast. "Have to take the chill off my boys," she said, cheerily. She seemed almost happy to have us back. "Nine o'clock tonight again. Be ready," announced Quinto. After gulping a quick cup of tea and swallowing some toast, with a "Grazie, Signora," he and his buddy slipped noiselessly out. Exhausted from physical exertion and disappointment, we all tumbled into our beds and were quickly asleep. No one cared to conduct a post mortem.

The next night was a replica of the first. This time, the Mas boat remained even farther out before deciding to leave without attempting the pickup. We couldn't believe it! In frustration and fury, some of the men wondered aloud about the ability of the Italian crews. Some of us, though, agreed with the thought expressed by Ranfurly. "It's no cakewalk to navigate one's way into a specific point, with no lights and no moon," he said. Another added the observation that "the Mas boat may have been warned off by radio." Others, less charitable, gave vent to their feelings with profanity, attributing the failure to nothing more than "sheer cowardice" on the part of the Mas boat crews.

Frustrated, I forced myself to remain optimistic. I felt sure the third night would be the charm. It would be the lucky night when everything would go right for us. When darkness fell that third night, not only was there no moon, there were no stars either. "That's a good omen," I commented to Ranfurly, as we prepared to leave. Clouds had drifted in during the afternoon, and the moon and stars slumbered beneath a thick quilt of gray wool, so dense it allowed no light to show through. Finding our way was extremely difficult, and we tripped and stumbled again and again in the pitch black. Once more we reached the beach at midnight. Some time around one-thirty, we heard the Mas boat. This time it was closer in. We flashed our signals, and the engines grew louder. Even though they were throttled back, their roar seemed to fill the night. We couldn't see the boat itself yet, but it had to be almost on top of us. It was definitely coming in! This is it, this time we're going to go, I thought exultantly.

Vaughn signaled us to move out across the beach, to the edge of the water, so we'd be ready to board quickly. We left the cover of the brush and started across the expanse of sand. I was at the north end of the group, in back, when out of the corner of my eye, I caught a quick flash from the direction of the railroad bridge. Quinto's partisan buddy, Angelo, who was standing only a few feet from me, suddenly had no nose. Then the rifle crack reached us. Screaming, he reached up to his face, then fell to the ground, and I did the same. I scuttled on all fours, crab-like, toward the others. More shots rang out from the bridge to the north of us. "Abort!" called Vaughn, as we broke for the bushes. "We've been spotted! Clear out! To the rendezvous, quickly!" There was no chance of getting to the boat. We heard its engines rev to full throttle as it turned and roared away. Zigzagging across the sand, I chanced a quick glance back and saw the gleaming phosphorescent curve of its wake break the inky darkness.

The shooting, still directed at the beach, continued as we silently worked our way back and across the railroad and highway, clambering up the embankment into safer territory. I figured it was probably coming from a German work party who had heard the boat and maybe saw our shadowy figures on the beach. It seemed to be limited to the one railroad bridge. I prayed there were no other patrols out in the area. When we finally re-grouped, we were out of breath. We had come so close! Quinto, who had grabbed up Angelo as we left the beach, dragging and forcing him along, had already disappeared, taking him for medical help. I couldn't believe we were back here. Just one minute, one more minute, and we'd have been on that boat and on our way back to Allied lines! Dammit all! So near, and yet so far. Our spirits were sagging, and my own morale fell to its lowest ebb. I'll never get out of here, I thought despairingly. The war will be over, and I'll still be wandering around these hellish hills all night! It was four o'clock in the morning by the time we dragged ourselves up the path to the villa again. No one was up. Silently, stealthily, so as not to wake the family, we groped our way along, in the dark, to our beds. None of us felt up to Signora Salvadori's cheerful ministrations, no matter how well-intended.

Cag arrived early the next day. "Sorry about last night," he said, clapping each of us on the shoulder. He brought us the welcome news that Angelo would be all right. He had lost a lot of blood, and the wound was grossly disfiguring, but not as serious as we had originally feared. "He is lucky it was his nose and not his brains," said Cag, with a philosophical shrug. "He can live with a stub of a nose. It could have been far worse. You were ALL lucky." We knew he was right, though we were still feeling frustrated about missing our big chance. "Do not despair, Signori," he said. "We'll try again on the twenty-third." We brightened somewhat at hearing that. The twenty-third was only three days away. "This time, though, we'll move to a different area of the beach for the pickup. The new pickup point will be on the beach north of the mouth of the river." He went on to give us new recognition signals and rendezvous points. Then he drew out a map, marked with the location of a dozen or more "safe" farmhouses within a five-mile radius. "If this next attempt fails, do not return to the villa here," he said. At our startled looks, he added, "it is too risky to keep all of you in one place for very long. We will split you up and billet you in pairs, or in fours, from now on. In one group, you make too lucrative a catch for the enemy. We'll still try to get you all out at the same time, but while you're waiting, we prefer that you be split up." I fully agreed with his reasoning. A group of ten, billeted together, was too easy to capture and too difficult to conceal for long periods of time. Three British Brigadiers, a member of the British House of Lords, an American Consul, along with four other Allied officers and one American flyer would make a nice haul for the enemy!

On the night of the twenty-third, with German patrols in the area, we had to backtrack and take a different route. We reached the beach later than planned, and I was sure we had completely missed the Mas boat. However, we had only been on the beach a short while, when out of the black came the chug-chug of a boat engine. Our spirits soared. Maybe we hadn't missed it after all! Quinto wasn't with us that night, and Gino, our man on the beach, was sending the signals. Flashes came back almost immediately, in the exact pattern of the signals being sent. That was not the pattern I thought we should expect to see. I began to feel misgivings, but no one else appeared concerned. The thump-thump of the boat's engines grew louder—it was coming in! Brigadier Vaughn once more ordered us down to the edge of the water, and we scampered across the sand and drew up with the waves licking at our boot tops. The night was not as dark as previous ones had been, and as the boat came nearer, Aldo, peering into the gloom, was able to make out the shape of the craft heading for us. "Hell!" came his sudden exclamation. "That's no Mas boat! That's a damned German boat!"

We turned and were all running pell-mell for the brush when the beam of the boat's searchlight swept the beach, brilliantly illuminating the exact spot where, only seconds before, we had been gathered! Gaining the safety of the brush, we dropped on our bellies, flattening ourselves down in it and slithering frantically away from the shoreline, praying we could make it out of range of the relentless searchlight. The light swept the beach three or four more times, then, finding nothing, flicked off. We waited, not moving a muscle. Finally, we heard the boat turn, its engine roar, and away it went. Silence reigned. I let my breath out in a whoosh, and once again Vaughn gave the all-too-familiar signal to retreat to the rendezvous point. This time, we ran almost all the way. Reaching its relative safety, in a thick copse of trees, we flopped down like a school of beached fish, audibly gasping for air.

Eventually, out of the dark came the voice of the irrepressible Ruggles-Brise. "Well, feather my britches! Nothing like signaling the bloody Jerry in for tea!"

"Hey, old boy," replied Todhunter. "Don't complain! At least we got the chance to find out the difference between an Italian Mas boat and a bloody German coastal freighter, and lived to tell about it, thanks to Captain Aldo's sharp eyes!"

There were weary grunts of assent. "Yeah, we sure were lucky that time," said Reiter. "If it weren't for Aldo, we'd all be lying back there on that beach, full of German machine gun bullets!" How close we had come to that fate was a sobering thought. It was early daylight by the time we reached the first of the safe farmhouses, where we began splitting up to go our separate ways. Now, we'd have to just sit tight and stay alert, waiting for Cag to notify us of a new pickup date.

Two nights later, Jack Reiter and I were awakened by the sound of a German motor patrol passing by, on the road not far from the farmhouse where we were staying. We got up and went to the window to watch it, returning to our beds only when we were sure it wasn't stopping. Vaughn and his three billet-mates were not as lucky—the patrol had decided to stop at their farm for directions, and they had to take to the bush to keep from being captured. Vaughn then decided we should move further inland, away from the mouth of the river, where there would be fewer patrols. We shifted about six kilometers further upriver. We had no more than made the trek to our new locations when a messenger from Cag arrived to inform us that there would be another sortie to the beach that very night!

We all groaned aloud on hearing that, and even the athletic Vaughn grimaced at the thought of the long walk ahead of us. Quinto arrived to escort us, along with another A Force agent I'd never seen, who introduced himself simply as Mario. As usual, we set out at about ten. As we neared the railroad and highway bridges close to the mouth of the river, we learned there were other dangers besides the Fascists and the Germans. This time it was our own—the British bombers, erstwhile subjects of Professor Salvadori's scathing ire. We heard the drone of their engines coming up the coast, no doubt bent on one of their attempts to knock out the Tenna railroad bridge and disrupt the rail lines. We were sitting duck—smack in the middle of their target area! We hit the ground, diving for whatever cover the intermittent clumps of bushes could afford us, as the three planes made a low pass directly over our heads.

"Jaysus!" I heard someone yell, "We'll go out bashed by our own blokes!"

"Shut up!" growled another. "Stay down, and say yer bloody prayers!"

Suddenly, we were thrust into the limelight, as Bengal flares, dropped by one of the planes, lit the landscape in an eerie, lime-colored glare. All thoughts except survival fled as the deafening concussions of bombs falling all around us filled our world. I felt my body being plucked into the air by unseen fingers, then I was slammed unceremoniously back down again, and I thought my eardrums had burst. Finally, all fell silent. The planes had gone. Slowly, painfully, I got up, and checked myself over to see if anything was broken or missing. There was a terrible ringing in my ears, and I was bruised and shaken and felt like I was still encased in a giant hollow steel drum, but I had no serious injuries. I was grateful to be alive. Bit by bit, one after the other, everyone reported in safely. Miraculously, no one was injured except for minor cuts and bruises. We looked around us, to assess what damage the bombs had done. Professor Salvadori would have had a field day. The bombers had missed their target completely, and by a considerable margin, too. "Bloody arses!" grumbled Ruggles-Brise. Not only had they done the enemy no harm, their clumsy attempt had caused us to miss our chance at escape! At that moment, no one among us, even their own countrymen, had a kind thought for the Royal Air Force!

As we trudged the long, weary distance back to the farmhouses, I remarked to no one in particular, "Well, I don't see why the Allies don't just send some explosives and some sappers up to the Cingoli Band by Mas boat, and let THEM knock out the bridges, instead of all this stupid hit-or-miss bombing they're doing!"

"You know, Orebaugh, that's not such a bad thought," said Rieter. "It would be a lot easier and cheaper, and probably the only way those damned bridges will ever be hit, from the looks of it!"

We all laughed in rueful agreement. "Hell, yes," Ruggles-Brise chimed in. "Cag and Quinto could handle a job like that in ten minutes. Maybe five. Those blokes up there can't find their own arses. Let's tell 'em that when we get down there, what?"

"Right-O!" snapped Brigadier Vaughn vehemently, surprising us. I could tell from his tone that there would be hell to pay for this when he saw the British commanders! He was royally pissed off at having missed this rendezvous, not to mention almost being killed by his own Air Force. That was bad enough, but understandable—such were the risks of war. However, to have had to witness such a poor show, confirming the professor's acerbic comments, really stuck in Vaughn's craw.

The moon had moved into its waxing phase, glowing brighter each night, and with its increasing light, our chances of getting off the beach grew correspondingly dimmer. The others were not gripped by my sense of urgency, but neither were they anxious to stay in danger one moment longer than absolutely necessary. No one was happy about sitting around, risking discovery, waiting for the next moonless phase. Reiter, Lord Ranfurly, and I, billeted together, had been doing a lot of thinking about our situation. To reach the beach on the north side of the mouth of the river, we had to pass through the tiny fishing village of Marina Faleriense. As I recalled, there had been several good-sized fishing boats pulled up on the beach, unused now that the Germans had banned all commercial fishing in the Adriatic north of the battle lines. "Why don't we try to buy one of the boats and use it for our escape?" I asked them. "I have money I'd be willing to put up for that."

"Hey, that's not a bad idea!" said Jack enthusiastically.

"Yes," agreed Ranfurly. "It sounds good, but how could we do it? We can't just go strolling up to them in broad daylight and ask to buy one of their boats."

"Yeah, I've heard those fishermen are a pretty mean and surly bunch, too," said Rieter. "Even though they're furious about the Germans cutting off their livelihood, I'm not sure we can trust them. Or that they'd sell."

"Well," said Ranfurly, with his usual practicality, "they probably hate the Jerries for taking away their livelihood. They must need money, and the boats aren't bringing them any income just lying around. Let's get Brigadier Vaughn to talk to Cag about it. Maybe A Force can do something."

Pleased that they both thought the idea was a feasible one, I said, "Let's go over to meet with Vaughn tonight, right after dark."

"Orebaugh the Impatient," teased Rieter, good-naturedly. "Sure, why not?"

We went to see Vaughn and outlined our idea. He thought it was a good one, too, and agreed to send for Cag for a meeting. Cag was interested. "You may be right," he said. "It's a possibility that we hadn't thought of. It might not be as chancey as the Mas boat. Let me explore it a bit."

Three days later, Vaughn came by to tell us he had received word that Cag had managed to negotiate the purchase of an old, twenty-four-foot wooden fishing boat, with a sail but no motor. A Force had agreed to pay for it. We were overjoyed! "Don't get your hopes up all that high yet, Orebaugh," cautioned Ruggles-Brise. "Cag says the bloody thing's a stinking mess and will take bloody what-all to make her seaworthy." That night, Rieter, Ranfurly, and I sneaked down to take a look. Cag was absolutely right—she was a mess. What a scow! It would take one helluva lot of patching just to get her to float. Beached for months, the sun and wind had taken their harsh toll, and had rotted her sails, beams and ropes. Her wooden hull had dried out, leaving wide gaps in the seams. Discouraged, we knew we had to do whatever it took to make her seaworthy again, because right now, she was our only hope for getting out. We were glad when we heard that Cag had hired two villagers to work on patching the boat at night.

About a week later, on May 2nd, Cag sent word that we had one more chance that night for a Mas boat connection. I had met Quinto in Grottazzolina on April 12th and thought then that I'd be on a Mas boat, headed for Allied lines, within a week. Now here it was May, and I was still cooling my heels, with no idea when I'd get out—if ever! We decided to go for it. We couldn't afford to pass up any chance, even though I winced at the thought of another long walk that might end in a blank. My feet had become a permanent mass of bloody, purple bruises. Pain knifed through my right shoulder whenever I moved my arm. Carrying the knapsack was agony. Once more we made our way to the beach and crouched in the brush, ears straining for the sound of a Mas boat engine, eyes trained on the unrelieved black of the shoreline, willing a boat to appear out of the gloom. Moonrise would come very late that night, so there was a good chance we could get away while the beach was still in blackness, if all went well. But this time, too, we were destined to draw a blank. We waited a full two hours past the designated pickup time, but no Mas boat appeared.

Finally, we gave up. Returning to out shelters, I drew the Earl of Ranfurly for my billet-mate. We peeled off from the rest of the group when we reached the farmhouse assigned to us. Our sleeping arrangements—the sheep stall—were a bit rougher than usual, and we exchanged a few joking remarks as we pushed and prodded the sleeping animals to clear a comfortable place to sleep. At least this stall, I noted, was a lot cleaner than some of the places I'd been forced to sleep in, and the sheep would help to keep off the chill. Unlike American farmers, the Italians never left their livestock out in the fields at night. They rarely had large herds of cows or sheep and always brought the animals in to stable them for the night. "Well, it ain't Buckingham Place, but it'll do," joked the Earl of Ranfurly, affecting a cockney accent. Pillowing his head on a clump of straw, he promptly dropped into deep sleep. I was not long in doing the same. We slept so soundly that the first passes of the British bombers failed to rouse us.

However, when the antiaircraft batteries at Porto San Giorgio opened up, and the hail of bombs dropping near the bridges began exploding, we were jolted from sleep. We quickly scrambled out and into the open field, momentarily dazed by the daylight. The bombers were making another pass at the target, coming in at low altitude, right above us. We looked up, shading our eyes against the dazzling early morning sunlight. Two planes came zooming in, making a run toward the bridges. As we watched, two round, dark objects, trailing smoke, detached from one of them and came tumbling down at us. We dived behind a nearby hedgerow and cowered there, arms over our heads, awaiting the horrendous explosion. We heard two almost simultaneous thuds as they hit the soft, newly plowed ground of the adjacent field. We cringed, but no explosion followed. Must be unarmed, or duds, I thought. Relieved, we got up, brushed ourselves off, and walked the few steps up to the farmhouse. The contadina welcomed us. She was a young woman, with a cherubic, curly headed little girl of about two toddling around the kitchen behind her. We were glad to have chairs to sit on, and a breakfast of bread and ersatz coffee. We were enjoying our meal, engaged in idle conversation with the woman, with me acting as translator for the Earl, when another little girl of about six came running into the yard from the adjacent field, screaming, "Tedeschi! Mamma, tedeschi!" (Germans! Mamma, Germans!) I jumped up and raced to the window. Four German soldiers were driving into the yard. The woman and I exchanged a terrified glance. It was too late to leave—we'd be seen. She pointed. The bedroom was our only hope! I pulled Ranfurly with me into the next room. Frantically, we shoved the big bed out from the wall a few inches and dropped down there, between the bed and the wall, concealed by the bedclothes. We heard the woman scoop up our dishes and mugs and drop them in a bucket, then the knock on the door and the scrape of chairs as the Germans seated themselves in the kitchen. We resigned ourselves to a long wait.

I knew they would probably take their time drinking the wine or coffee the contadina would offer them. The murmur of their voices rose and fell, suddenly interrupted by a piercing shriek from the toddler. My hair stood on end. I heard the soothing voice of the mother, and the child quieted. Several minutes dragged by, and suddenly we heard a soft, insistent tapping at the window right above our heads. I jumped in panic, and the Earl's sharp intake of breath showed he had heard it too. Then I realized the tap could only be intended for us. Screwing up my courage, I turned my head to look, and there was the woman, up on a ladder, looking in, her finger to her lips for silence. I got to my knees, and she quickly backed down the ladder, making signs that we were to climb out, go down the ladder, and head for the trees nearby. I nodded. Her skirts flew as she raced around the corner of the building to return to the kitchen and attend to her unwelcome visitors. I could hear her enter and speak in a somewhat louder tone. At the same time, she began making noise with dishes and glasses, to cover any sound we might make. Slowly, cautiously, we pushed the window up, just enough to squeeze through the opening. Barely daring to breath, we scrambled rapidly down the ladder, expecting any moment to hear "ALT!" shouted in German, or feel bullets ripping into us. Once on the ground, we shoved the ladder under the foundation of the house, then turned and dashed across the short yard, sliding down the gentle slope behind it, to the safety of a small stand of trees growing beside a tiny stream. We accomplished it all without making a sound. I looked up to the yard and saw that newly washed laundry had been hung out to dry. She must have used that as her excuse to go outdoors, so that she could put the ladder up and get us out! What quick thinking! The woman's courage was astounding! She knew that her life, and her childrens', was as much at stake as ours. My watch told me only an hour had passed. It seemed like four. Finally, the six-year-old came down to the stream looking for us. "The tedeschi are gone," she informed us, with great seriousness. "La mamma says you can come back to the house now."

We found the young woman in the front yard, calmly throwing feed to the ducks and chickens. "Grazie, Signora," I said fervently, "you saved our lives today!"

"Who were they? What did they want?" asked the Earl. I translated his questions to her.

"It was three Germans and an interpreter," she said. "They were interested in what fell from the plane. It landed in our field."

"Did they say what it was?" I asked.

"Nothing. They looked, but it was only half empty oil drums. They took them with them."

The two "bombs" had been nothing more than reserve oil drums, probably hit by antiaircraft fire and jettisoned by the pilot. While the woman and I were talking, the Earl had wandered to the far side of the yard. He looked up and saw Ruggles-Brise and Brigadier Combe heading our way, coming across the fields from a nearby farm. "Hullo! Here come two of our blokes," he called to me.

I whirled. "Are they nuts," I said, "wandering around in broad daylight like that? What the hell do they think they're doing? Something must be up." I signaled them to head for the stand of trees over to their right, that we'd meet them there. This poor woman had been jeopardized enough for one day!

Thanking her warmly, Ranfurly and I set off to meet Combe and Ruggles-Brise. Their farmer had told them of the arrival of the Germans at our place, and they were coming to investigate what had happened to us. "It's dangerous, being out in the daylight like this," I commented.

"Well, never mind that now," said Combe. "Tell us what happened! We saw the duds hit in the field."

"They weren't duds," I said. "They were just . . ." I got no further.

A farmer came running, gesticulating wildly. He was trembling. "Militia! A squad is coming! They are here!"

We looked in the direction he was pointing, and saw the last six of the squad of Facist militiamen, weapons unslung, jump the stream about 400 meters below us. "Christ!" I said. "Let's get the hell out of here!" We took to our heels as the militiamen, spotting us, gave chase. In this terrain, it was up one hill and down the other, which, luckily for us, gave our pursuers only an occasional glimpse of us. Resolutely, we raced on, alternately appearing for seconds and then disappearing, as we traversed the mosaic of wheat fields and hedgerows. The chase continued for fifteen or twenty minutes, and all four of us were nearing exhaustion. Frantically, I looked from side to side for a hiding place. The wheat was only about eighteen inches high, not tall enough to conceal us well, and the trees were all cut back to little more than stumps, to allow sun to reach the grapevines strung along them.

For everyone, there comes a time when he can physically do no more. I had reached mine. The others, although younger and more conditioned by military training, were unable to do much more either. "Go on! Leave me!" I gasped, as I dropped to my knees and wiggled, snake-like, towards the thickest, tallest stands of wheat. Seconds later, I could hear our pursuers close by. I wished myself into the dirt, but had my Colt clasped in hand and ready, so I could come up firing and get in at least one good lick before they got me. I knew the Colt would be no match for a submachine gun. My body tensed as a voice, so close it seemed to be speaking directly to me, called, "Guardi nel mezzo del grano!" (look over there—in the middle of the field!). Another few steps, and he'd have stepped on my head! I could hear the wheat being trampled underfoot nearby. I held my breath and waited, sweat trickling down my face, the wheat dust choking me. Fearing I'd sneeze, I pressed my nostrils together with my left hand. Agonizing seconds ticked by. All sound stopped. I didn't dare raise my head to look. They might be standing there, silently waiting for us to pop up so they could blow our heads off, or capture us. For a half hour or more, I remained perfectly motionless. Finally, I felt I had to risk a look. I raised my head to where I could just peep through the tips of the wheat stalks and looked around.

There was no sign of the militiamen. The wheat field was deserted. In the next field, a couple of young peasant farmers were calmly working the soil. I stood up and walked over to them. They looked at me with broad smiles. "Rallegramenti, we are glad to see you, Signore," said one. "We saw what happened, but we did not dare interfere. They would have killed us all."

"That's okay," I said, "you have risked enough for us today."

"We were glad to see them leave," said the other, and he spit disdainfully on the ground to show how he felt about the Fascists.

"What about my friends?" Did you see what happened to them?" I inquired.

"They're gone. They eluded the bastards too," said the first farmer. "The Fascisti had to give up and leave empty-handed!" They both laughed and, clapping me happily on the back, hurried me along to a nearby farmhouse.

"This is an occasion for celebration," said Renzo, as he poured each of us a glass of wine. I was parched, and gulped mine gratefully. Several hours, and several glasses later, I bid them a fond farewell, relaxed, and with a hearty hot meal from Renzo's wife in my stomach.

I walked back to the farm where I was sheltering, enjoying the pungent smell of the budding bushes and trees and the newly plowed earth. I was weary, but God, it felt good to be alive! Today had been the closest call yet. It was dark when I arrived, and the contadina and her husband were glad to see me. Ranfurly was there, too, and he pounded me on the back. "What a relief to see you, Orebaugh! We were worried about you," he said sincerely. "We hid out in the wheat, too, but we were a pretty good distance away from where you stopped. We didn't hear any commotion from back your way, so we figured you probably got away."

"Yeah," I said, picking up the little one and sitting her on my lap. Curious, she tugged at my beard. "Stupid of them, but lucky for me, they only searched the middle of the field."

We all discussed the events of the day. The dropping oil drums had been seen by many eyes. The Fascists, always eager for booty, thought it was an airdrop of supplies for the partisans. Like the Germans, they had come to investigate and see what there was for the taking. Of one thing we were certain. Now that our presence in the area was known, it was dangerous for us to stay around any longer.

We shifted billets again, to some farms farther away. A soggy weather front settled in, and we anxiously waited for it to pass, hoping there would be a northerly wind following it—the wind we needed to push us down the coast in what we jokingly referred to as our "yacht." Finally, the weather began to break. A messenger came from Cag. "Be at the assembly point on the beach, near Marina Faleriense, at nine o'clock tonight," he said. "We'll be leaving at nine-fifteen." My excitement over the prospect of actually making an attempt to get out was tempered by the nagging fear that this, too, might prove fruitless. With Giorgio, who would be our A Force escort for the voyage south, and three other Allied officers we had picked up along the way, our number had swelled to fourteen. We were all at the designated assembly point well ahead of time. Promptly at nine-fifteen Giorgio gave the whispered order for us to "proceed to the boat, and get it into the water as quickly and quietly as possible."

Our "yacht"—all twenty-four feet of her, carvel-planked, with solid oak knees for the ribs—was no light racing affair, to be lifted easily and tossed quickly into the water. While Brigadier Todhunter and two others stood guard, Giorgio and the rest of us literally manhandled the cumbersome hulk into the water. "Okay, LIFT," came a hoarse whispered command, and we lifted. "Stern up more!" came another whisper. "PUSH!" We pushed and prodded mightily, sweating and straining, not daring to speak, except for necessary commands. Foot by agonizing foot, we pried her loose from her mulish foothold in the sand. Slowly, painfully, we prodded and tugged and shoved her stubbornly resistant bulk toward its natural home—the sea.

A full forty-five minutes of struggle were spent before she dipped her pointed prow, like a bird's beak, into the river and took a sip. She found it to her liking, and, with the water buoying part of her weight, and all of us heaving mightily from the stern, she slid in the rest of the way. Scrambling, we dumped our gear in and clambered aboard, two at a time, as quietly as we could. Giorgio gave one last mighty shove, then swung into the boat as she floated seaward. Nothing broke the sound of the waves lapping at the sandy shore, not even a dog's bark. We were away.

Then "Sweet Christ!" whispered Rieter, urgently. "There's water coming in everywhere!" Sure enough, she was taking on water from at least twenty leaks in the hull!

"Give me one of those those pitch buckets—we need to bail!" I said, urgently. "Hurry!" Feverishly, we bailed. As we drifted further out to sea, water was spurting into the boat from all sides, and already sloshing ankle deep at our feet. The two fishermen Cag had paid to caulk the boat had had to work only at night, and without any light. They had missed a lot of open spots. The only bailers aboard were the two empty pitch buckets they had left behind, which still had pounds of half-dried, heavy black pitch stuck to them. The added weight of the water made bailing an arduous task. After a half hour or so, I was spent, and lathered in sweat. I felt like I had a dagger in my shoulder, and someone was turning it every two minutes to increase the pain.

I turned my bucket over to Ruggles-Brise. "Hell's fire, Orebaugh, this bloody thing weighs a ton!" he complained. "How the hell did you do this?"

"Just shut up and keep bailing or we'll sink," I groaned. "Don't waste energy talking. It's a damned long way from here to the Allied lines!" Giorgio was already down on his knees in the sloshing water, plugging leaks with raveled hemp and globs of black tar. He worked methodically, silently, emitting only an occasional grunt as he pushed and pressed the stuff into the leaks. Occasionally, he'd use a screwdriver to punch the strands of hemp into place. Thank God someone aboard knew something about boats!

While two of us were bailing, and Giorgio was plugging leaks as fast as he could, the others manned the two lengthy oars—four to a side. With help from the northerly wind, the oarsmen managed to get the boat far enough out to sea to be out of gunshot range from shore. No one wanted to turn back. We, and our leaky craft, were committed. The sea was black and choppy, with two- to three-foot waves pushing against the hull. I heard several groans as the boat alternately rose then dropped with a sickening lurch, yielding to the motion of the waves. Giorgio had finally made some real headway against the leaks, reducing them to a mere trickle. Feeling safer, we laid off and relaxed a bit, while Vaughn, Todhunter, and Ranfurly hoisted the loose-footed lugger sail. They seemed well schooled in the gentlemanly art of sailing, jumping to with alacrity as Vaughn called out crisp commands. This was certainly not like blueblood sailing on the Thames—out on a breezy Sunday afternoon, in impeccable whites, the Union Jack snapping merrily at the top of the mast, everything shipshape and spotless. But they turned to with a will, and we let out a cheer as the north wind filled our patched and weathered sail and began bowling us down the Adriatic at a good clip.

By midnight, we were scudding swiftly southward. The sea, only moderately choppy at first, became more agitated as the offshore wind became stronger. By then, most of the group were heaving and retching with seasickness—several so violently they couldn't even lift their heads. For me, there was no respite. The leaks were gaining on the patching, and bailing was not only necessary, it was a matter of life or death for us all. My stomach felt queasy, too, but the constant need to shift my weight as I bailed, in order to keep my balance and not go overboard, kept my mind off it. Finally, the leaks seemed to be under control. I had stopped bailing and had flopped down, exhausted. I was taking it easy, enjoying the ride. For the first time, I allowed myself to think it might work. That I might, this time, make it down the coast to Allied-held territory—if we encountered no enemy patrol boats along the way.

Just then, there was a loud crack, closely followed by shouts of "Damn!" "What the hell?" "Oh no!" and the mast, sail and all, whizzed past my ear and crashed into the water. The brace that had been rigged to hold the rotted old mast had snapped under the combined stress of the weight of the sail and the pull of the strong wind. At the same moment, I felt the chill of cold water around my ankles. There was a new leak—a big one! I grabbed my bucket and began bailing again. "Rieter! Man the other bucket!" I yelled. He sprang to help me. Meanwhile, Giorgio and two of the others, leaning precariously over the side, grabbed the waterlogged sail. Bit by bit, with Herculean effort, they pulled it, and the broken mast, back aboard. That done, Giorgio attacked the new leak, and with great effort, brought it under control. I glanced around. What a pathetic cargo of almost drowned rats we were! Soaking wet, streaked with pitch, sick, and half-frozen from the cold north wind which, even without a sail, continued to move us southward. Teeth chattering, I grabbed a bucket and began bailing vigorously, trying to warm myself. Giorgio sprang into action with the mast. He was amazing! Following his instructions, with Vaughn, the tallest and strongest, pushing, and several others holding, they managed to re-secure the broken mast. We held our breath as Ranfurly carefully hoisted the sail again. We gave him a rousing cheer as the sail gulped a bellyful of air, and the mast held! We were once more running before the wind. A faint smattering of applause came from the seven or eight men whose spasms of seasickness had them almost beyond caring whether or not they drowned.

Bailing, checking sail and mast, keeping watch, and tending to the sick men kept us busy, although we stayed wet, freezing, cold, and utterly miserable for the rest of that seemingly endless night. I knew we were moving fast, but had no idea how far down the coast we might have traveled. I was both anxious and fearful for what daylight might bring. We were far enough out to sea not to be visible from shore, I was certain, but we didn't know, with any degree of certainty, at what point along the coast the battle lines were drawn. We'd have to trust the judgement of Giorgio on that.

Like a bugler signaling retreat, the night wind blew one final blast at the onrushing dawn, then slackened and died, as from behind the veil of the dawn mists, daylight chased it. Glancing toward shore, we could see, silhouetted in the distance, the peaks of a high mountain range. "The Abruzzi?" I asked Giorgio.

"Sì, Signore, I think so," he replied. "It has to be them—we've come a good distance in the night."

That gave us the will to resume rowing. Not knowing what the day would bring, or how long we'd be without a breeze, we decided to put only two to each oar, in half-hour shifts, to conserve energy. Even those who had been immobilized with seasickness for most of the night manfully took their turn at the oars. No one looked to Giorgio or me to row, since we had spent the night bailing and repairing, and were completely spent. Around nine in the morning, a tiny gust nipped at us, ushering a moderate breeze along behind it, and the rowers gratefully shipped the oars. "Water and food are getting low," Rieter murmured, as he turned to the bail buckets once more. We had not accurately calculated what it would require to supply fourteen men for more than twelve hours on the water, doing hard physical work all the way. We had to give the seasick men extra water, so they didn't become dehydrated. Our water supply was dwindling fast. We could do without food for a while, but water was a grave concern.

"We'll have to ration water," I informed Vaughn.

He nodded, anxiously scanning the horizon for any signs of life. "I hope we're behind the line of battle," he said wearily. "We're sitting ducks out here in broad daylight! I'd hate to get this far and be picked up by the damned Jerries!"

"God, don't even think about it!" I said.

He glanced at the water jug. "Men!" he called. Everyone looked up. "We're conserving our supplies. Limit water to two sips an hour, each. A mouthful each after a rowing stint. An extra mouthful every hour for the sick men." A murmur of alarm went through the group. "Ssh! Quiet!" Vaughn called suddenly. Everyone fell silent. "Hear that? That's artillery fire!" Sure enough, as we listened we could hear the rumble and occasional "crump!" of an artillery battle in progress.

I turned to Ranfurly. "We must be parallel with the battle lines!" I said excitedly. "Another hour or so at most, and we'll be in Allied territory for sure!"

"Another hour or two, d'you think?" groaned Kerine, who was desperately seasick. "God, I don't know if I can stand it!"

"Sure you can, old man," said Rieter. "You'll make it. Before you know

it, you'll be home having tea and toddies, and being nagged by your wife."
We had to chuckle at Rieter's parody of the English.

Shortly after eleven in the morning our fickle breeze deserted us again,
and it was back to the oars. The grunts of the rowers as they heaved and
pulled at the heavy oars, the splash as the oars broke the water in a steady,
monotonous rhythm, the slosh of the bailing buckets, and an occasional
weary groan or empty-stomached retch were the only sounds we heard
until almost two o'clock that afternoon. We had been at sea for seventeen
hours. No one had energy left to talk. Then, just as a slight breeze teased
at the edge of the sail, flipping it a bit, giving us hope we might see our
friendly breeze again and get a respite from the detested rowing, there was
a roar overhead, and two Allied aircraft buzzed us! We nearly capsized the
"yacht" as we all rushed to one side to wave at them. Two men whipped
off their shirts and frantically waved them, too. However, the planes flew
on, without dipping their wings or giving us any signal that they had seen
us. Dejectedly, we turned back to the oars. Breeze and sail finally finished
flirting and decided to mate, so with full sail we were once again zipping
along in a southerly direction.

After about an hour, Ruggles-Brise spotted several boats to the west of
us, also under sail. "Look—sails! Another boat!" he called out, pointing,
and I felt my heart leap. I understood how the early explorers must have
felt. Using the oars, we altered our direction slightly and attempted to
steer our clumsy, leaky craft toward the sails that billowed enticingly in
the distance. A cheer went up as we saw the men on one of the boats pull
in the nets it was dragging, then turn and head toward us. They closed
the distance rapidly. We knew the boat was a friendly one. All nonmilitary
boats were banned by the Germans in areas they controlled. The vessel
approaching was a civilian fishing boat, which meant we were in Allied-
held territory!

"It's a friendly! It's a friendly!" shouted Rieter, pounding me excitedly
on the back. "We made it! We made it!"

The two men on the other boat waved happily at us. When they were
close enough, they hove to and tossed a line to Giorgio, which he looped
firmly around the wooden cleat at the prow. Their boat had an auxiliary
motor, which would tow us in to port.

I called, "Where are we? What port are you from?"

"Ortona, Signore," they replied. Ortona! Ortona had been liberated by
the Allies only a few weeks ago! We cheered, shouted, hugged and pum-
meled each other. We had made it to the Allied lines! By the skin of our
teeth, to be sure, but who cared?

Artillery fire, both incoming and outgoing, roared deafeningly all around
us as we were towed into the devastated port of Ortona. As we prepared
to dock, we were greeted by British Marines. "Hullo! Who is this?" they
inquired. On hearing the high rank of the British officers aboard, they

snapped to attention and saluted, then rushed to help us. "Welcome back, sir!" they greeted Vaughn, as senior in command. "We'll see to your needs, and your people's needs, immediately, sir!"

"Thank you corporal," said Vaughn. Despite his filthy, unshaven, ragged appearance, he was every inch the Brigadier. "Carry on."

The corporal lost no time in hustling us over to the beach hotel that served as headquarters. Situated in the lee of a hill, it had escaped major damage from shelling. The British officers in command of the Ghurka regiment, which was manning this important sector of the front, saluted our distinguished companions smartly, welcomed us cordially, and immediately showed us to facilities where we could bathe and shave. While we were enjoying that welcome luxury, clothing and personal items were procured for us. My clothes were little more than shreds, and they, and my body, were coated with black pitch. I hardly recognized some of the fellows once they had shaved and cleaned up! In fact, everyone had shaved, except me. I was determined to keep my "beard of many colors," as Amy had dubbed it, at least until after Marguerite had seen it. One of the British officers looked in on us. "Well, that's a lot better, eh? But now, I imagine you gentlemen must have a bit of a hunger and thirst. How about some dinner?"

"Captain, you've got yourself a deal!" I said, jumping up with alacrity. The others, laughing heartily, followed suit. We were ravenous! Although the meal was field rations—tinned meat, canned vegetables and fruit—it was just the ticket to us, and we dived right into it.

I was almost finished with my meal, and just starting to think about asking where I could get a cigar to enjoy a relaxing smoke, when a messenger appeared to inform us there was transportation awaiting us outside and we were to come with him immediately. Bidding the others a hasty farewell, not sure where we were being taken—or when, or if, we'd be back—I followed the young soldier to the front of the building and climbed into the command car with Vaughn and the other two brigadiers. The others followed in other vehicles.

I had survived my capture and detainment in Italy, my raids with the San Faustino Band, my trek across the mountains, and the boat trip down the Adriatic, but I wasn't sure I'd survive the ride across Ortona to my destination. Because of the danger from constant German shelling, the British driver, declining to pick his way carefully around the shell and mortar craters and the piles of rubble on the main road south, floored the accelerator and charged ahead at breakneck speed. Several times we were in danger of literally being thrown from the car. "Slow down!" I roared, but he paid no attention. As we sped along, bounding in and out of deep potholes with tooth-jarring regularity, Allied artillery pieces, aligned along the south side of the road, were laying down a continuous barrage of fire. The shells cleared the roof of our vehicle by a margin of only inches! It

was May 10, 1944, the first day of the major Allied offensive that culmi-
nated in the liberation of Rome.

Sometime after midnight, we arrived at Torino del Sangro, an advance
Allied army base on the banks of the Sangro River. We slept on army cots
that night and in the morning enjoyed our first hot showers. I felt almost
human again, despite my purple, blood-congested feet and the sores from
hundreds of bedbug bites on my neck and body, which were to plague
me with intermittent infection for years to come. While at Sangro, we
were interrogated by Nile McNally of British Intelligence. He, like many
who came after him, was astounded to hear the details of our escape odyssey. It was there that Rieter and I said a fond farewell to our British
friends. They had all been supplied with uniforms, and to see them spiffed
up, in their khakis, bathed and shaved, brought a rush of warmth to me.
We had all made it back safely. We shook hands all around, determinedly
keeping a "stiff upper lip," although there was a trace of mist in every
eye. We went through the ritual of parting wherein everyone vows eternal
friendship and constant communication, vows that are the formula of the
ritual—sincerely spoken, rarely kept.

"Good luck," said Vaughn, "take care of your friends in Umbria." He
shook my hand warmly, as did Ranfurly.

"Call when you're in London, and we'll have a dram together."

"You'd bloody well better write," growled Ruggles-Brise, gruffly,
pressing a missive with everyone's home address in England into my hand.
That done, we climbed into the car, they all saluted us, and we drove
away in a cloud of dust.

The British driver delivered us to the American forces at 12th Air Corps
Headquarters in Foggia. After being passed through a succession of American army officers of succeedingly higher rank, and finally establishing my
identity beyond a doubt, I sent telegrams to the Department of State and
to Marguerite, informing them of my escape and of my intention to proceed to Algiers, which is where I thought the nearest American Embassy
was situated. I had no idea then that an American Embassy, under Ambassador Alexander Kirk, as well as a Consulate General, had been opened
in Naples. Rieter and I parted, both to begin a whirlwind of interviews,
interrogations, and debriefings. I asked everyone I spoke with to help me
get an airdrop arranged. I was told that I would have to handle that at
Allied Headquarters in Caserta, and was reminded constantly not to discuss any of the details of my escape with anyone outside of military intelligence. The following day I was flown to Naples, where I conferred with
Ambassador Kirk and Consul General George Brandt. A day later, I was
taken by jeep to Caserta, where I was to report to, and be the guest of,
General Harold Alexander, the ranking Allied Commander.

A kindly man, with graying hair, a clipped mustache, and erect, military bearing, the general greeted me cordially. He had heard some sketchy
details of my ordeal and immediately offered me his personal trailer for

my accommodations. When I politely refused, he insisted on giving me sleeping quarters in the headquarters building. Never had I dreamed I would one day sleep in a royal bedchamber. But that night, chuckling at the thought of my leap from cow and sheep stalls to this, I slept in one of the luxurious bedrooms of the House of Savoy Royal Palace, which served as the headquarters of the Allied Command. There, tucked in a massive, gilded, canopied bed, under a satin goosedown comforter, cosseted by sheets of the finest, softest linen, I curled up alone, in a room bigger than the whole Bruschi farmhouse, and slept like a baby.

"Good to see you, Orebaugh," General Alexander greeted me warmly the next morning at breakfast. "Did you sleep well?"

"Well? I would say I slept exceedingly well, in absolute royal luxury, sir," I answered, smiling.

"I imagine you must have quite a tale to tell us," he said, leaning back in his chair, an interested gleam lighting his blue eyes.

"That I do, sir," I replied, "I most certainly do! I think you'll find it an interesting one." He listened with rapt attention as I briefly described my activities since being captured in Monaco.

That afternoon, as I rested in my room, and prepared reports, an aide knocked on the door, and informed me that the general sent his compliments and requested that I join him at dinner. I felt incongruously out of place in the glittering assemblage of polished, beribboned, high-ranking officers General Alexander had invited in to dine with him. My shaggy beard and nondescript clothing stood out like a sore thumb in those regal surroundings. The dining room of the Savoy Palace was the most enormous room I had ever seen, other than in the Palace of Versailles in France. It was a Renaissance great hall. Ornately carved, gilt borders outlined large portions of the room, and light from the hundreds of thousands of prisms in the twelve huge crystal chandeliers, each roughly the size of a jeep, danced off the mirrors and the gleaming table. The dining table, richly laid with fine china and crystal, ran the length of the center of the room. It could seat fifty with ease, and that night every seat was taken. I was placed to the right of the General, in the position of honor. A memorable five-course dinner was served. First a light spinach soup, then a simple pasta course of ravioli—but what ravioli they were! With the first mouthful, I knew my fate was sealed—I would love Italian pasta for the rest of my days. This was followed by enormous platters of sliced roast veal in a delicious wine sauce, accompanied by an assortment of vegetable dishes— peas, artichokes, eggplant, tiny potatoes. It was all topped off by a magnificent "zuppa Inglese," the liquor-laced Italian version of English trifle. With each course, an appropriate wine was offered. The military always knew how to "liberate" the best supplies for its tables! I had not seen a dinner like that, ever. It was such a far cry from supper at the Bruschis' as to be almost unimaginable.

After dessert was cleared, as the servants poured real espresso into our delicate china demitasse cups and cordials into tiny crystal flutes, the General rose. I had my coffee cup up to my nose, inhaling the aroma. I didn't know if I'd be able to bring myself to actually consume such a rare treat. "Gentlemen," he began, "today I have heard a most amazing and interesting story. A very touching story, of the fortitude and courage of a young American, and of the bravery of the Italian people behind the lines. I think you'll find it an interesting story too, and that is why I am now going to ask Mr. Walter Orebaugh, an American Foreign Service Officer, who has just escaped after sixteen months behind enemy lines, to tell you some of his incredible story." Startled, I almost dropped my cup. All eyes turned to me. I tried to demur, but there was strong applause from the assemblage, and strong urging from General Alexander. I stood up, feeling unkempt and insignificant, and skipped through the highlights of my story, in as few words as possible. When I finished, there was stunned silence. Then the group of officers rose, to a man, and gave me a resounding ovation. I flushed with pride. The joy of actually being back struck me, and I felt a lump rise in my throat, as tears flooded into my eyes.

The next day, I was asked to meet with a Mr. Proctor and several Office of Strategic Services (OSS) officials. "Orebaugh," said Proctor without preamble, "I'm almost sorry to see you here."

I looked at him, shocked. "What do you mean?"

A well-groomed man in a gray, double-breasted suit, he perched casually on the corner of the desk, one leg up, pipe in hand. "We had counted on using you to our advantage in that district around Perugia. On May 2nd, we broadcast your code signal to you telling you you were authorized to draw consular drafts for two-thousand dollars a month for partisan activity. Unfortunately, you had already left the area, so you never got the message."

My heart fell. If only I had delayed a few more days! "But sir," I protested, "does that mean I can't get help—ammunition and money and supplies—to the Band at San Faustino? What I want, more than anything else in the world, is to get help to my partisan comrades immediately."

"No, no, Orebaugh," Proctor hastened to reassure me. "Don't worry about that! We're getting ready to make an airdrop there within the week. You just tell us what's needed."

I jumped up eagerly. "I have the list in my knapsack," I said. "I can go get it now, if you don't mind."

Proctor smiled, puffing on his pipe. "Tomorrow morning will be time enough. We have a pretty good idea of what's probably on the list."

I was elated. An airdrop to Morena within the week! Bonfigli's smiling face flashed before me, and Pierangeli's. Giovanni's, and Ruggero's. They'd be elated! "What about a radio transmitter, and someone to operate it? Can we get someone up there. Maybe someone from A Force?" I asked, thinking immediately of Cag.

"As a matter of fact, we have two operatives who will shortly be dropped behind the German lines. One of them is intended for San Faustino."

"Thank you, sir," I said sincerely. "Any Allied effort on behalf of these people will not be wasted, I can assure you." Then, briefly, I described the battle between the united Bands of San Faustino and Cantiano, and the Waffen SS troops. He whistled softly in admiration, making notes, when I gave him the details and the numbers involved. As I was to learn later, the Germans had retaliated fiercely for that encounter.

The next day, I talked to the two operatives who were scheduled to be dropped behind the lines and set up the airdrop for Morena. Then, I flew to Algeria. I found out much later that, as I was winging my way across the Mediterranean, my friend and companion Giovanni Marioli, monitoring the BBC at his neighbor's home in Pietralunga, heard the magic code words, "abbia fede" (have faith) and "puoi gioire" (you can rejoice), crackle from the radio. He raced to notify Pierangeli. Darkness was falling as a squad of partisans arrived at the church in Morena, and informed Don Marino Cecarelli, the bandit priest, that Il Console had succeeded in reaching Allied lines and that an airdrop for the partisans was on its way! Don Marino, after saying a quick prayer of thanksgiving, hurried out to round up help to gather materials for the six huge bonfires, which were to be built in the field across from the church, then lighted to identify and outline the drop area. Don Marino, the partisans, and the villagers worked feverishly against the ten-thirty deadline for the drop. By ten-fifteen the bonfires, and the torches to light them, were ready.

At ten-twenty on May 18, the lookout called to those gathered in the field, "Attenzione! Ascoltate!" (Attention! Listen!) In the distance, the faint drone of an airplane motor sounded.

"Light the fires!" commanded Bonfigli. A dozen torches were lit and touched to the six tall piles of dried brush and branches that lined the field. With a whoosh and a crackle, the bonfires blazed up in the night. A plane roared in low, and as they strained their eyes to see, twenty-three voluminous dark objects tumbled from it, down to the center of the flame-edge field, followed by a parachutist.

"God be praised!" murmured Don Marino Cecarelli, as he, the squad of partisans, the peasants, and the townspeople of Morena rushed in to gather up the vital store of ammunition and supplies dropped from the heavens, courtesy of Il Console and the Allies. Within ten minutes the bonfires had been extinguished and the debris cleared away. The field across from the church at Morena was nothing more than a field again. As Don Marino Cecarelli and some of his flock knelt in the tiny church, reciting prayers, silence settled on the Umbrian hills once again. But not for long—no, not for long.

11

Epilogue: Welcome Freedom

From the moment I was arrested by the Italians in Monaco on November 20, 1942, I had lived in a round-the-clock culture of fear. From that day, until I reached U.S. 12th Air Force Headquarters at Foggia on May 12, 1944, and saw the Stars and Stripes waving at its entrance, I was never able to let down my guard or enjoy a completely carefree moment. Fortunately, very few people in our free society know what it's like to live like a hunted animal, or a fugitive, over a long period of time. Even in the relative luxury of the Hotel Brufani, the fear that the Germans would arrive and deport us to prison camps was always with us. At the Bonucci flat, we couldn't set foot outdoors, and the prospect of random house searches by the enemy kept us on the alert day and night. In the hills of San Faustino, the lurking shadow of danger dogged my every move. During the trek to the Le Marche region with Giovanni, we repeatedly ran the gauntlet of terror and impending disaster. The disappointments of the many times we wended our way to the seaside at night, trying to escape, and the harrowing journey by boat to reach Allied lines, was hardly an exercise in relaxation. I had borrowed heavily against my physical reserves and my nerve centers for over a year and a half. Reaching the front lines at Ortona, in the midst of a raging battle, afforded no immediate relief, either, despite our elation at having reached Allied-held territory. For me, one kind of stress was merely exchanged for another. I was subjected to an endless round of debriefings, and meetings, interspersed with hours of report writing. Readjusting to living by day and sleeping by night was no small feat, after months of doing just the opposite. Added to all that were long, drawn-out luncheons and dinners at which, inevitably, I was called upon to "say a few words about your experiences."

My world for more than two years had been one of stealth, silence, and terse whispers. Now, the ceaseless noise of vehicles, machinery, and people, which went on twenty-four hours a day, kept my nerves on edge. I slept little. When I finally boarded the plane for Algiers, I was almost a basket case. I vaguely remember saying goodbye to Consul General Brandt, who saw me off. After that came a complete blank. I probably slept the full four hours of the flight across the Mediterranean. I remember that I was greeted personally on my arrival in Algiers by Ambassador Robert Murphy—he had been notified I was coming and insisted I be his house-guest.

It was at the Ambassador's serene, luxurious residence in Algiers that I finally began to relax and make the first tentative moves toward becoming a normal human being again. Bob Murphy, the antithesis of a stuffed shirt, was a genial, charming and very considerate host. Almost as an order, he charged me to sleep late and to order breakfast to be brought to my room at any hour that suited me. At lunch, and during some after-noon meetings, he introduced me to a number of high-ranking Allied of-ficers, both British and American, who were based in Algiers. I had a long session with the head OSS man in Algiers, who took copious notes on what I had to say about conditions behind the German lines. To him, and to others, the story of the partisans, and particularly the story of the blan-ket raid, was fascinating.

Late on the second morning I was there, the OSS man dropped by to see me. "I have some news you'll be glad to hear, Orebaugh," he said, smiling. "The airdrop to your friends at Morena went off without a hitch! They have their supplies. The radio operator we sent made it, too, and he has been in touch." He would never know how welcome those words were to me! I thought of my "buddy" Mario Bonfigli, of Captain Pier-angeli, Giovanni, the Bruschis, Don Marino—and Bonuccio Bonucci. Would I ever see any of them again? They had become so much a part of my life. I wondered what had happened after the airdrop and what raids the Band would make, now that they had ammunition and supplies. I missed being there, missed them all. It was as if I were two people—Walter Orebaugh, U.S. diplomat, Consul, married to Marguerite, father of young Howard, anxious to get back to them, and resume my former life. And I was also Michele Franciosi, 'sfollato clerk from Naples, peasant, fugitive, the guer-rilla fighter known as "Il Console." Would I ever be able to reconcile the two personalities and become one person—my real self—again?

Relaxing at Ambassador Murphy's house, with the knowledge that the airdrop at Morena had been successfully accomplished, I was finally able to sleep and to shed some of my weariness and tenseness. The Ambassa-dor's other house guest, the famous actor Douglas Fairbanks Jr., was every bit as suave, urbane, and witty as I had imagined him to be, and he was fascinating company. After a couple of days of this relative indolence, however, I was restless again. I wanted to get back home, to my family. That was quickly arranged.

My flight to New York was at night, and I slept most of the way, arriving at sunrise on May 21, 1944. Forehead pressed to the window next to my seat, looking out like an excited child, I wept unashamedly as the pilot swept past the Statue of Liberty, still holding aloft her torch of freedom, then made a banking turn that revealed the skyline of New York, bathed in the soft light of dawn. I had been away two years and three months. I purchased a bus ticket to Centerville, Virginia, then went to the Western Union station in the terminal and sent Marguerite another telegram. "Arrived New York today, stop. Meet me Trailways stop, Centerville, tomorrow, May 22, 4 P.M. stop. All my love, Walter." Little did I know that that telegram would be Marguerite's first word that I had escaped, left Italy, and was back in the United States! The telegram I had sent from Naples didn't arrive until after I did. The next afternoon, with pink and white helmeted dogwoods forming a guard of honor along the country roads, I arrived at the tiny hamlet of Centerville, not far from Washington, D.C.

As I stepped down, the lone passenger to alight, the expression on the face of the lovely, dark-haired young woman waiting there shifted, with kaleidoscopic speed, from surprise, to shock, to dismay. I can only imagine how Marguerite must have felt—the man who stepped off that bus bore scant resemblance to the man she had kissed goodbye more than two years ago! I was considerably thinner, and the rugged Italian winters had left their mark on my face above the long, scraggly beard that camouflaged the Walter of old. The cane in my hand was also a surprise. Her first thought was that I had been wounded. She didn't yet know the story of the "man with the cane," or about the treasure in rolled-up bills concealed in its hollowed-out stem. After those initial very brief reactions passed, Marguerite smiled the radiant smile that had attracted me to her when we were still in high school and lifted her arms in welcome. On cue from his mother, little Howard, now a sturdy young boy, cried "Daddy!" and followed her into my arms. I gathered them to me and held them close, tears streaming down my face. I was home again, at last.

By the end of June, I had been interviewed, quizzed, and debriefed by several ambassadors, generals, and everyone in the State Department who mattered—including Dean Acheson, who for several days insisted that I spend hours with him while he wrestled with, and grumbled about, lend-lease problems with the Soviet Union. There were several luncheons and dinners given in our honor, and I was treated very kindly by Assistant Secretary of State Adolf Berle and by my immediate boss, Nathaniel P. Davis, Chief of Foreign Service Personnel. As soon as I could, I sent word by diplomatic pouch to Nancy in Rome, letting her and Amy know that I had escaped and was safe in Washington. I asked her to send a postcard to "my friend in Trieste, telling him that Felice is visiting Marguerite." I fervently hoped that somehow Manfred had managed to escape, would receive it, and know I was safe.

With Marguerite's loving care and tender ministrations, and after a month of respite from walking and carrying heavy gear everywhere I went, my feet were vastly improved, and my shoulder had begun to heal, too. I had shaved off my beard and looked more like my old self, much to my wife's relief. I had finished my meetings and debriefings at the State Department, and we were ready to take some leave, to become a family again. Howard, initially extremely reserved with me, was beginning to accept the idea of having a Daddy around, but I needed to spend more time alone with him before the reunion would be complete.

In late June, I was happy to learn that I was being assigned back to Italy—to Florence—and that this time, even though the war was far from being over, I'd be allowed to take my family with me—AND a car. I was given ninety days of leave, and we spent most of that in Oregon, visiting family, and resting. On our return to Virginia in late August, I found a letter waiting for me—from my friend Captain R. D. G. Ramsay. It had been forwarded, through the OSS and the State Department, from the presidio at Morena. In it, he gave me my first information on the aftermath of the SS battle and the airdrop on May 18th:

For various reasons I cannot give you any details of what happened after you left, but there was absolute hell to pay! Morena was burnt and blown up by the Germans, and one or two people shot, but fortunately we all got away after the airdrop, and after the Allied offensive started in earnest, we returned to Morena with 500 well-armed partisans, and got a bit of our own back. . . . All of our party [the British officers living at Acqua Viva farm] got through safely on July 9th and are back home in England. I have elected to stay here in Italy, and have been given command of the 273rd Armored Delivery Squadron—also a promotion to major! Incidentally, I received your message by parachute along with the arms—thank you.

I also learned, much later, that the euphoria created in San Faustino by the arrival of the airdropped supplies was beyond description. Rebounding from a death-rattle state, the Band of San Faustino increased the tempo of its activities and was able to carry out a number of daring raids during May and June. The Allies liberated Perugia and the surrounding areas of Umbria in the final weeks of June 1944.

When stories of my adventures behind the lines, and my clandestine escape by boat, were released in the fall of 1944, I was hailed as a national hero. Unaccustomed to such publicity, I found it all rather embarrassing, and at times somewhat of a nuisance. I received letters and accolades from many high-ranking government officials, along with a good deal of attention from the media. After my secretive, Spartan existence in the Umbrian hills, it was disconcerting to find myself so often in the limelight. I was featured in True Comics, and I was the main character in a popular radio adventure program.

In October 1944, with the war in Europe still raging, Marguerite, Howard, and I arrived in Rome. I couldn't wait to see Nancy and Amy again. I phoned Nancy at the Vatican. "Walter!" she screamed happily, "how wonderful to hear your voice! Where are you? When can I see you?" We agreed to meet for dinner that same evening at a small restaurant on the Via Veneto. As soon as she saw me, Nancy threw herself into my arms, and, much to my surprise, the normally cool, reserved Amy burst into tears and hugged me warmly.

I felt tears in my own throat. "Here, let me look at you," I said, huskily, holding them both at arm's length. They looked wonderful—far better than when I had seen them last. Amy was less gaunt, though still rangy, and her blue eyes were clear and bright. Nancy was prettier than ever. She had regained her normal weight, lost the dark circles under her eyes, and looked positively radiant. She had cut her hair and still wore her girlish grin, but she had acquired an air of sophisticated maturity, which only added to her attractiveness. As I looked them over, I couldn't help but chuckle, remembering the "make do" outfits both had worn in Gubbio and Perugia. Now, they were attired in the latest designs—walking proof that the Italian fashion industry had somehow managed to survive both the German occupation and the Allied invasion.

As soon as we were seated and had ordered our meals, Nancy turned to me. "You first, 'Felice,' " she teased. "We want to hear everything that happened to you after you left us!" We barely touched our food, so absorbed were we in catching up. Hours later, we were still lingering over coffee. After I finished with my tale, it was a contest between them as to which one could do the most talking. It was like old times again, and there were a few tears, and many laughs, that evening.

It was well past one o'clock in the morning when we finally said good night. As I gave them a farewell hug, I remarked, "You know, you're both looking great—years younger than when I last saw you, in Perugia!" They smiled delightedly. Nothing I could have said would have pleased them more. Before we left Rome, we all had dinner together again, and this time Marguerite and little Howard were with us.

Our promised car arrived, creating an unbelievable sensation. In Europe, there had been no production of cars for the civilian market since 1939. The brand new, shiny gray DeSoto had the additional distinction of being the only civilian car permitted to circulate in Italy, and it drew swarms of humanity wherever it appeared. It was such a curiosity, it even rated mention on the front page of the *New York Times!* As we were getting ready to leave Rome for Florence, I remembered the diplomatic pouch full of French francs that I had given to Alex Manz, the Swiss Vice Consul in Nice, just before I was taken to Italy from Monaco. I decided to drop by the Swiss Legation in Rome, and inquire, just to see if anyone there knew anything about what had happened to it. I really didn't know what to expect.

"May I help you, sir?" asked the young Swiss clerk.

"Perhaps you can," I replied, showing him my identification. "Could you possibly check and see if, by chance, a diplomatic pouch for Walter Orebaugh might have been sent here for safekeeping? It would have been sometime late in 1942."

"Certainly. Just a moment, sir, and I'll check," he said. In less than five minutes, he was back, with the very pouch that I had turned over to Alex Manz!

Surprised and pleased, I signed the receipt for it. "I never expected to see this again," I remarked. It was his turn to look surprised, a look that said how could one even think such a thing?! The Swiss rarely lost anything—and NEVER money!

I was in for an even bigger surprise. While it had remained quietly in the custody of the Swiss, the money's value had grown considerably. General De Gaulle, in his determination to restore France to a position of dignity as a world power, had insisted on revaluing the French franc to be exchangeable against the Italian lira at two lire to the franc. My hoard had more than doubled in buying power!

My next stop was the American Embassy. I went to the finance office and explained that I had purchased some francs in Lisbon with my own funds and I wanted to exchange them. "No problem, sir," said the officer in charge. "Go to any U.S. Army exchange office, and they will change them for you." I exchanged my French francs, receiving enough lire in occupational scrip to more than cover our living expenses for a year or two. I proceeded to Florence, my pockets bulging. If only the Portuguese money changer in Lisbon could have known what finally happened with those hundreds of thousands of "worthless" French francs that "crazy American" had insisted on buying. I could just picture the look on his face!

A few days later, I visited the jewelry mecca of Florence—the Ponte Vecchio. Dating from before the time of Michelangelo and the Medicis, the narrow covered bridge over the Arno was home to scores of goldsmiths and jewelers, crowded together in tiny shops that lined both sides of the bridge. With part of my windfall of lire, I commissioned a very extravagant brooch as a special gift for Marguerite. A week later, it was ready. When she opened the box, the beauty of it took her breath away. Lying there, nestled on black velvet, winking up at her, was a finely wrought, jeweled rose. Icy diamonds sparkled from the center of petals made of dazzling red rubies. The graceful stem and leaves of the flower were set with glittering emeralds. It was an artist's masterpiece in red, white, and green—the colors of Italy.

We settled in and I reopened the United States Consulate in Florence, with four veteran Italian employees of its prewar staff. It was November 1944, almost two years from the day I had opened the ill-starred U.S. Consulate in the Principality of Monaco, which was never reopened. Finally, I had time to begin checking up on old friends. Through the Consulate in Nice, I received word that Marino Sales, my former driver, was doing well and was once again employed as the Consulate's driver there. Mmes. Eme and Goff-Lowenstein had made it through the war, somewhat the worse for wear. The latter, being a Jewess, had had a scary time of it, in hiding for months, but was grateful to be alive. The advancing Allied forces were just beginning to uncover the horrible results of Hitler's relentless persecution of the Jews of Europe. In Gubbio, the banker Meletti had been arrested and imprisoned, based on what I had told the OSS about him. I informed the city officials, who came to me to plead for him, that I would request his release if he donated 12,000 lire to the Civilian Hospital in Perugia. Meletti complied at once, and was freed.

Bonuccio Bonucci somehow survived the brutalities of his imprisonment by the Fascists. Released by the arrival of the Allies in June of 1944, he was in terrible physical condition, the result of the torture he had endured. His back was striped with scars from the lash, and his eyes were dark-rimmed and sunken. He was, in truth, but a shadow of his former self. Nevertheless, he meticulously accounted, to the penny, for the 100,000 lire that Manfred had sent me for use by the Band. My copy of that accounting is a treasured souvenir of my all-too-brief friendship with Bonuccio Bonucci. After he was freed, he returned to his prewar occupation as an agriculturalist. His loyal Gigi, who had faithfully looked after his interests during his imprisonment, remained in his service. The cache of weapons Bonucci had buried was never accounted for. It is believed they were probably discovered and "appropriated" at some point, by the peasants or the Germans.

Widely acclaimed as a partisan hero, Bonucci became president of the Agrarian Union of the Province of Perugia, a post he was successively reelected to annually, almost to the date of his death in 1977 at age 73. Throughout his life, he bore, in the black, congested condition of his legs, the signs of horrendous torture at the hands of his neo-Fascist captors. Bonuccio Bonucci's name and works are forever enshrined in the memories of those of us who, with him, laid the foundations for, and shared in, the San Faustino partisan movement. His villa has been restored, and, ironically, it is now owned and occupied by a German family. A memorial plaque of dedication to Bonucci and the Brigata d'Urto di San Faustino (Band of San Faustino) is affixed to an outside wall of the villa (see photographs).

For about a year following the cessation of hostilities, Nancy Charrier stayed in Rome as clerical assistant to the U.S. president's personal representative to the Vatican. We kept in close touch. Later, she returned home to her mother's in New Jersey and eventually married industrialist Sherman Burling. They have three children. Nancy pursued graduate studies both at home and abroad and has remained an active and inquisitive observer of life. Between Nancy and me there remains an affectionate bond that neither time nor distance will ever extinguish.

Amy Houlden never married. She stayed on at the Vatican until 1947, as a member of the same staff as Nancy. After her stint at the Vatican, she returned to the French Riviera, her favorite playground. I rarely heard from her after she left Italy. Her life was to be brief—she died of natural causes less than ten years later, in 1956. Lester Maynard was arrested in Perugia by the Germans and sent to a prison camp in Spoleto, where he was strenuously interrogated about me and my whereabouts. It was a good thing I had told him nothing, so he was unable to give them any useful information. In early June of 1944, he managed to escape from the German military hospital in Spoleto, where he had been confined to await deportation to a concentration camp in Germany. He reached Perugia again and went into hiding. Lester was the first person to meet the British advance patrol that arrived to liberate Perugia at dawn on the 20th of June, 1944. After the war, he and his wife and daughters lived in Perugia for several years before returning to their home in Monaco. He died there in the early 1950s.

Mr. Scheck, the helpful manager of the Hotel Metropole in Monte Carlo, wrote to me in Florence in December 1945: "We then had a hard time, and I was on the 'black list,' and slept for several months with my bag, containing the most essential things, ready to go when forced to. Fortunately it did not happen. We have just reopened the Metropole." To this day, the Metropole remains a landmark hotel in Monte Carlo.

In Gubbio, the Albergo San Marco still endures, though much renovated and improved; Signorina Vera has gone on to her reward. The Piazza Italia, where Nancy and I often walked, has been renamed Piazza di Quaranta Martiri, in honor of the forty innocent citizens of Gubbio—heads of household—who were chosen at random, lined up against a wall, and machine-gunned to death by the Germans, in reprisal for partisan activities in the area.

Soon after we arrived in Florence, at my request, Vittoria Vechiet moved there to join our household staff. We enjoyed having her with us, and she was the same loyal, closemouthed Vittoria, worthy of implicit trust, that I had known in the Hotel Brufani and at Margherita's apartment in Perugia. She continued in service in Florence until her retirement, then returned to Gorizia—her birthplace. I also sent word to Ruggero Bruschi, asking him to pack up his family and come to Florence to join us. They were overjoyed! "Oh, Signore, Signore," Adalgisa exclaimed to me again and again, "Grazie, grazie! Never in my dreams did I imagine such beauty, such luck, at this!" They loved the picturesque old city. Marguerite and I had a twenty-five room apartment in a wing of the Palazzo San Clemente. We installed the Bruschis in a couple of the large rooms downstairs, and they remained there with us until an apartment was ready for them in the annex to the Palazzo Canevaro—the new home of the Consulate. Adalgisa and Ruggero were loyal, devoted members of my staff, and, along with Vittoria, they managed to spoil the three of us outrageously—especially little Howard, whom they all loved on sight.

Ruggero remained with the U.S. Consulate in Florence until his retirement at age sixty-five. The family prospered and, with the marriages of Concetta and Pepe, grew in size. They were able to buy an apartment building in Sesto Fiorentino, a suburb of Florence, where they live to this day—one family to each floor. To our great sorrow, Adalgisa died of a heart attack at Christmas time in 1986. At her suggestion, Assunta (the young girl who lived down the hill from the Bruschis and watched out for approaching Fascists or Germans) was brought to Florence and she, too, joined our household staff. I felt fortunate to have so many friends around me. Their honesty, and their fierce and unwavering loyalty, were, in those trying times, beyond price. Assunta and her husband now live on a farm on the outskirts of Pietralunga. I visit them whenever I'm in Italy, and we remain in touch by letter.

Our beloved friend Margherita Bonucci remained in Perugia. Always a proud and independent woman, she steadfastly refused any money or assistance from me. She was eventually reunited with her husband, Gregorio, who had miraculously survived his imprisonment in Germany. We visited them as often as we could during our stay in Florence. Little Lucia was overjoyed to see her "Zio Gualtiero" again. She loved to come to Florence to visit us and play with little Howard, but alas, those visits were to be few. In 1945, at age fourteen, Lucia contracted typhoid fever. Despite all the effort I could expend, despite the best medical care available, years of undernourishment and deprivation took their toll. She could not marshal the strength in her frail body to combat the ravages of the disease. She died, and I felt as if I had lost my own beloved daughter. She is buried in the Campo Santo in Perugia. Valentina Bonucci grew up to be an outstanding beauty, and in her early twenties she married a British noncommissioned officer and moved to England. Young Franco Bonucci married a neighborhood Perugina and now lives in Perugia with his family, in the apartment where we all stayed.

In the late 1970s, Nancy went back to Perugia to visit Margherita and wrote me:

Walter, my shock at seeing her cannot be described. My last memory was of a sturdy, fast moving, woman . . . Instead, a bent, white-haired old woman came hobbling toward us! Her smile was warm, her eyes still bright, but old, as the contadine do become. My dear Walter, when I saw those rooms again, I could not believe it was possible we were ever able to stay there! The dank cold was terrible, and it was April! Nothing had changed. The old kitchen table was still there. The smell from the sanitary arrangement permeated the rooms. How did we all stand it? I was profoundly moved. . . . Margherita and I talked about Lucia and shed a few tears together. I looked at the spot where we kept the can of condensed milk. I can still remember how good that one teaspoon a day tasted! She insisted on walking with me to the bus stop—'only a short walk,' she said, but you of all people know how the "short walks" are here; it seemed like miles!—I hugged her goodbye, and left with tears, and sad, mixed emotions.

Our beloved Margherita Bonucci died a few years later, in 1976.

Jack and Florence Kutsukian returned to Trieste in the fall of 1945. They lived only a few years after the war ended.

After my intercession on his behalf, and his release by the partisans, Leonard Mills disappeared. I heard nothing more from him until one day in January 1945, when he turned up, unannounced, at my office in the Consulate on the Via Tornabuoni in Florence. "Hello, Walter," he greeted me, in his usual lackadaisical manner, as though nothing had transpired in the interim and that finding me ensconced as Consul, instead of running around the hills bearded, and in rags, was the most ordinary thing! He asked me for a job. Given his high academic credentials, and his knowledge of several languages, I knew he would make a useful addition to my staff. Leonard did his job well, and some months later he played a role in my acquisition, for the United States Government, of the massive Canevaro Palace in Florence. The acquisition of that valuable Palace, situated on the Arno river, in the very heart of the city, ranks as one of the best deals ever consummated for the benefit of the United States. To this day, it houses not only the various offices of the Consulate but also provides living quarters for the entire American staff.

My buddy Lieutenant Mario Bonfigli stayed in the Italian Army following the cessation of hostilities. Later, he achieved recognition as director of the Provincial Postwar Assistance Program. Cultured and well-educated, he eventually attained his degree of doctor of economics. I was overjoyed to be reunited with him and with Don Marino Cecarelli, "il prete bandito," in 1986, when I returned to Pietralunga for the 43rd anniversary of the organization of the Band of San Faustino. Although white-haired like the rest of us, and somewhat heavier, Mario was still the same bright and jovial person I had known in those perilous days of 1944. Don Marino is, incredibly, still serving the parish of Morena, as he has done for more than half a century. Stelio Pierangeli received widespread recognition for his bravery in the Northern Italian campaign, and after the war he returned to private practice as an attorney. He refused numerous offers to accept official posts. He died in 1980.

My traveling companion, Giovanni Marioli, and I shared many a happy hour during my years in Florence, and I enjoyed watching his two young sons grow. I did not forget my deep debt to him and his family and did everything possible to make life pleasant for them. Of all my gifts to Giovanni, the most popular by far was a light motorcycle I gave him for a birthday. I can still see him, as he sat happily astride it. "Signor Console!" he exclaimed, bowled over with surprise and delight, "this is not 'just a gift'—it's a regalone! (a very big gift!)" In March of 1969, Giovanni's delightful, mischievous sense of humor and unabashed zest for life were snuffed out when a car, traveling too fast to stop, hit and killed him as he walked behind his cart on a narrow country road. To this day, I remain in touch with his family. Oreste Ortali, who courageously provided us with bicycles, and arranged food and lodging to begin our journey, is still living and working in Pietralunga, Italy.

Although valiant old Francesco Rossi and his wife died long ago, the Rossi family was never far from my thoughts. When I was last in Italy, in 1990, I drove into Le Marche to search them out. We were eventually steered to Fermo, where we found a grandson, Nello Rossi. At his home, my companions and I were joyously welcomed by Nello and his wife, his brother, Leonardo, and their parents. I learned that the family had abandoned the farm near Grottazzolina many years ago. I spent two days with them and was once more extended the famous Rossi affection and generous hospitality.

"Cag," Lieutenant Cagnazzi of A Force in Bari, survived the war and returned to his home in Durban, South Africa. We corresponded for a number of years, and, from his letters, I learned he was quite successful in several business ventures. Quinto Silenzi was killed in an accident in the late 1940s. Despite our promise to stay in touch with each other, except for the note from Ramsay, I never heard from any of the Allied officers who escaped with me.

This postscript would not be complete, of course, without mention of Manfred Metzger. Dear Manfred! No one could ever hope for a more loyal or conscientious friend. When we returned to Washington from leave in August of 1944, not only was there the letter from Ramsay, there was also one addressed to me, care of the State Department, from Manfred, postmarked Switzerland. Anxiously, I tore it open. "Dear Felice," he wrote. "You will no doubt be surprised to learn we are now residing in Switzerland." He went on to tell me that, upon being notified he was being conscripted into the German army, he and his wife had managed to escape to Switzerland. They had taken up residence in Geneva, and he was running the family tank car business from there. I was happy to hear he was safe and well. He had no idea, of course, that I had escaped from Italy. I immediately dashed off a reply to him, telling him the good news about my posting back to Florence. Strangely, I didn't hear from him. Then, one evening in June of 1945, Vittoria came in to announce we had "a distinguished visitor."

"Who is it?" I asked.

"I suggest you go see for yourself," she said, with a mysterious smile.

Curious, I followed her to the front door, and there was Manfred. We embraced joyously, and after much handshaking and backslapping, we sat down over a brandy to catch up on our lives. I noticed that Manfred seemed uncharacterisitically nervous. "What's wrong?" I asked, concerned.

"Well," he said, "I may need your help, if you can do anything. My company and I have been blacklisted. It's dangerous for me to even be here visiting you." That was probably true. Being an important German business, it was not surprising they had been placed under economic sanctions by the Allies.

"Of course I'll help you, Manfred," I said immediately. "Why didn't you come to me sooner? I'll report the details of your help to us right away, to the powers that can change that. It's little enough, considering all you've done, and the risks you've taken on our behalf." The next day, on Consular stationary, I prepared and signed a declaration, attesting to Manfred Metzger's assistance to me, and to the Allied cause. He and his company were immediately removed from the "blacklist" and were able to resume trading. From that day on, rarely did more than a month or two pass without some contact between us.

During the decades that followed, as I continued my career in the State Department, no matter where I was in the world, Manfred visited me at least once a year. We often relived our youthful adventures in Italy, and, although he protested modestly, he was always pleased when the high point of his long and eventful life—his heroic role in arranging the escape of Nancy and Amy—came up. In May of 1985, it was my pleasure to be in Switzerland for Manfred's eightieth birthday. From the time we met in 1937, until his death in January of 1986, Manfred was my closest friend. As a special memorial to our friendship, we established the Metzger–Orebaugh Friendship Fund for Youth, to provide worthy youth activities and projects in the Naples, Florida, area. The affinity that existed between us for almost half a century knew no limits, and was sealed with life's most precious gifts—mutual respect and love. I miss him, very much. His widow Nerina and their two daughters Héliane and Adrienne and their families still live in Geneva, where Héliane runs their tank-car business.

January 1947 brought the highlight of my wartime experiences. I was summoned to Rome, where, in the presence of my wife Marguerite, my dear mother (who was living with us at that time), and Generals C. H. Lee, commander of the U.S. Forces in the Mediterranean Theater of Operations, and Raffele Cordona, Chief of Staff of the Italian Forces, I was presented with the Medal of Freedom, the highest civilian award of the

United States of America. Chargé d'Affaires David McK. Key made the presentation, on behalf of President Harry S. Truman. No honor before, or since, in my life has given me such an intense feeling of awe, or such a sense of pride.

In 1948, while still in Florence, Marguerite and I decided to adopt a little sister for Howard. The addition of four-year-old Edith to our family made it complete and has kept our cup of happiness overflowing ever since. Howard and Edith are grown, married, and have families of their own now, and their children, our grandchildren, are a deep reward and fulfillment in our lives today.

Now, in my eighty-first year, as I look back over my long and eventful life and review those turbulent times of my youth and the events of World War II, I can still recall the one brief encounter that was the pivotal point in finally restoring my life to its prewar balance. It was mid-1946, a year after the end of World War II. I had stepped out of the Consulate in Florence, bent on some errand not far away (on foot, even though I had vowed never to walk anywhere again!), and was making my way down one of the narrow, cobbled, pedestrian-only streets that branch off the Via Tornabuoni. As I threaded my way through the lunchtime crowds in the street, I saw coming toward me a dark-haired man, rather ordinary looking, pushing a bicycle. He was staring hard at me, with his brow wrinkled as though trying to recall something. As we drew abreast, his eyes suddenly lit with recognition. "Signor Console! Signor Console!" he exclaimed, startling me. I stopped, and he grabbed my hand and shook it warmly, smiling. "How are you, Signore? What in the world are you doing here? How is your beautiful secretary?" I stared at the man. A faint tinge of recognition stirred in the back of my brain. Then it dawned on me. The man facing me was one of the four callous OVRA guards who had transported us from Monaco to Gubbio. He was the guard who had been totally indifferent to our comfort and our basic human needs during that long, miserable journey. He was the guard who had kept all of us, including "my beautiful secretary" (Nancy), freezing on the station platform for hours, dressed only in our thin summer clothes. He, like Meletti, was one against whom I had vowed to some day square accounts, if ever I had the chance.

And here he was—standing before me, smiling happily. He was obviously genuine in his pleasure at seeing me, when he could easily have passed me by. For an instant, I stood frozen, then all rancor drained from me. Totally disarmed, I found I was able to smile back and engage in polite conversation with him. As we talked, I realized that I was not talking to a Blackshirt Fascist bastard, but to a newborn Democrat. He, like so many of his countrymen, had "cambiato la camicia" (changed his shirt), to borrow a familiar Italian expression. As a member of Italy's postwar democratic society, he had changed the color of his shirt and dismissed the dismal past. I too, had changed the color of my shirt. I had become a diplomat again, not a guerrilla fighter. All desire for vengeance had finally left me. It was in that moment that World War II ended for me. There was no longer any trace of Michele Franciosi, 'sfollato, guerrilla fighter, in me—there was only Walter Orebaugh, diplomat—"Il Console."

During the nearly five decades that have passed since that day, no matter where I have gone in the world, or what I have experienced in life, the words uttered by a seventeen-year-old girl, sitting at a poor kitchen table in Perugia, have echoed in my heart and remained my watchword as I served my country and raised my family:

It is better to be in danger, and hope to live
than to be safe, and pray to die.
Valentina Bonucci
December 1943

Appendix A

Selected Portions of the Report of Colonel Guerrizzi and Stelio Pierangeli on Partisan Activities of the Brigade of San Faustino in Umbria

(Translated from Italian by Walter W. Orebaugh)

GIVEN TO THE ALLIED COMMAND, JULY, 1944.

Our Program

To fight without quarter against the German invader, to fight against Fascism, to obstruct recruitment by them for the so-called Republican Army, to impede the collection of foodstuffs by them, and to educate the masses about the principles of a free society, devoid of partisan bias.

The first secret meeting to lay the foundation of the movement took place at San Faustino, Pietralunga, where tasks were assigned to various officers and recruits. As stated above, it was my wish, shared by everyone present, that the movement be kept free of political party coloration.

As a result of these various meetings, a number of nuclei (initially without arms) were created in the Zone, steps were taken toward gathering arms and funds necessary for the struggle, and assistance was extended to numerous Allied prisoners of war who drifted into our Zone.

I traveled to other localities in Umbria, in turn, to help organize more resistance centers: Città del Pieve, Umbertide, Città di Castello, Spoleto, etc. . . .

At a later meeting (January 1944), I got to know the American Consul Orebank [Orebaugh] who earlier had hidden out in Perugia. Spontaneously he offered to collaborate with us, and to join our movement in the San Faustino-Morena zone, being willing to share our discomforts and dangers as well. He offered us the sizable sum of 100,000 lire toward the initial financial needs of the movement and promised additional help and funding if we could help him get a message through to the Allies.

At another meeting in San Faustino, attended by the above-named Consul and other English and American officers who had fled from concentration camps, it was agreed to transmit a message soliciting money and arms from the Allies by means of a clandestine transmitter-receiver radio located in the Garfagnana [Tuscany area]. . . . I must state here that Consul Orebank [Orebaugh] was of tremendous help to us at a later date when, after suffering through harrowing vicissitudes, he managed to make it through the German battle lines and get the Allies to send us the various supplies and types of help we needed and had requested.

In December [1943], at a meeting in Perugia, eighteen officers took the oath in my presence, and each was assigned a nucleus of patriots. In January [1944] through the Florence Committee of National Liberation, where I often went, contact was established with the Allies, and code phrases were agreed upon as signals for airdrops of arms. Unfortunately, our cause was severely damaged at a high level by the betrayals of several men.

One Paciotti, caught carrying arms, fearful of being shot, to save his life spilled all he knew about our organization, naming me as its leader and also naming others of my command. Warned that an arrest warrant had been issued for me and Bonuccio Bonucci, who was my civilian advisor, we both went into hiding. I found refuge on a farm at M. Tezio, while Bonucci went to his villa at San Faustino. Shortly thereafter, he was arrested there by a Fascist patrol. Six days later, I miraculously escaped arrest after the Fascist militia received an anonymous tip about where I was. It was then that I moved to Florence, where I continued resistance activities under the aegis of the Committee of National Liberation. In reprisal, the Fascist Prefect of Perugia—Rocchi—arrested my wife and my eighteen-year-old son, who was also active in our organization, and imprisoned them for a period of two months. A Fascist order was issued that, when apprehended, I was to be "skinned on sight."

On the day after my arrival in Florence, I dispatched my cousin, Capua, a disabled army major, to Perugia to the law offices of Angeli, of our organization, to let the Committee of National Liberation know of my whereabouts, and to authorize Angeli to assume command of our movement. . . .

Conclusion

In addition to the results previously reported in the Bulletin of the Fronte Della Resistenza, the brigade has for six long months kept an area of more than 400 square kilometers out of the control of the Germans and Fascists, thereby forestalling the conscription of thousands of young men, as well as the forced donation of large quantities of foodstuffs to the use of the German armed forces. These results were made possible by the support given by the Allies and by the inhabitants of the Zone where the Brigade operated.

The Brigade's leadership cooperated closely with Captains Fitzgerald and Ramsay of the British Army, in accordance with instructions emanating from Allied military headquarters. We owe the precious help provided by airdrops to the intervention made for us by the Consul of the United States, Guglielmo Orebaugh, who also arranged for the sending of the American Fifth Army special mission. From the start, promoters of the (resistance) movement were:

Lt. Col. Mario Guerrizzi	Bonuccio Bonucci
Lieut. Mario Bonfigli	Lieut. Vittorio Biagotti
Don Marino Ceccarelli	Lieut. Livio Dalla Ragione
Lawyer Salcerini Gaetano	. . . and others

Statement of Pierangeli

Throughout the occupation, Lt. Col. Guerrizzi has carried out intense liaison and coordination with the anti-Fascist Committee of Florence, with particular attention to the airdrop of arms and supplies.

Brigade Statistics

Total Strength: 4 Battalions
Officers: 11; Men: 300
Killed: Officers: 2; Patriots: 35
Wounded: 27
Signed:
Colonel Mario Guerrizzi
and
Commander of the Brigade
Stelio Pierangeli

Appendix B

The Medal of Freedom (Now the Presidential Medal of Freedom)

Established by order of President Harry S. Truman July 6, 1945, amended by Executive Order 11085, issued February 22, 1963, and Executive Order 11515, issued March 13, 1970. Only about 300 people have received this prestigious award, the country's highest decoration for a civilian, in the 47 years since its inception—among them the author, Walter W. Orebaugh, and the following:

Dean Acheson	Duke Ellington	Jesse Owens
Marian Anderson	Arthur Fiedler	Ronald Reagan
Neil Armstrong	Gerald M. Ford	Artur Rubenstein
Irving Berlin	John Ford	Jonas Salk
Eubie Blake	Philip C. Habib	Beverly Sills
Omar Bradley	Pope John XXIII	Ludwig Van der Rohe
Ralph Bunche	Lyndon Johnson	E. B. White
Alexander Calder	Helen Keller	Andrew Wyeth
Rachel Carson	John F. Kennedy	
Jimmy Carter	Martin Luther King, Jr.	
Aaron Copland	Margaret Mead	
Michael DeBakey	George Meany	
Will and Ariel Durant	Richard M. Nixon	
T. S. Eliot	Eugene Ormandy	

Sources: The White House
               Information Almanac
               Executive Orders

CITATION TO ACCOMPANY THE AWARD OF
THE MEDAL OF FREEDOM

to

WALTER W. OREBAUGH

Walter W. Orebaugh, Consul of the United States, for exceptionally meritorious and courageous service in gathering military and political information behind the German lines during the Italian campaign of 1943. Mr. Orebaugh, Consul at Monte Carlo in November 1942, was captured after successfully destroying the codes and other confidential material entrusted to him. After a period of internment at Gubbio and Perugia, Italy, he joined a band of guerrilla troops, and, rejecting the opportunity to appeal to the protecting power for exchange, remained with the guerrilla band and became its leader. After harassing German communications in January, February, and March, 1944, at frequent risk to his life, he crossed territory constantly patrolled by German forces and made his way by foot and small boat to Ortona, within the Allied lines. There he gave the first accurate and detailed report on the guerrilla movement as well as other valuable military and political intelligence. Mr. Orebaugh voluntarily performed services beyond his normal duty as a Foreign Service officer, and displayed courage, resourcefulness and coolness under fire, worthy of the best traditions of the Foreign Service.

Dean Acheson (signature).
Acting Secretary of State.

Washington, December 11, 1946.

Text accompanying the Medal of Freedom.

Selected Readings

Alpini, Antonio. *La Resistenza Armata nella Zona Libera di Pietralunga* (Armed Resistance in the Free Zone of Pietralunga). (Gazetta Ufficiale No. 33 del 3 October 1953).

Barzini, Luigi. *The Italians*. New York: Atheneum, 1965.

Eisenhower, John S. D. *Allies: Pearl Harbor to D-Day*. New York: Doubleday, 1982.

Hytier, Adrienne Doris. *Two Years of French Foreign Policy: Vichy, 1940–1942*. New York: Greenwood Press, 1974 (Reprint of the author's thesis, Columbia University, 1958).

Jackson, Stanley. *Inside Monte Carlo*. New York: Stein and Day, 1975.

Kauffman, Richard and Field, Carol. *The Hill Towns of Italy*. New York: Dutton, 1983.

Keegan, John. *The Second World War*. New York: Viking Penguin, 1989.

Kennedy, John F. *Profiles in Courage*. New York: Harper & Brothers, 1955.

Lawson, Don. *The French Resistance*. New York: Messner, 1984.

Leeds, Christopher Anthony. *Italy under Mussolini*. New York: Putnam, 1972.

Lisagor, Peter and Higgins, Marguerite. *Overtime in Heaven: Adventures in the Foreign Service*. New York: Doubleday, 1964.

Marrus, Michael Robert and Paxton, Robert O. *Vichy France and the Jews*. New York: Basic Books, 1981.

Monticorre, A. *Cattolici e Fascisti in Umbria*. Bologna, Italy: Il Molino, 1946.

Mulvihill, Margaret. *Mussolini and Italian Fascism*. New York: Franklin Watts, 1990.

Spaziani, Carlo. *Orrori e Stragi di Guerra*. (Horrors and Massacres of War). Gubbio, Italy: Edizioni Melos, 1946.

Torguato, Sergenti. *L'Altra Resistenza* (The Other Resistance). Città di Castello, Italy: Edizioni Confronto, Tipografia Legatori, 1990.

Vaughan-Thomas, Wynford. *Anzio*. New York: Holt, Rinehart & Winston, 1961.

Villari, Luigi. *Italian Foreign Policy under Mussolini*. Greenwich, Connecticut: Devin-Adair Co., 1956.

Wallace, Robert. *The Italian Campaign*. New York: Time-Life Books, 1978.

Index

About the Authors

Originally from Kansas, WALTER W. OREBAUGH was selected for the United States Foreign Service in 1932 and was promoted to consul in 1941 and transferred to Nice, in Vichy-controlled France. Orebaugh spent a harrowing nine months helping people flee Europe and emigrate to the United States. In early November 1942, Orebaugh opened the first U.S. Consulate in the Principality of Monaco. A few days later, Italian Sixth Army troops surrounded it, taking Orebaugh and the female employees of the Consulate prisoner. Orebaugh, Lester Maynard, and two young female clerks from the Consulate were taken to Gubbio, Italy, and interned there.

Hailed as a hero in the United States following his escape and repatriation in 1944, he was awarded the Medal of Freedom, the nation's highest civilian award, by President Harry S. Truman.

In 1945, Orebaugh again returned to Italy—as U.S. Consul, and continued his distinguished career in the Foreign Service. He left the Foreign Service from 1950–1955, at the behest of CIA chief Allen Dulles, to serve as Chief of a branch of the CIA.

On his return to the Foreign Service, Orebaugh served as U.S. Consul in several countries before retiring in 1962 from his post as Senior Counselor of Career Development. He then accepted a position as Vice-Director of the Bologna Center of the School of Advanced International Studies for Johns Hopkins University. After two full careers marked by national and international recognition, Walter Orebaugh retired permanently in 1975.

CAROL JOSE is a free-lance writer and journalist. She has edited and collaborated on several books, writes a weekly newspaper column on food and cooking, and has written feature articles on cooking, education, travel, and current issues. She lives in Satellite, Florida.